CYBER SECURITY AND SUPPLY CHAIN MANAGEMENT

Risks, Challenges, and Solutions

Trends, Challenges and Solutions in Contemporary Supply Chain Management

ISSN: 2737-5390

Series Editors: Steven Carnovale, *Rochester Institute of Technology, USA*
Sengun Yeniyurt, *Rutgers University, USA*

Published

Trends, Challenges and
Solutions in Contemporary
Supply Chain Management
Volume 1

CYBER SECURITY AND SUPPLY CHAIN MANAGEMENT

Risks, Challenges, and Solutions

editors

Steven Carnovale
Rochester Institute of Technology, USA

Sengun Yeniyurt
Rutgers University, USA

NEW JERSEY · LONDON · SINGAPORE · BEIJING · SHANGHAI · HONG KONG · TAIPEI · CHENNAI · TOKYO

Published by

World Scientific Publishing Co. Pte. Ltd.

5 Toh Tuck Link, Singapore 596224

USA office: 27 Warren Street, Suite 401-402, Hackensack, NJ 07601

UK office: 57 Shelton Street, Covent Garden, London WC2H 9HE

Library of Congress Cataloging-in-Publication Data

Names: Carnovale, Steven, editor. | Yeniyurt, Sengun, editor.

Title: Cyber security and supply chain management : risks, challenges, and solutions /
    editors, Steven Carnovale, Sengun Yeniyurt.

Description: Hackensack, NJ : World Scientific, [2021] | Series: Trends, Challenges and Solutions
    in Contemporary Supply Chain Management, ISSN: 2737-5390 |
    Includes bibliographical references and index.

Identifiers: LCCN 2021005317 | ISBN 9789811231568 (hardcover) |
    ISBN 9789811233128 (ebook for institutions) | ISBN 9789811233135 (ebook for individuals)

Subjects: LCSH: Business logistics. | Computer security. | Risk management.

Classification: LCC HD38.5 .C94 2021 | DDC 658.70285/58--dc23

LC record available at https://lccn.loc.gov/2021005317

British Library Cataloguing-in-Publication Data

A catalogue record for this book is available from the British Library.

For any available supplementary material, please visit
https://www.worldscientific.com/worldscibooks/10.1142/12140#t=suppl

Desk Editor: Lum Pui Yee

Typeset by Stallion Press
Email: enquiries@stallionpress.com

Printed in Singapore

Contents

INTRODUCTION

Cybersecurity & Supply Chain Management: What's the Big Deal?

Steven Carnovale* and Sengun Yeniyurt†

*Rochester Institute of Technology, Saunders College of Business
† Rutgers University, Rutgers Business School

I do not fear computers. I fear the lack of them.

Isaac Asimov

Isaac Asimov, the prolific science fiction writer, made an unmistakable mark on our notion of what science fiction should be and, in the process, advanced many predictions about the future and about computing. He discussed topics such as "mobile computing objects" and terminals through which mankind is able to access all information at any time and place. He described the power of computing to democratize information, and how it would benefit humanity by leveraging robotics to tackle rudimentary tasks so humans can add value to the world. Indeed, it appears that his predictions have largely become reality. As of 2019, there are an estimated two billion computers in the world (Loisy, 2019), and these numbers will only continue to grow. However, with this vast number of interconnected devices comes a series of problems that even Asimov would have had trouble fathoming.

The largest issue with such a vast number of interconnected devices is information security concerns. A recent Accenture (2019) study established that over two-thirds of business leaders feel that cybersecurity concerns are growing, while a separate study revealed that, on average, only 5% of the time are data security protections for key folders/information correctly handled (Varonis, 2019). Furthermore, this proliferation of computers and computing, more generally, has enabled nefarious actors to hack into one of those computers/servers approximately every 39 seconds (Maryland, 2020), with the approximate (average) cost of a data breach at US$3.92 million per incident (Zorabedian, 2020). As a result of the increasing use of cloud computing in the banking, finance, and government sectors, one of the largest and perhaps most nefarious hacks occurred. In 2017, over 147 million people had their social security numbers, dates of birth, and other personal information stolen by malicious actors (Equifax, 2017). All told, because of the pressing threat to information security, the size of the industry tasked with protecting these data will likely grow to over US$170 billion dollars a year (Gartner, 2018).

Then, couple this (truncated) list of concerns with respect to data and information security, with the complexity and scale of modern supply chains. Take, for example, the production of an Apple iPhone. It has been reported that manufacturing one such phone involves suppliers (e.g. raw materials suppliers, contract manufacturers, logistics providers, etc.) from approximately 43 different countries across 6 different continents (Mpetrova, 2018). If we think about the supply chain as encompassing all processes relating to the sourcing of raw materials, the transportation and storage of inventory (work in process and finished goods), the planning of production/value added processes, and ultimately delivering finished goods and services to the end consumer, there are some serious cybersecurity vulnerabilities that arise. In any number of industries, data about production volumes, costs, engineering specifications, product design, margins, marketing plans, release dates, process flows, etc. are being shared internationally across numerous servers and data centers. A recent example of this potential vulnerability to the extended enterprise is the Target data breach of 2013, which involved hackers accessing confidential information via one of Target's suppliers: an HVAC supplier that performed service on one of their locations. This breach resulted a cost of over US$200 million (FacilitiesNet, 2017) and significant reputational damage.

All these issues noted above, taken together with such broad and expansive supply chains, lead to one glaring conclusion: the extended supply chains of firms are a major source of cyber vulnerability that require further scrutiny. Hence the impetus behind the creation of this book. We chose the title *Cybersecurity and Supply Chain Management: Risks, Challenges, and Solutions* deliberately to provide light on three core areas at the intersection of cybersecurity and supply chain management:

(1) **Risks**: In this new modus operandi, what risks do supply chains face as it relates to cybersecurity?
(2) **Challenges**: Knowing that new risks exist, what challenges do they place on normal operations for global supply chains?
(3) **Solutions**: What can be done?

We are fortunate to have leading scholars in the field as well as prominent practitioners provide a balanced view and approach on the topic. Chapter 1 provides a philosophical treatise that formally grounds cyberspace. The chapter covers an interesting history of the first known cyberattack in 1971, which impacted interconnected machines on ARPANET by printing the text "I'm the creeper: catch me if you can." Innocuous enough of course, but it set the stage for a whole new world of chaos. The chapter then grounds cyberspace by dichotomizing it into the body and the mind of cyberspace. This distinguishes the physical from the intangible, all of which intersect to form cyberspace as we know it. The chapter is critical, as it sets the stage for thinking about how a cyberattack on an Internet of Things (IoT) device may be different from, say the core physical infrastructure of a bank. Though the chapter answers several questions about cyberspace, it leaves the reader wondering about ownership of information and the ways it can (perhaps cannot) be protected.

The focus of the book comes into full force in Chapter 2, when the connection between supply chain management and cybersecurity are developed. Effectively, the chapter argues that increasing complexity, expansiveness, and size of modern supply chains have opened up new vulnerabilities, particularly given the increasing use of technology in such supply chains. The chapter then frames what may constitute a cyberthreat and risk, as well as some critical frameworks that are out there for understanding cyber risks.

Chapter 3 provides an earnest and practical assessment of cybersecurity risks and supply chain vulnerabilities and provides a series of clear recommendations for improving cybersecurity. The author provides examples of high-profile cyberattacks, including NotPetya and the ASUS supply chain attack, explains the methods used for the hack, and recommends that companies take a germ-theory–based approach to cybersecurity. According to this perspective, invisible cyberthreats should be regarded as germs, and organizations should implement good cyber hygiene practices to neutralize and avoid infections. The chapter also discusses cyber liability insurance policies, the NIST Cybersecurity Framework, third-party cyber risk management, cloud computing vulnerabilities, and specific measures that need to be implemented to protect organizations from malicious code.

Chapter 4 focuses on the human component and its role in supply chain cybersecurity. It provides an overview and discussion of the importance of the human factor from a social sustainability perspective. The chapter highlights that one of the main vulnerabilities is the human element of the supply chain, i.e. persons that utilize and engage with the cyber systems. The author brings attention to the fact that cyberattacks often are attacks on humans, their identities, assets, and personal information using cyber tools, resulting in worry, anxiety, and damage. Companies are urged to take a socially responsible approach to cybersecurity by setting and maintaining clear expectations of societal impacts and empowering users and consumers to make informed decisions and consumption choices.

Chapter 5 provides a comprehensive overview of the extant literature in cybersecurity, supply chain risk management, and supply chain security. This comprehensive review results in clear definitions of supply chain cybersecurity and key concepts related to cyber supply chain risks. Key concepts covered include cyber disruptions and cyber harm; cyber risk and risk management; risk identification, measurement and assessment; cyber risk management frameworks and best practices; supply chain cyber resilience; Industry 4.0/5.0, blockchain, and IoT; and the cyber supply chain. Specific variables discussed and defined include cyber capabilities, supply chain cyber visibility, supply chain cyber distance, risk propagation, robustness, and resilience. Further, the chapter provides guidance for future research in this domain.

Chapter 6 provides insights from Mærsk Line's experience with NotPetya, a cyberattack that incapacitated their entire network within minutes. The chapter provides a first-hand account of the events through Andy Jones, the former Chief Information Security Officer. This major cybersecurity case provides invaluable insights for managers and delineates how they can prepare and respond to such inevitable cyberattacks in the future.

Chapter 7 focuses on the pharmaceutical supply chain and proposes a Cyber Security Maturity Model (CSMM). The authors indicate that the

CSMM framework can be employed to ensure effective monitoring, training, and compliance. They further state that blockchain would allow tracking throughout the supply chain, enhancing cybersecurity and guarding against criminality, counterfeiting, falsification, and tampering.

Chapter 8 provides a review of the recent cybersecurity breaches and explains how supply chains face a unique combination of vulnerabilities. Cases reviewed include Target and Home Depot, and cyberattack strategies explained include brute force attacks, compromised passwords, phishing, spear phishing, supply chain hacks, SQL injection, and distributed denial of service. The chapter then describes some simple cyber protection tools such as password managers, as well as more comprehensive approaches such as new ANSI-approved 12N QR codes, and explains how these tools can be used to mitigate cyberthreats.

Chapter 9 focuses on cybersecurity in logistics. It first reviews the traditional cybersecurity challenges that are related to the centralized information systems used to manage logistics activities. Next, the author explains the novel attack planes that arise from the instrumentation used to track vehicles and shipments. The author also provides concrete suggestions regarding how instrumentation can be utilized as a physical security solution.

Overall, the book provides a broad as well as deep overview of the supply chain cybersecurity risks and challenges, as well as concrete risk management solutions that managers can implement to protect their supply chains. The book presents rich perspectives from industry experts and academics, thereby providing a comprehensive overview of the field, along with practical, readily applicable solutions and mitigation strategies. The question remains: if Asimov were here today, would he still fear such a lack of computers?

References

Accenture (2019). Cost of cybercrime. Available at: https://www.accenture.com/_acnmedia/PDF-96/Accenture-2019-Cost-of-Cybercrime-Study-Final.pdf#zoom=50. Accessed November 11, 2020.

Cukier, M. (2007). Study: Hackers attack every 39 seconds. Available at: https://eng.umd.edu/news/story/study-hackers-attack-every-39-seconds. Accessed November 11, 2020

Equifax (2017). Equifax announces cybersecurity incident involving consumer information. Available at: https://investor.equifax.com/news-and-events/press-releases/2017/09-07-2017-213000628. Accessed November 11, 2020.

FacilitiesNet (2017). Target settles HVAC data breach for $18.5 million, May 25. Available at: https://www.facilitiesnet.com/hvac/tip/Target-Settles-HVAC-Data-Breach-for-185-Million--39237. Accessed November 11, 2020.

Gartner_Inc. (2018). Forecast Analysis: Information Security, Worldwide, 2Q18 Update. Available at: https://www.gartner.com/en/documents/3889055. Accessed November 11, 2020.

Loisy, N. (2019). How many computers are there in the world?, August 9. Available at: https://www.scmo.net/faq/2019/8/9/how-many-compaters-is-there-in-the-world. Accessed November 11, 2020.

Maryland (2020). https://www.securitymagazine.com/articles/87787-hackers-attack-every-39-seconds.

Mpetrova92 (2018). We traced what it takes to make an iPhone, from its initial design to the components and raw materials needed to make it a reality. Available at: https://www.cnbc.com/2018/12/13/inside-apple-iphone-where-parts-and-materials-come-from.html. Accessed November 11, 2020.

Varonis (2019). Varonis Global Data Risk Report. Available at: https://www.varonis.com/2019-data-risk-report/?__hstc=51647990.be9d744a9ecca03569441f5b54 28c63f.1604764262655.1604764262655.1604764262655.1&__hssc=5 1647990.1.1604764262655&__hsfp=3557980309. Accessed November 11, 2020.

Zorabedian, J. (2020) What's new in the 2020 cost of a data breach: Report. *Security Intelligence*, July 28. Available at: https://securityintelligence.com/posts/whats-new-2020-cost-of-a-data-breach-report/. Accessed November 11, 2020.

CHAPTER 1

A Philosophical Examination on the Definition of Cyberspace

Myles D. Garvey

*Marketing Group, D'Amore-Mckim School of Business Northeastern
University 360 Huntington Ave, Boston, MA 02151, USA*

1.1. Introduction

Cybersecurity in the supply chain is of the utmost importance. Manufacturing, logistics, and the various operational processes throughout the supply chain today looks nothing like what it did just 10 years ago. Assembly lines, manufacturing facilities, as well as trucks delivering products and materials between the various intermediaries in the supply chain are now all Internet-enabled. Put simply, our modern supply chains have not only emerged as key economic components in our global ecosystem of commerce but have also graced their presence in what is often referred to as "cyberspace." But what is "cyberspace"? Much like any new word that emerges in its massive colloquial usage in any culture or society, it appears that this term has taken on various de facto meanings without a proper and thorough philosophical examination of "what is."

It is actually quite shocking how few, if any, have taken on the task to examine this complicated yet ubiquitous term. Since the first usage of the word itself in the 1980s, and its conceptual meaning being present even before then, and its usage throughout modern society up to today, many have struggled to understand the concept of cyberspace. As with any concept that undergoes scientific examination, the academic must first begin with a philosophical examination as to the concept's definition and description of "what is." Scholars of supply chain management have recently taken an interest in examining the various facets of cybersecurity in the supply chain. Interestingly enough, even the concept of cybersecurity is still in its infancy despite the calls from many to undertake its study and application in practice.

As a result of these calls for additional study and integration into practice, many have put forth "best practices" and definitions of cybersecurity that are either too general or too specific. Many tools have been proposed and designed, procedures and roles created, to secure the Internet and other information-technology–related assets, and even products and services to achieve this goal. Yet, while many have suggested the various practices, procedures, roles, products, and services to achieve cybersecurity, few have actually defined what exactly is to be secured in the first place. Many have suggested that it is "cyberspace" that is to be secured. According to *Merriam-Webster* dictionary, cyberspace is defined as "the online world of computer networks and especially the Internet." But even this definition is arbitrary.

What is an "online world"? Is it all-encapsulating in the sense of "computer networks"? If two computers are networked together, can it be called "cyberspace"? The definition apparently also appears to draw a distinction between "Internet" and "computer networks." So, would cyberspace thus apply to networks that are not the "Internet"? We notice that we come to a level of ambiguity here with this basic definition. Thus, it is argued here that the concept and the term "cyberspace" necessitates a philosophical examination that will drive deeper into each of these questions before its proper usage in a scientific context, as done in this chapter. First, a brief history of both the concept and the phrase of cyberspace is presented. Next, an examination on the definition of "cyberspace" and an argument that its definition is composed of two smaller dimensions, what the author call the "mind" and the "body" of cyberspace, is put forth. This chapter concludes with a deeper examination of both of these areas and provides a definition of cyberspace that is not too general but also not too specific, but "just right" for future examination of its security.

1.2. How Did We Get Here? A Brief History of Cyberspace

"I'm the creeper: catch me if you can." This is often considered as one of the first tangible cyberattacks against the fetus of the Internet, scilicet

ARPANET. Robert Thomas, an engineer at BBN Technologies, invented the first virus in 1971, which moved on the various computer systems connected to the ARPANET (Benford, 2011). While the attack itself was not malicious in nature and only printed the aforementioned text to the screen, the event is often hailed as the first attack on cyberspace. A second iteration of the virus was developed by Raymond Tomlinson, another engineer at BBN Technologies who is often attributed to designing the first email system (and arguing in favor of removing the hyphen between "e" and "mail") (Metcalf, 2014). Instead of Creeper simply moving from computer to computer on ARPANET, it self-replicated itself, and was hence a realization of John Von Neumann's ideas of self-replicating software theorized only a few decades prior (Von Neuman *et al.*, 1966). It equally is often hailed that the first counter-measure to Creeper was a program named Reaper. Reaper was another self-replicating program designed by Tomlinson that had the intent to transition across all of ARPANET to remove Creeper.

However, the first attack that was spread throughout the nascent Internet at the time that amounted to tangible costs would not occur until November 2, 1988. The first (accidental) denial-of-service attack came from a worm that was coded by a graduate student at Cornell University by the name of Robert Morris (Mello, 1993). Morris' worm originally was intended to be released to specifically illustrate security loopholes that were present on various UNIX systems throughout the Internet. However, Morris accidentally programmed a worm that self-replicated itself multiple times per machine. The result was a shutdown of a large portion of the Internet, and the "estimated cost of dealing with the worm at each installation ranged from $200 to more than $53,000" (Dressler, 2007).

Similar "tests" were later performed by rogue computer programmers, although not necessarily in the same manner or spirit. For example, one of the founders of ARPANET, Jon Postel, in January 1998, had emailed a majority of the owners of the organizations that ran a majority of the name servers of the Internet at the time. His request was to redirect traffic from their servers to his. Given his legendary status of being one of the effective founders of the Internet, these owners complied. The result was a near total shutdown of the Internet overnight (Bridis, 1998). The shutdown led to many questions of the intent of Postel's request, mainly since it was during a time when the government was handing over many of its operations to the private sector (Singer and Friedman, 2014).

The history of these so-called "cyberattacks" illustrate the various loopholes that many new innovative information systems tend to have in their canonical forms. They illustrate that while some actors may have non-malicious intent, the intent does not justify the potential cost that firms face as they expose their technological systems to other computer systems, devices, or actors. In order to understand the costs of having or not having a strong "cybersecurity," one must first define this term. However, before defining the term cybersecurity, one must first have an understanding of what exactly is being secured, namely the presence of an actor in cyberspace. Put simply, in order to define cybersecurity, we need to first define cyberspace.

1.3. Defining Cyberspace

Interestingly enough, many academics, practitioners, and even governments struggle with the definition of "cyberspace." In fact, the Department of Defense had struggled with over 12 iterations of the official definition of cyberspace, even though it is often considered to be the founder (Singer and Friedman, 2014). Finally, it landed on the official definition of cyberspace being the "global domain within the information environment consisting of the interdependent network of information technology infrastructures and resident data, including the Internet, telecommunications networks, computer systems, and embedded processors and controllers" (Theohary, 2020). The term "cyberspace" was first coined in 1982 by William Gibson, a science fiction author. In his short story *Burning Chrome*, he refers to a custom-built computer simulator as the "Ono-Sendai VII, the 'Cyberspace Seven'" (Gibson, 2014, p. 240). Gibson had later commented on its origin, where "cyberspace" was "a word that first saw the light in red Sharpie on a yellow legal pad. It was the first time I ever quite got something else to work in fiction, though I still don't know exactly what that is" (Gibson, 2014, p. 17).

Two years after his first usage of the word, Gibson attributed a conceptual meaning to it and had leveraged its usage in his now seminal novel *Neuromancer*. The story about a drug-abused ex-hacker brought out of punishment for one more job against a powerful form of artificial intelligence set in a dystopian future in Japan, *Neuromancer* set the conceptual picture of the concept of "cyberspace." More specifically, Gibson had described it as a "consensual hallucination experienced daily by billions of legitimate operators, in every nation, by children being taught mathematical concepts…

A graphic representation of data abstracted from the banks of every computer in the human system. Unthinkable complexity. Lines of light ranged in the nonspace of the mind, clusters and constellations of data. Like city lights, receding ..." (Gibson, 2000, p. 65).

However, this definition is too conceptual for practical purposes. That is, it is not precise enough. Natural questions must follow from this. Who is an "operator"? What criteria constitutes them as "legitimate"? Does one's "mind" need to be "connected"? Or is this only metaphorical to intend to say that data is a reflection of the mind? Alternatively, the Department of Defense's definition is too restrictive in scope. What constitutes an "embedded" processor or control? Is being connected to the Internet really a necessity? What constitutes "technology infrastructures"? And what of software, is this now no longer part of "cyberspace"?

Others have offered similar definitions. Historically, in the 1990s, "cyber-space" essentially became the de facto word to refer to the Internet and the World Wide Web (Mueller, 2017). As we have seen, this was not precise enough for the government to enact proper security measures and procedures, hence the many iterations (Singer and Friedman, 2014). Since then, many countries, professional organizations, academics, and governments have attempted to define this strange concept, often bouncing from definitions that begin to resemble the Internet to other definitions that are more expansive than just "the Internet." As Pilarski (2020) argues in their review of the concept, despite all the definitions, cyberspace is a medium primarily used for human communication and social interaction.

We argue that cyberspace is so challenging to define precisely because it involves elements that are both abstract and concrete. The definition of cyberspace thus is less of a scientific problem and more of a philosophical problem. Cyberspace is challenging to define in much the same way that the human mind is challenging to define. When discussing the philosophy of the mind, there tends to be two primary schools of thought: the mind is part of the body and is something that is physical (i.e. materialism), or the mind is separate from the body and each person is a combination of a mind and a body (i.e. dualism) (Taylor, 1963). Ryle (2009) argues that the mind is nothing more than the logical conclusion of an argument, often posed by dualists, that is dependent on what he refers to as a "category mistake."

Ryle puts forward the illustration of such a mistake. He uses the example of a university tour being provided to a foreigner who visits Oxford or Cambridge. They visit the numerous office buildings, classrooms, administrative offices, sporting fields, and laboratories. They see and witness the various students, the books in the library, and the buildings within which the various colleges are identified. Yet after the tour, the foreigner claims to have seen the buildings, students, and colleges, but inquires as to when they will see "the university." Of course, the university is just a name that is given to organize all of the concepts of the buildings, colleges, books, etc. The university and the college, students, books, etc., are not separate entities, but rather the former is just a category within which all the latter entities lie.

Putting aside the debate of materialism versus dualism, Ryle's example actually gives us a baseline to use for defining "cyberspace." Analogous to the mind and the body of a person, cyberspace has a "mind" and a "body." The "body" is the collection of all of the physical pieces of infrastructure. Similar to the human being, whose various organs such as the heart, liver, and kidneys, as well as the veins that connect these organs, the skin within which all the organs and veins run, and the blood, electrical signals, and air that flows through them, constitute "the body," cyberspace has an analogous organization. It is the hardware that is used to store the various pieces of information, the wires that are used to transmit the information, and any device that communicates in its own manner, analog or digital, base 2 or some other numerical system, to store and transmit the information.

Analogous to the person, cyberspace also has a "mind." It is an organization of these physical properties that constitute what we call the "mind" of cyberspace. While on the physical plane, this information may be nothing more than electrical signals representing 0s and 1s; on an abstract plane, they represent some concept when the 0s and 1s are organized together. Analogous to how the concept of the word "concept" flowing to the author's mind while typing this at the moment is nothing more than just blood and electrical signals flowing through the brain and being transmitted to fingers to move in specific ways to strike certain letters on the keyboard to create the word "concept," the brain's organization of this information, namely the electrical signals, is what gives the word "concept" meaning. Thus, the organization of the information flowing through the "body" of cyberspace into differing concepts and categories, various ontologies, and taxonomies is the "mind" of cyberspace.

What differs between the mind and body of cyberspace versus that of a human is twofold. First, the mind is unique to each person that is a human, while "the mind" in cyberspace is not a property of the individuals in space but is rather a property of the space itself. The second difference is that the "body" of a human is fixed. Every human, with rare exceptions, needs the same organs to "live." Put differently, in most humans, we can expect to see a heart, a brain, bones, skin, etc. This is not necessarily true for all physical devices in "cyberspace." While it is true that most computer systems need a processor, memory, and power to operate, the types of processors, memory, and power all differ. Gaming computers will likely have different components than a smart-enabled home thermostat, or a manufacturing machine, yet these devices connected to the Internet all form a physical infrastructure. Put differently, the devices that constitute the "body" of cyberspace are always changing and of many different forms, thus leading to the dynamic nature of cyberspace.

Thus, we can define cyberspace as a two-dimensional space that is paradoxically abstract, concrete, and evolves over time. Similar to a human, all of cyberspace has a "mind" and a "body," both of which evolves over time. The first dimension, the body, is always changing as a result of humans adding, modifying, updating, or removing technological devices and entities from it. This dimension is a physically connected network of devices of all kinds, analogous to how the human is a connected network of organs. The second dimension of cyberspace, the mind, is the collection of information, organized concepts, and general processes that manipulate, generate, or remove information that is stored and transmitted throughout the "body" of cyberspace. Both of these dimensions change over time.

They also consistently interact with each other, similar to how the mind and body of the human interact. The first dimension could change as a result of a change in the second dimension. A human recording a video to "the cloud" is appending an information artifact to cyberspace, but this change to the collective mind of cyberspace results in a physical change to the space, since the information is being recorded and converted to physical symbols representing 0 and 1, with physical electric current transmitted from the web camera, to the local computer's RAM, into packets transmitted via signals over WiFi, subsequently converted into light over fiber optic wires, then converted back to electric and/or radio signal, to eventually be converted back to electrical current to another physical machine, and physically etched into a hard disk or held as an electrical charge in a transistor. Put simply, cyberspace is a generalization of the human mind and body. Humans, machines, and computers interact with the mind and body of cyberspace. Cyberspace is the collective mind and body of digital human society and intelligence.

1.4. The Body of Cyberspace

Now that we have defined cyberspace as a space of two dimensions, we will dive more into each individual dimension. Some of the extant academic work on the matter will help guide us in further clarifying our dimensions. As for the "body" of cyberspace, we defined this more generally as the so-called physical plane that is analogous to the human body. However, it is a generalization of the human body, where the complicated information artifacts that exist and are formed in the collective mind of cyberspace are themselves physically generated, removed, manipulated, or stored, albeit in a highly complex manner and form. Inglis (2016) argues in favor of a framework where multiple physical layers exist in cyberspace. These layers are people, circuits, control logic, and devices.

People are necessary for cyberspace to exist. They are the reason why the environment changes, as well as why information is generated, stored, manipulated, and reported. Then there is a circuit layer, which comprises the physical pathways of communication between people and devices. These include technologies such as network wires and fiber optic cables, as well as the circuitry itself which connects the individual components of a computer. The control logic layer, as they define it, is the layer that dictates how information flows not only between people but also between devices and circuits. It is the controlling mechanism that directs the physical information traffic between devices. Lastly, they argue in favor of a device layer, which "is perhaps the most visible component of cyberspace" (Inglis, 2016, p. 22). This layer comprises the physical devices that generate and report the information, such as mobile phones and computers, as well as more recently the Internet of Things (IoT), such as smart thermostats and production machinery.

Similar frameworks have been proposed that are tangential to the one presented above. Ning *et al.* (2018) argue that cyberspace is an amalgamation of three separate spaces: physical, social, and thinking. Their description of the physical space conveys the idea that human communication can be achieved not only by connecting computers to each other, but also a diverse collection of devices. Lambach (2019) suggests that cyberspace is also a collection of hardware that enable the exchange of data over electronic networks. Likewise, it has been suggested that the physical layer of digitalized information, represented by computer codes, and transmitted over networks of computers, enable people to interact with "cyberspace" (Vieira and Ferasso, 2010). Thus, the body of cyberspace can be conceptualized as the collection of people and devices who have a need to generate, manipulate, remove, or obtain information by way of specific and physical forms of logical control, connected to each other via some form of modern technology, be it electrical, optical, or some other physical means.

1.5. The Mind of Cyberspace

Just as the human has a mind, we have argued so too does cyberspace. This is the so-called "hallucination," as Gibson (2000) describes. We have physical representations of information in highly complex forms such as binary-based information. However, the information itself is conceived in the minds of humans. The "mind" of cyberspace is thus the collection of information artifacts, in human-readable represented form, that constitutes a general body of knowledge as well as a collection of behaviors that are the cause for the creation, manipulation, deletion, and curation of the information. The general mind of cyberspace can be categorized into one of two categories, as our definition here implies: knowledge and behavior.

The first is the collection of concepts and knowledge in cyberspace itself. These are the various human ontologies of knowledge such as mathematics, science, social constructs, business, politics, sports, etc. They are the sum total of not only the knowledge of a single human, but all humans connected to cyberspace. The second category of information is the behavior itself that interacts with this information. These are the processes and procedures that enable the curation, generation, manipulation, and removal of information. Extant literature has suggested that what we refer to as the "mind" of cyberspace comprises information ontologies and processes. For example, Ning *et al.* (2018) suggest that cyberspace comprises a social and "thinking" dimension, respectively. Likewise, Bauwens (1994, p. 42) suggests that one of the levels of cyberspace is the "mental map that we have of the information landscape when we are using our computers to find information or to communicate with others." Likewise, it has been characterized as the "3-D cyberspacial environment which humans can 'enter' and 'move through', interacting with both the computer and other human beings" (Bryant, 2001, p. 139). In a similar framework to ours, Woolley (2006) suggests that cyberspace lies in three domains: physical, information, and cognitive.

Thus, the "mind" of cyberspace is analogous to that of a human, namely that it comprises knowledge and behaviors. While we have sought to model cyberspace after that of the human body and mind, we will reserve a philosophical discussion on the ability of cyberspace to so-called "think" for itself. Such an intellectual inquiry, while interesting and necessary for philosophers, is far outside the scope of this discussion. However, regardless of whether or not the mind is separate from the body or one and the same, we argue that the distinction provided by the analogy to human psychology is a useful one for characterizing what many refer to as "cyberspace."

1.6. Conclusion

So to put it simply, cyberspace is a two-dimensional space, consisting of a body space, which is itself the physical infrastructure that enables the physical representation of information, and a mind space, which is itself the organization and existence of concepts and various behaviors (i.e. processes) in an abstract conceptual representation. The body space is meaningless without the mind space, and vice versa. What good is it to speak of a "cyberspace" that is merely just physical computers and network wires with no organized information stored on that infrastructure? Likewise, the mind space exists primarily due to the existence of the body space. The mind space of cyberspace is the collection of all information curated, created, and recorded.

So why is this distinction important? Understanding cyberspace as a combination of a body and mind space allow us academics to more easily identify not only what should be secured but also how to secure it, and whether or not it should be secured in the first place. This distinction also raises other interesting questions that should be addressed. For example, if cyberspace has a body and a mind, does anyone own this body or mind? Or, more appropriately, who owns which portions of the body and of the mind space? Understanding the body space as a physical space and the mind space as an abstract space also aids in our ability to construct the processes that will enable the security of cyberspace.

References

Bauwens, M. (1994). What is cyberspace? *Computers in Libraries*, **14**, 42–48.

Benford, G. (2011). Future tense: Catch me if you can. *Communications of the ACM*, **54**, 112–111.

Bridis, T. (1998). Internet reconfiguration turns out to be rogue. *The Daily News*, 2B.

Bryant, R. (2001). What kind of space is cyberspace. *Minerva-An Internet Journal of Philosophy*, **5**, 138–155.

Dressler, J. (2007). United States v. Morris. *Cases and Materials on Criminal Law*.

Gibson, W. (2000). *Neuromancer* (New York, New York: Penguin Publishing Group).

Gibson, W. (2014). *Burning Chrome* (Harper Voyager: HarperCollins).

Inglis, C. (2016). Cyberspace — making some sense of it all. *Journal of Information Warfare*, **15**, 17–26.

Lambach, D. (2019). The territorialization of cyberspace. *International Studies Review*, **22**, 482–506.

Mello, S. M. (1993). Administering the antidote to computer viruses: A comment on United States v. Morris. *Rutgers Computer & Technology Law Journal*, **19**, 259.

Metcalf, J. (2014). Core war: Creeper & reaper. Available at: https://corewar.co.uk/creeper.htm (Last Accessed Feb 12, 2021).

Mueller, M. (2017). Is cybersecurity eating internet governance? Causes and consequences of alternative framings. *Digital Policy, Regulation and Governance*, **19**, 415–428.

Ning, H., Ye, X., Bouras, M. A., Wei, D. & Daneshmand, M. (2018). General cyberspace: Cyberspace and cyber-enabled spaces. *IEEE Internet of Things Journal*, **5**, 1843–1856.

Pilarski, G. (2020). Cyberspace as a tool of contemporary propaganda. *Safety & Defense*, **6**, 95–108.

Ryle, G. (2009). *The Concept of Mind* (New York, NY: Routledge).

Singer, P. W. and Friedman, A. (2014). *Cybersecurity: What Everyone Needs to Know* (USA: Oxford University Press).

Taylor, R. (1963). *Metaphysics* (New York, NY: Taylor and Francis).

Theohary, C. A. (2020). Defense primer: Cyberspace operations. Congressional Research Service. Available at: https://fas.org/sgp/crs/natsec/IF10537.pdf (Accessed Feb 12, 2021).

Vieira, L. M. M. & Ferasso, M. (2010). The rhizomatic structure of cyberspace: Virtuality and its possibilities. *International Journal of Networking and Virtual Organisations*, **7**, 549–559.

Von Neuman, J., *et al.* (1966). Theory of self-reproducing automata.

Woolley, P. L. (2006). Defining Cyberspace as a United States Air Force Mission. Technical Report, Wright-Patterson AFB School of Engineering, Air Force Institute of Technology, OH, USA.

Chapter 2

Connecting Supply Chain Management to Cybersecurity

Michael Herburger[1,2,4,5,*] and Ayman Omar[3,6]

[1]*Copenhagen Business School, Denmark*
[2]*University of Applied Sciences Upper Austria, Logistikum Steyr, Austria*
[3]*Kogod Cybersecurity Governance Center*
Kogod School of Business, American University, Washington DC, USA
[4]*mihe.om@cbs.dk*
[5]*michael.herburger@fh-steyr.at*
[6]*omar@american.edu*

2.1. Introduction

Over 20 years ago, scholars discussed the seriousness of cyberattacks on supply chains (e.g. Warren and Hutchinson, 2000), yet research on this topic is still rare and at a nascent stage (Ghadge *et al.*, 2019). This topic is important given the fact that cyber risks are ranked as top risks for companies and supply chains and has been a fast-growing trend over the last few years (Riglietti and Aguada, 2018). Almost daily media reports on cyber incidents create awareness and show the criticality of these risks for practitioners, but research across various academic disciplines has not paid much attention on this topic despite its significant implications for supply chains (Davis, 2015; Eling and Wirfs, 2019).

---

*Corresponding author.

Supply chains that continue to expand globally with additional links and partners have increased their vulnerability and exposure (Boone, 2017). Advancements in IT systems and methods of information sharing have facilitated not only growth and expansion of the supply chains but also an increase in cyberthreats, with cyberattackers using advanced techniques that has resulted in increased impact on companies and supply chains (Sokolov *et al.*, 2014). The increased use of IT systems can also add complexity and become a huge challenge for managers (Kunnathur, 2015). Although there is a lack of research in this area, companies realized the significance of such risks and possible negative impacts due to the complexity of their supply chains and have increased their cybersecurity investments. This has been fueled by the changing nature of the global supply chain landscape.

Today's supply chains operate in challenging times with an increased level of complexity, uncertainty, and unpredictability of what might happen in the future, such as catastrophic climate events, pandemics, bankruptcies, terrorist attacks, price fluctuations, or the lack of raw material availability. In the light of current trends related to the digitalization, these vulnerabilities have the potential to become more pronounced in the future. Several scholars have focused on investigating specific supply chain disruptions caused by catastrophic events such as earthquakes, terrorism, or financial crises. However, the theoretical knowledge of supply chain risk management or supply chain resilience has rarely been used to deal with cyber incidents. Although several scholars have addressed specific supply chain risks, their connection with cyber risks is unclear, because cyber risks are different from conventional risks. First, the main difference is the anonymity of cyber risks: they can remain undetectable until they impact business (Renaud *et al.*, 2018). Second, the IT or IT-security department plays a vital role, while they do not have a role in managing other supply chain risks. Third, IT systems have reduced the traditional layers that often were barriers between companies, leading to an increase in the possible ripple effects of an attack to multiple supply chain partners (Nasir *et al.*, 2015). This area of research is currently underdeveloped and needs further exploration (Colicchia *et al.*, 2019; Ghadge *et al.*, 2019).

The contemporary literature from other research areas addressing cyber risk typically focuses on the technical or security perspectives (Gaudenzi and Siciliano, 2017) or just consider single companies (Biener *et al.*, 2015). This focus has led to less attraction to the human elements of these risks, although the human/behavioral parts within cybersecurity are very critical (Ghadge *et al.*, 2019). Several scholars emphasize that there is a lack of research focused on the management of cyber risks explicitly taking a supply chain perspective (Colicchia *et al.*, 2019; Soomro *et al.*, 2016). This is a cross-disciplinary topic by nature where it intersects multiple domains of research (Ivanov and Sokolov, 2012; Davidson and Shankles, 2013). It lies at the intersection of several areas, such as supply chain management, operations management, security, cybersecurity, cryptography, telecommunications, computer science, information systems, and risk analysis (Linton *et al.*, 2014), which gives supply chain management the opportunity to break those silos.

The remainder of this chapter is organized as follows. Section 2.2 defines terms around the phenomenon of "cyber risks" and provides an overview of the relevant literature on cyber risks, their definition, and ways of classifying them. Section 2.3 outlines the implications for supply chains, followed by Section 2.4 showing ways of managing cyberthreats in supply chains. Section 2.5 gives an overview of international standards of cybersecurity that already address supply chains.

2.2. Cyber Risks

Due to the interdisciplinary nature of the underlying phenomenon, it is important to first clarify the definitions of cyber, cyber risks, and related management approaches. In literature, cyber risk and information risks are often used interchangeably (e.g. Kache and Seuring, 2017; Colicchia *et al.*, 2019, Ghadge *et al.* 2019). The computer science literature demonstrates that there is a substantial overlap between information security and cybersecurity, but they are not completely analogous (Von Solms and Van Niekerk, 2013).

The term "cyber" is short for cyberspace, with no agreed official definition, although several definitions can be found in the literature. In the literature, the terms "cyberspace" and "information technology" (IT) has often been used interchangeably (Von Solms and van Niekerk, 2013), or in a related manner (Ward, 2012). One basic definition of cyberspace by Choucri and Goldsmith (2012) describes it as an integration of "complex networks into global internet." Cyberspace is characterized by anonymity, low price of entry, and asymmetries on vulnerability (Nye, 2011). One more detailed and most recent definition of cyberspace is provided by Mayer *et al.* (2014, pp. 1–2):

> Cyberspace is a global and dynamic domain (subject to constant change) characterized by the combined use of electrons and electromagnetic spectrum, whose purpose is to create, store, modify, exchange, share and extract, use, eliminate information and disrupt physical resources.
>
> Cyberspace includes:
>
> a) physical infrastructures and telecommunications devices that allow for the connection of technological and communication system networks, understood in the broadest sense (SCADA devices, smartphones/tablets, computers, servers, etc.);
>
> b) computer systems (see point a) and the related (sometimes embedded) software that guarantee the domain's basic operational functioning and connectivity;
>
> c) networks between computer systems;
>
> d) networks of networks that connect computer systems (the distinction between networks and networks of networks is mainly organizational);
>
> e) the access nodes of users and intermediaries routing nodes;
>
> f) constituent data (or resident data).
>
> Often, in common parlance, and sometimes in commercial language, networks of networks are called internet (with a lowercase i), while networks between computers are called intranet. Internet (with a capital I, in journalistic language sometimes called the Net) can be considered a part of the system a). A distinctive and constitutive feature of cyberspace is that no central entity exercises control over all the networks that make up this new domain.

The term "cyber risk" refers to multiple different sources of risks affecting different assets of a company. Also, for this term, there is no agreed official definition, although several definitions can be found in the literature. Biener *et al.* (2015) define cyber risk as "operational risk to information and technology assets that have consequences affecting the confidentiality, availability or integrity of information or information systems." Mukhopadhyay *et al.* (2005) define this type of risk as "the risk involved with malicious electronic events that cause disruption of business and monetary loss." To our best knowledge, there is yet no publication in supply chain management that clearly defines cyber risk. Some scholars defined similar terms, such as cybercrime (Urciuoli *et al.*, 2013) or cyber events (Boyes, 2015). Ghadge *et al.* (2019) provide multiple definitions of cyber-related supply chain risks, although some of them are just definitions of information risks (e.g. Faisal *et al.*, 2007) or information security (Smith *et al.*, 2007), or IT-security incidents, such as that provided by Deane *et al.* (2009), or operational cybersecurity risks (Cebula and Young, 2010). These examples also reflect the interchangeable and synonymous use of information and cyber risk, although both are similar but not analogous (Von Solms and Van Niekerk, 2013). Because of this synonymous use without clarification, it is also unclear how studies related to supply chain information risks are also applicable for supply chain cyber risks (e.g. Sindhuja, 2014). We define supply chain cyber risks as follows:

Supply chain cyber risks are those events that may lead to a negative outcome(s) that are caused by internal or external vulnerabilities in the cyber environment of supply chains. Possible impacts are on information and operation technology and can cause disruption(s) of business and monetary loss for supply chain partners. These kind of risks can be classified by SC-impact (e.g. dyadic, triadic, n-tier), activity (e.g. criminal or non-criminal), type of attack (e.g. malware, spam, distributed denial of service, ransomware, phishing), and the source (e.g. criminals, individuals, organizations, government).

2.3. Theoretical Frameworks for Cyber Risks

Several scholars have provided a variety of theoretical frameworks for classifying cyber risks. Based on the framework provided by the National Institute for Standards and Technology (NIST), Cebula and Young (2010) posit four categories of actions of people, systems and technology failures, failed internal processes, and external events. Gordon and Ford (2006) use Type I and Type II for classifying cybercrimes. Type I covers phishing, theft, or manipulation of data or services by hacking or the use of viruses. Type II includes cyberstalking and harassment, espionage, online terrorist activities, or blackmailing. Ghadge *et al.* (2019) identify five categories of cyber risks: physical threats, breakdown, indirect attacks, direct attacks, and insider threats. Physical threats include disruptions of tangible physical infrastructure components, such as switches, servers, routers, and other ICT devices, and natural disasters as sources of cyber risks. Breakdown refers to systems or resources breaking down, such as firewalls and landing pages. They differentiate between indirect (denial of services or password sniffing) and direct attacks, such as virus attacks, hacking attacks, and counterfeit products. Their last category of insider threat covers the human effect, such as carelessness, lack of awareness, and intentions or accidents attributed to employees. The same authors also provide a possible classification by using different "points of penetration" as failure points where cyber risks can emerge. The three categories are technical, human, and physical "points of penetration." A third way of classifying cyber risks is according to their propagation zones, which differentiate between the consequences of cyber risks, from focal company, supply chain, and society. NCSC, UK (2016) used un-targeted and targeted attacks as classification for cyber risks. Un-targeted attacks target multiple devices or users includes phishing, ransomware, and scanning, while targeted attacks cover spear phishing, denial of service, and subverting supply chains, as they target single devices or users.

Boyes (2015) differentiates between threats and vulnerabilities that affect the resilience of supply chains in case of cyber incidents. Threats cover hacktivism, corporate espionage, government driven, terrorism, criminal, and nature. Vulnerabilities include accidental or those caused by poor design and/or operation, such as people, process, physical, and technical. On the risk side, he refers to possible impacts on assets, economy, reputation, life/health, environment, and national security.

Nasir *et al.* (2015) differentiate between various departments within an oil supply chain which can be affected by cyberattacks. They identify potential cyberthreats for each department and list potential countermeasures. Warren and Hutchinson (2000) use four different categories of password sniffing/cracking software, spoofing attacks, denial of service attacks, and direct attacks to show potential cyberthreats for supply chains. There are many more theoretical frameworks used in literature for classifying cyber risks, such as Kim *et al.* (2011), Smith *et al.* (2007), and Estay and Khan (2015), to name a few, or Colicchia *et al.* (2019), who differentiate between internal and external sources of cyber and information risks in the supply chain. Internal sources cover current and former employees, while external sources include suppliers/contractors, customers, competitors, foreign nation states, domestic intelligence services, and hackers/hacktivists. Internal sources of risks, such as fraud by employees, are becoming more important and difficult to detect, stop, or prevent (Boyson, 2014). On the other hand, the sources of external cyber risks are hidden in most cases beyond Tier 1 and can have a huge impact on the entire supply chain system.

As this section provided an understanding of the types of risks, Section 2.4. explains the relevance and possible implications of risks for supply chains.

2.4. Implications for Supply Chains

This section provides insights on why it is necessary to broaden the perspective, from the focal company only, to the supply chain. Supply chains have numerous possibilities of targets for incidents caused by cyberthreats. This can result in the records of customers, suppliers, and employees becoming compromised (Riglietti and Aguada, 2018) and sensitive data breaches on processes, products, data flows, governance, and operations (Boyson, 2014). Other cyber risks discussed in the literature on supply chain management are theft of intellectual property, counterfeits, crashing of websites, and the failure of firms' IT infrastructure and networks, leading to unavailability of critical services (Riglietti and Aguada, 2018).

Williams (2014) identifies four different streams of concerns for supply chains. First, the supply chain itself is recognized as a source of vulnerability and risk to the operation of the critical computer systems themselves. These systems could be invisibly infiltrated by a malware lodged deep in silicon that can then control computing devices that everyone in that supply chain depends on. Second, the supply chain could be used by hostile actors, such as criminals and intelligence agencies. An example is the theft from the port of Antwerp by drug traffickers who used cyberattacks to breach IT systems that control the movement of shipping containers (Bateman, 2013). Third is a disrupted supply chain unable to continue the supply of technology-related services or products. Fourth is the infiltration by counterfeits and forgeries of trusted brands products.

Other forms of security compromises include backdoors in software or hardware, allowing a third party to access information that is considered critical and confidential by supply chain members. This is similar to the unintended access to supply chain information by unauthorized third parties (Linton and Boyson, 2014). The challenge in dealing with such a risk in supply chains also includes the ability (or lack of) to accurately assess and identify the source of the risk.

Global supply chains have complex structures which make it challenging to assess the risk of compromised information at every stage of a supply chain. Malicious entities are constantly looking for weak links. Such links may not be on the radar of different supply chain managers focused mainly on operational kind of risks. Cyberattacks on supply chains are the most destructive way to damage many linked entities due to their interdependency (Guerra and Estay, 2018).

Some examples of highly visible cyberattacks with impact on supply chain partners are the cyber breach at the financial services group JPMorgan in 2014, which affected 76 million customers (Caruthers, 2014), the security breach at the retail company Target in 2013 with an estimated 40 million payment cards stolen and upwards of 70 million other personal records compromised (Kirk, 2014), and the data breach at SONY Pictures in 2014 (Lewis, 2014). Recent examples are WannaCry and NotPetya in 2017, which had a huge impact on the car manufacturer Renault, leading to production halts; logistics service provider TNT, with customer complaints coming still months after the attack; and the global leader in the shipping industry, Maersk, which plays major role in global supply chains. The latest example from 2019 is the cyberattack on Norsk Hydro, the world market leader in aluminum production, where a ransomware attack was realized. These are just a few known and documented attacks, while other attacks may be ongoing without the companies being aware of it.

Identifying the weak links and the entity that may be vulnerable to an attack is challenging across all sectors. No industrial sector is immune to cyberattacks. However, some sectors such as financial services, healthcare, high technology, energy, and the public sector, including different government agencies, are especially attractive targets (Nagurney, 2015). In today's networked economy, many businesses are dependent on their globalized supply chains, with their IT infrastructure increasingly spread out and, at the same time, vulnerable to cyberattacks. For example, the 2013 Target data breach occurred when the cyberattacker took advantage of the vulnerability in the remote diagnostics of the HVAC system supplier connected to Target's IT-system and entered a vulnerable supply chain link.

2.5. Ways of Managing Cyber Risks in Supply Chains

Extant literature provides a variety of approaches for managing risks in supply chains. Supply chain risk management (SCRM) and supply chain resilience

(SCRES) are some of these approaches for managing supply chain risk that have risen to prominence in the last decade because of growing turbulence, volatility, and complexity in supply chains. While considering SCRM and SCRES as ways of managing cyber risks, it is important to know that both concepts are fundamentally different (Linkov *et al.*, 2018). Section 2.6. explains the concept of SCRM, followed by Section 2.7 discussing SCRES in the context of supply chain cyber risks.

The aim of SCRM is to develop strategies for identification, assessment, treatment, and monitoring of risks in supply chains (e.g. Manuj and Mentzer, 2008; Tummala and Schoenherr, 2011; Ho *et al.*, 2015). The first phase contains the identification of risks and sources. In this phase, it is important to know the potential points of penetration in the supply chain in order to identify the weak points where these risks are most likely to happen (Smith *et al.*, 2007; Ghadge *et al.*, 2019). These points of penetration can be classified into technical, human, and physical dimensions. The second phase focuses on the assessment of the probability of occurrence and the possible impact of incidents on business. Additionally, the risk propagation model proposed by Ghadge *et al.* (2019) may be used in assessing supply chain cyber risks. They differentiate between primary propagation, with impact only on a focal company; a secondary propagation zone with consequences for the supply chain network; and a third zone with impact on the society. The last two are influenced by cascading or ripple effects. The third phase of SCRM involves the design, selection, and implementation of strategies to manage and mitigate risks. Possible strategies are avoidance, postponement, speculation, hedging, control, sharing/transferring, and security (Manuj and Mentzer, 2008). The fourth phase includes the monitoring of the supply chain and the implementation of metrics and measures for the early detection of potential risk signals.

Based on SCRM, new approaches have been developed, such as cyber supply chain risk management (CSCRM) (Boyson, 2014; Windelberg, 2016, Colicchia *et al.*, 2019) or managing cyber risk in supply chains (Gaudenzi and Siciliano, 2017, 2018; Ghadge *et al.*, 2019; Guerra and Estay, 2018). While the first approach focuses on IT networks, hardware, and software systems, the second approach seems to also include conventional supply chains addressing cyber risks, not only cyber supply chains. The book chapter's authors argue that CSCRM is different from supply chain cyber risk management. The first focuses on cyber supply chains considering all supply chain risks, while the second focuses on supply chains with narrow focus on supply chain cyber risks. There is no agreed official definition of both, although several definitions can be found in the literature, and the existing publications also seem to use the terms interchangeably. Future research could consider this and clarify their research focus.

2.6. Supply Chain Cyber Risk Management

The term cyber supply chain risk management (CSCRM) was introduced by Boyson (2014) and is defined as "the organizational strategy and programmatic activities to assess and mitigate risk across the end-to-end processes (including design, development, production, integration, and deployment) that constitute the supply chains for IT networks, hardware, and software systems." This concept was introduced as an addition to cybersecurity, adding managerial and human factors to the purely technical means of cybersecurity. The author (Boyson, 2014) developed a CSCRM capability model based on three key factors of governance, systems integration, and operations, leading to three maturity phases of emergent, diligent, and proficient. Based on this CSCRM definition, Colicchia *et al.* (2019) explore how firms manage information and cyber risks in their supply chain and the initiatives undertaken.

For managing cyber risks in supply chains, based on their literature review, Guerra and Estay (2018) identified 12 themes with different approaches for managing cyber risks: compliance, situational awareness, governance, pre-event knowledge management, cybersecurity, visibility, velocity, ability to adapt, recovery management, market position and financial strength, post-event knowledge management, and social capital.

The primary focus of CSCRM is on cybersecurity, with security as one of the strategies for mitigating supply chain risks (Manuj and Mentzer, 2008), due to the focus on technical aspects while addressing cyber risks. Cybersecurity is identified as one of the major challenges at the supply chain level in our digital business world and must be considered from a focal firm and supply chain perspective for managing and mitigating cyber risks (Kache and Seuring, 2017). Knowing the difference between information and cybersecurity, the aim of the first is to secure information together with the underlying technology, while second is definitely not to secure cyberspace but rather secure functions in cyberspace, such as individuals, organizations, or nations (Von Solms and Van Niekerk, 2013). To address cyber risks in supply chain, a supply chain cybersecurity system could be used, where IT security system, organizational security system, and supply chain security systems are linked (Ghadge *et al.*, 2019). This becomes challenging when the scope of interest becomes the supply chain as opposed to just one organization.

Making the entire supply chain secure is challenging because of the conflicting interests or priorities of the different supply chain partners. The breadth of supply chains and associated costs renders total security difficult. Based on these budget constraints, Nagurney *et al.* (2017) propose a model of supply chain cybersecurity investment including budget constraints. Attackers expand their techniques continuously, exploring new ways of breaches, making purely technical cybersecurity approaches difficult to keep up with cyber risks (Boyson, 2014). If large firms comply with security standards and use certified hardware and software, most of their supply chain partners (including smaller companies) are still mainly focused on reducing costs. Hence, there is a growing interest in developing rigorous frameworks for cybersecurity investments. According to PWC (2014), mid-sized and large companies reported a 5% increase in cybersecurity budgets, whereas small companies reduced security costs by more than 20%. Whether in retail, financial services, government settings, energy, healthcare, or others, it is essential to recognize that the cybersecurity investments of one member of a supply chain in terms of cybersecurity may impact the probability of a successful cyberattack on another. The IT infrastructure may be shared, suppliers may be common, and the members may have similar vulnerabilities. The need for an effective strategy for cybersecurity investments, given budget constraints, is a very timely problem. 100% cybersecurity is impossible, which means supply chains must also be prepared for inevitable cyber incidents, underlining the need for cyber resilience in supply chains.

2.7. Supply Chain Cyber Resilience

Several studies have discussed Supply Chain Cyber Resilience (SCRES) more broadly. SCRES, in a broad sense, refers to the ability of supply chains to prepare for, respond to, and recover from disruptions (Pettit *et al.*, 2010; Ponomarov and Holcomb, 2009; Sheffi, 2005), ideally leading to a phase of growth in order to emerge as stronger entities (Hohenstein *et al.*, 2015). Based on SCRES, a new approach of cyber resilience have been developed (Khan and Estay, 2015; Jensen, 2015; Urciuoli, 2015) and can be defined as "the capability of a supply chain to maintain its operational performance when faced with cyber-risk" (Khan and Estay, 2015). The same authors also show how new this concept is because they have identified no single publication in SCRES addressing the phenomenon of cyber risks. Unexpected disruptions caused by cyberattacks and the dynamism around it should be managed by taking several steps through a systematic perspective (Estay and Khan, 2015). In the same way, Davis (2015) suggest several steps in order to create a cyber-resilient supply chain.

There are several ways for managing cyber risks in supply chains. For all three approaches, it has to be summarized that the discussion in the literature with special focus on cyber risks are conceptual, hardly empirical, and highly disconnected from the main literature of supply chain risk management, supply chain resilience, and supply chain security, barring a few publications (Colicchia *et al.*, 2019; Ghadge *et al.*, 2019). In addition to the general discussion about cyber risks in supply chains, several standards exist. Section 2.8. highlights some of the standards that are currently used in industry.

2.8. Supply Chain Aspects of IT-security Standards

In addition to the academic literature, there are several standards and industry-based frameworks for managing cyber risks. Table 2.1 gives an overview of how different IT-security standards (COBIT 5, ISA 62443-3-2013, ISO 27001:2013, NIST-SP-800-53 Rev. 4, BSI) have included supply chain aspects by showing the underlying tasks. There are several areas that are usually mentioned in the different frameworks, such as the supply chain risk management elements; the personnel, including sensitization and training; and the detection part. The supply chain risk management area includes several categories that organizations should focus on, such as identifying the priorities and areas of vulnerabilities, establishing a clear process involving the relevant stakeholders, mapping out the critical links, and establishing a dynamic monitoring and audit process. This also includes clear requirements that are communicated to the suppliers as well as a recovery and a response mechanism in place in the event of a successful breach. The sensitization and training areas of the different frameworks focus on the personnel for the focal company as well as those of its critical links in its ecosystem. This is essential for effective supply chain cyber risk management to minimize, and ideally prevent, breaches due to intentional or unintentional insider actions.

Table 2.1:   Supply Chain Aspects of IT-security Standards

Supply chain risk management	• Identify the priorities, limitations, and maximum risks your organization is willing to take in relation to supplier risks.[a, b, d] • Establish clear processes for managing supply chain risks. All stakeholder should review and approve these processes. [a–e] • Identify and prioritize suppliers and service providers of your critical systems, components, and services using the defined processes of the previous mentioned task. [a–e] • Require your suppliers and service providers to take appropriate actions to develop and implement the goals and specifications from the supply chain risk management process. [a–e] • Establish a monitoring system to ensure that all your suppliers and service providers are fulfilling their obligations as specified. Check this on a regular basis using audits or technical tests.[a–e] • Define reaction and recovery processes after cybersecurity incidents with your suppliers and service providers. Test these processes in exercises. [a–e]
Sensitization and training	• Arrange regular training and education on all aspects of cybersecurity for your employees and external partners.[a–e] • Ensure that your employees and external partners carry out their security-related tasks according to the associated specifications and processes. [a–e] • Ensure that all stakeholders outside your company (supply chain partners) are aware of their role and responsibility. [a–e]
Detection process	• Processes and procedures for the detection of cybersecurity incidents are maintained and tested.[a–e] • Communicate detected incidents to appropriate authorities (e.g. supply chain partners). [a–e]

[a]COBIT 5; [b]ISA 62443-3-2013, [c]ISO 27001:2013, [d]NIST-SP-800-53 Rev. 4, [e]BSI.

Finally, the detection part should be constantly evolving to ensure that new threats are detected and that organizations are aware of any successful breaches that have taken place. A quick response to a successful breach may minimize the damages resulting from that breach.

2.9. Conclusion

Managing cyber risks in supply chains is a huge challenge for companies, especially in times where every organization tries to fulfill the wishes for digitalization, Industry 4.0, or Internet of Things. This chapter shows the relevance of cyber risks for supply chains and that there is the need to enlarge the view from a single company's point of view to the supply-chain view. We provide a definition of supply chain cyber risks in order to shed light into the underlying topic as no single agreed definition exists in the literature. We identified the current literature of the underlying topic and show that there are a lot of different research streams with many confusing and different terms and definitions. There is a need for future studies to consider the proper use of different terms, e.g. addressing information and/or cyber risks and not using them just interchangeably. SCRM and SCRES and supply chain security are concepts that help to manage cyber risks in supply chains, but it is yet unclear whether the existing approaches in the literature are also valid for cyber risk, because of the different nature of cyber risks compared to other supply chain risks, as we have shown. In particular, the vital roles of IT and IT-security while addressing supply chain cyber risks are unclear; they have almost no role in managing other supply chain risks. Finally, we show how current available IT-security standards already address supply chain aspects and identify the appropriate managerial and theoretical implications.

References

Bateman, T. (2013). Police warning after drug traffickers' cyber-attack, *BBC News*. 16.10.2013, Available at https://www.bbc.co.uk/programmes/p01jtsgw (Accessed 12 April 2020).

Biener, C., Eling, M. & Wirfs, J. H. (2015). Insurability of cyber risk: An empirical analysis. *The Geneva Papers on Risk and Insurance-Issues and Practice*, **40**(1), 131–158.

Boone, A. (2017). Cyber-security must be a C-suite priority. *Computer Fraud & Security*, **2017**(2), 13–15.

Boyes, H. (2015). Cybersecurity and cyber-resilient supply chains. *Technology Innovation Management Review*, **5**(4), 28.

Boyson, S. (2014). Cyber supply chain risk management: Revolutionizing the strategic control of critical IT systems. *Technovation*, **34**(7), 342–353.

Caruthers, R. (2014). JPMorgan will double cybersecurity spending but many other companies may cut costs. *Fierce Financial IT*, October 14, 2014.

Cebula, J. L. & Young, L. R. (2010). A taxonomy of operational cyber security risks (No. CMU/SEI-2010-TN-028). Software engineering Institute, Carnegie-Mellon University, Pittsburgh, PA, USA.

Colicchia, C., Creazza, A. & Menachof, D. A. (2019). Managing cyber and information risks in supply chains: Insights from an exploratory analysis. *Supply Chain Management: An International Journal*, **24**(2), 215–240.

Choucri, N. & Goldsmith, D. (2012). Lost in cyberspace: Harnessing the Internet, international relations, and global security. *Bulletin of the Atomic Scientists*, **68**(2), 70–77.

Davidson, D. & Shankles, S. (2013). We cannot blindly reap the benefits of a globalized ICT supply chain! Chief Information Officer, Department of Defense, Washington DC, USA.

Davis, A. (2015). Building cyber-resilience into supply chains. *Technology Innovation Management Review*, **5**(4), 19–27.

Deane, J. K., Ragsdale, C. T., Rakes, T. R. & Rees, L. P. (2009). Managing supply chain risk and disruption from IT security incidents. *Operations Management Research*, **2**(1–4), 4.

Eling, M. & Wirfs, J. (2019). What are the actual costs of cyber risk events? *European Journal of Operational Research*, **272**(3), 1109–1119.

Estay, D. A. S. & Khan, O. (2015). Extending supply chain risk and resilience frameworks to manage cyber risk. *22nd EurOMA Conference: Operations Management for Sustainable Competitiveness*. 28.06.2015, Neuchâtel, Switzerland.

Faisal, M. N., Banwet, D. K. & Shankar, R. (2007). Information risks management in supply chains: An assessment and mitigation framework. *Journal of Enterprise Information Management*, **20**(6), 677–699.

Gaudenzi, B. & Siciliano, G. (2017). Just do it: Managing IT and cyber risks to protect the value creation. *Journal of Promotion Management*, **23**(3), 372–385.

Gaudenzi, B. & Siciliano, G. (2018). Managing IT and cyber risks in supply chains. In *Supply Chain Risk Management* (Singapore: Springer), pp. 85–96.

Ghadge, A., Caldwell, N. & Wilding, R. (2019). Managing cyber risk in supply chains: A review and research agenda. *Supply Chain Management: An International Journal*, **25**(2), 223–240.

Gordon, S. & Ford, R. (2006). On the definition and classification of cybercrime. *Journal in Computer Virology*, **2**(1), 13–20.

Guerra, P. J. & Estay, D. S. (2018). An impact-wave analogy for managing cyber risks in supply chains. *2018 IEEE International Conference on Industrial Engineering and Engineering Management (IEEM)*, pp. 61–65.

Ho, W., Zheng, T., Yildiz, H. & Talluri, S. (2015). Supply chain risk management: A literature review. *International Journal of Production Research*, **53**(16), 5031–5069.

Hohenstein, N. O., Feisel, E., Hartmann, E. & Giunipero, L. (2015). Research on the phenomenon of supply chain resilience: A systematic review and paths for further investigation. *International Journal of Physical Distribution & Logistics Management*, **45**(1/2), 90–117.

Ivanov, D. & Sokolov, B. (2012). The inter-disciplinary modelling of supply chains in the context of collaborative multi-structural cyber-physical networks. *Journal of Manufacturing Technology Management*, **23**(8), 976–997.

Jensen, L. (2015). Challenges in maritime cyber-resilience. *Technology Innovation Management Review*, **5**(4), 35.

Kache, F. & Seuring, S. (2017). Challenges and opportunities of digital information at the intersection of Big Data Analytics and supply chain management. *International Journal of Operations & Production Management*, **37**(1), 10–36.

Khan, O. & Estay, D. A. S. (2015). Supply chain cyber-resilience: Creating an agenda for future research. *Technology Innovation Management Review*, April, 6–12.

Kim, W., Jeong, O. R., Kim, C. & So, J. (2011). The dark side of the Internet: Attacks, costs and responses. *Information Systems*, **36**(3), 675–705.

Kirk, J. (2014). Home Depot says attackers stole a vendor's credentials to break in. *PCWorld*, 6 November. Available at: http://www.pcworld.com/article/2844832/home-depot-says-attackers-stole-a-vendors-credentials-to-break-in.html (Accessed 28 November 2019).

Kunnathur, A. S. (2015). Information security in supply chains: A management control perspective. *Information & Computer Security*, **23**(5), 476–496.

Lewis, D. (2014). Sony Pictures data breach and the PR Nightmare. *Forbes*, December 16.

Linkov, I., Trump, B. D. & Keisler, J. (2018). Risk and resilience must be independently managed. *Nature*, **555**, 7694.

Linton, J. D., Boyson, S. & Aje, J. (2014). The challenge of cyber supply chain security to research and practice–An introduction. *Technovation*, **34**(7), 339–341.

Manuj, I. & Mentzer, J. T. (2008). Global supply chain risk management strategies. *International Journal of Physical Distribution & Logistics Management*, **38**(3), 192–223.

Mayer, M., Martino, L., Mazurier, P. & Tzvetkova, G. (2014). How would you define cyberspace. *First Draft Pisa*, 19 May.

Mukhopadhyay, A., Saha, D., Chakrabarti, B. B., Mahanti, A. & Podder, A. (2005). Insurance for cyber-risk: A utility model. *Decision*, **32**(1), 153–169.

Nagurney, A. (2015). A multiproduct network economic model of cybercrime in financial services. *Service Science*, **7**(1), 70–81.

Nagurney, A., Daniele, P. & Shukla, S. (2017). A supply chain network game theory model of cybersecurity investments with nonlinear budget constraints. *Annals of Operations Research*, **248**(1–2), 405–427.

Nasir, M. A., Sultan, S., Nefti-Meziani, S. & Manzoor, U. (2015). Potential cyber-attacks against global oil supply chain. *2015 International Conference on Cyber Situational Awareness, Data Analytics and Assessment (CyberSA)*, June, pp. 1–7.

National Cyber Security Centre, UK (2016). Common cyber attacks: Reducing the impact. Available at https://www.ncsc.gov.uk/files/common_cyber_attacks_ncsc.pdf (Accessed 12 April 2020).

Nye Jr, J. S. (2011). *Nuclear Lessons for Cyber Security* (Montgomery, AL: Air University Press, Maxwell AFB).

Pettit, T. J., Fiksel, J. & Croxton, K. L. (2010). Ensuring supply chain resilience: Development of a conceptual framework. *Journal of Business Logistics*, **31**(1), 1–21.

Ponomarov, S. Y. & Holcomb, M. C. (2009). Understanding the concept of supply chain resilience. *The International Journal of Logistics Management*, **20**(1), 124–143.

PwC (2014). Managing cyber risks in an interconnected world. https://www.pwc.com/gx/en/consulting-services/information-security-survey/assets/the-global-state-of-information-security-survey-2015.pdf (Accessed 12 April 2020).

Renaud, K., Flowerday, S., Warkentin, M., Cockshott, P. & Orgeron, C. (2018). Is the responsibilization of the cyber security risk reasonable and judicious? *Computers & Security*, **78**, 198–211.

Riglietti, G. & Aguada, L. (2018). BCI Supply Chain Resilience Report 2018.

Sheffi, Y. (2005). *The Resilient Enterprise: Overcoming Vulnerability for Competitive Advantage* (Boston, MA: MIT Press).

Sindhuja, P. N. (2014). Impact of information security initiatives on supply chain performance. *Information Management & Computer Security*, **22**(5), 450–473.

Smith, G. E., Watson, K. J., Baker, W. H. & Pokorski Ii, J. A. (2007). A critical balance: Collaboration and security in the IT-enabled supply chain. *International Journal of Production Research*, **45**(11), 2595–2613.

Sokolov, A., Mesropyan, V. & Chulok, A. (2014). Supply chain cyber security: A Russian outlook. *Technovation*, **34**(7), 389–391.

Soomro, Z. A., Shah, M. H. & Ahmed, J. (2016). Information security management needs more holistic approach: A literature review. *International Journal of Information Management*, **36**(2), 215–225.

Tummala, R. & Schoenherr, T. (2011). Assessing and managing risks using the supply chain risk management process (SCRMP). *Supply Chain Management: An International Journal*, **16**(6), 474–483.

Urciuoli, L., Männistö, T., Hintsa, J. & Khan, T. (2013). Supply chain cyber security—potential threats. *Information & Security: An International Journal*, **29**(1), 51–68.

Urciuoli, L. (2015). Cyber-resilience: A strategic approach for supply chain management. *Technology Innovation Management Review*, **5**(4), 13–18.

Von Solms, R. & Van Niekerk, J. (2013). From information security to cyber security. *Computers & Security*, **38**, 97–102.

Ward, J. M. (2012). Information systems strategy: Quo vadis? *The Journal of Strategic Information Systems*, **21**(2), 165–171.

Warren, M. & Hutchinson, W. (2000). Cyber attacks against supply chain management systems: A short note. *International Journal of Physical Distribution & Logistics Management*, **30**(7/8), 710–716.

Williams, C. (2014). Security in the cyber supply chain: Is it achievable in a complex, interconnected world? *Technovation*, **34**(7), 382–384.

Windelberg, M. (2016). Objectives for managing cyber supply chain risk. *International Journal of Critical Infrastructure Protection*, **12**, 4–11.

https://doi.org/10.1142/9789811233128_0003

CHAPTER 3

Cyber Hygiene Leadership in Organizations

Kip Boyle

Chief Information Security Officer
Cyber Risk Opportunities LLC

3.1. NotPetya

In the spring and summer of 2017, a piece of malicious code, eventually named NotPetya, stormed across Europe (Nash *et al.*, 2018). It caused over US$10 billion in total damage to global law firm DLA Piper, pharmaceutical manufacturer Merck, small package delivery company FedEx, the shipping giant Mærsk, and hundreds of other organizations all over the world. In addition, it caused even more damage to the supply chains of thousands of other companies who could not send, receive, or track their shipments for weeks.

At first, it looked like NotPetya was a type of ransomware. However, evidence now suggests that NotPetya was in fact a weapon of state-sponsored cyber warfare whose goal was to delete all the data on the computers it accessed (Greenberg, 2018). The attack was designed around a flaw in Microsoft Windows that was discovered and weaponized by the NSA into an exploit called "Eternal Blue." The attack was released when a compromised update to M.E. Doc — a Ukrainian tax preparation program — was automatically distributed to all its users (Greenberg, 2018). In other words, it was *a software supply chain attack* that was ushered right through the network firewalls of all its victims. However, the exploit code was so virulent that it quickly spread beyond the Ukrainian borders and across Europe. DLA Piper,

Merck, FedEx, and Mærsk were not the intended targets, yet they suffered tremendous collateral damage during this cyber battle (Nash *et al.*, 2018). Know who was hit but was not hurt badly? DHL, the small package delivery competitor to FedEx (*Reuters*, 2017). In fact, DHL has thrived in the wake of NotPetya because they took in customers who defected from FedEx. Without running a special promotion, but just by staying in business when others could not, DHL showed that good cybersecurity can provide a competitive advantage even when one is not a direct target of a supply chain cyberattack.

3.2. Company-wide Risks of Cybersecurity in Supply Chain

Increasingly, cyber risk materializing in supply chains has brought about disastrous results for organizations of all sizes around the world. Disk-wiper worms like NotPetya and ransomware like WannaCry have already paralyzed operations and caused reputation-ruining data breaches to hundreds of organizations. In addition, privacy violations due to cyber supply chain failures will continue to result in large fines, penalties, and other regulatory sanctions.

Often, when they materialize, these cyber risks result in massive financial losses, sometimes bankrupting organizations when the costs of recovery become out of reach. As a result, executives need to manage cyber risks as thoughtfully and intelligently as other major business risks, such as those to sales, order fulfillment, and accounts receivable.

3.3. Germ Theory

In spite of the possibly paralyzing effects of cyberattacks on organizations, executives sometimes struggle to take cyber risks seriously, probably because they cannot easily see or touch their digital assets or visualize the risks. However, there is something else that we cannot see, that is very risky to us, and we take very seriously: germs!

In fact, the idea of germs is very new to humans. It is only been about 200 years since we started believing that something so small and invisible makes us sick. In response, we have adopted some regular habits of good hygiene: to protect ourselves from germs, we wash our hands; go to the dentist twice a year for a check-up; get our annual flu shot; and, thanks to COVID-19, we practice social distancing. We even take precautions to protect other people from our germs, such as covering our mouths when coughing, wearing a face mask when we are sick, and wearing gloves when making food.

It is stunning that cyber risks so often approach us invisibly and strike without warning like germs do. So, let us borrow from our 200-year-old, anti-germ playbook and find ways to neutralize or avoid the "digital cooties." Let us call it "practicing good cyber hygiene."

We will explore many good cyber hygiene practices later in this chapter, such as faithfully using an attack-resistant password manager every day; installing security updates on computers to protect oneself and others; performing reliable data backups; and conducting an annual risk assessment. We will also tackle how to effectively spread good cyber hygiene practices across an organization.

3.4. Supply Chain Cyber Risk is a Third-Party Risk

NotPetya was an example of a software supply chain failure. There are other types of cyber risks when acquiring technological supplies. Vendor software updates are an ideal way for attackers to deliver malware to systems after they are sold, because customers trust vendor updates, especially if they are signed with a vendor's legitimate digital certificate.

In contrast, supply chain attacks can also focus on malicious implants added to hardware or software during manufacturing. In October 2006, McDonald's and Coca-Cola did a promotion in Japan. They gave away 10,000 USB-stick MP3 players. Each music player was loaded with 10 free songs. However, each player also had one free virus, the QQPass Trojan. Upon plugging it into a computer, it started logging the person's keystrokes, collecting passwords, gathering personal data, and sending it all over the Internet back to the criminals (Marke, 2016).

Let us see a more recent example of malicious implants added to during manufacturing involving ASUS.

3.5. ASUS Supply Chain Attack

In January 2019, Kaspersky Labs, the anti-malware company, discovered that cyberattackers had broken into the servers that belong to ASUS, the large Taiwanese computer maker (Kaspersky, 2019). ASUS makes desktop computers, laptops, mobile phones, smart home systems, and other electronics (ASUS, 2019). They are the fifth largest computer maker in the world (Gartner, 2018).

Reminiscent of NotPetya, it was a two-pronged attack:

(1) First, once inside, the attackers silently broke into the ASUS developer tools and injected malicious code into digitally signed code.
(2) Then, the attackers pushed out a malicious software update tool signed with a legitimate digital certificate to thousands of ASUS customers, affecting up to a million computers.

This went on for at least five months in 2018. The fake update tool created a secret backdoor into the systems that received it.

Kaspersky Lab, which discovered the attack, calls it "Operation ShadowHammer." It estimated that around 500,000 people received this update. However, the cyberattackers were only targeting 600 of them (Securelist, 2019).

Why the name ShadowHammer? The idea behind the name is that silently releasing malicious code that hits tens of thousands of targets when the targets are only a few is really going after something small with a big hammer. This was an incredibly well-planned and well-executed attack that relied on compromising a trusted channel: ASUS's product update system.

In one way this was unlike NotPetya: the attackers wanted to get into a very specific list of computers and they already knew in advance the hard-coded address of each Ethernet card, which is more evidence this was a targeted attack. It also means other ASUS computers could have been compromised to reveal the sales records of the targets. Where else would that list of 600 hardware addresses come from?

The issue highlights the growing threat from so-called supply chain attacks, where malicious software or components get installed on systems as they are manufactured or assembled, or afterward via trusted vendor channels.

3.6. Compromising Technology Services

A managed service provider (MSP) is a company that remotely manages a customer's IT infrastructure and/or end-user systems, typically on a proactive basis and under a subscription model.

Why are IT service companies targeted for cyberattack? To the attackers, an MSP is seen as the weak link in a supply chain to get to their targets.

After all, the MSP is a single point of attack, and therefore a single point of failure, for all their customers. A single exploited MSP can open a number of simultaneous paths to illicit profits.

How long has this been going on? At least since 2009, when the Advanced Persistent Threat 10 Group (APT10) was first discovered and tracked by US law enforcement. It turns out that APT10 is actually a team in the Chinese Ministry of State Security. And, in 2018, the US DOJ indicted two members by name (FBI, 2018).

So, what do the cyberattackers specifically want? Well, a group like APT10 wants intellectual property to give Chinese companies greater economic advantage. "Made in China 2025" is a strategic plan of China to move away from being the world's "factory" and produce higher value products and services (Crawford, 2019).

Here is a walkthrough of a typical attack by APT10 as part of "Operation Cloud Hopper," a campaign against MSPs designed to steal intellectual property.

(1) The initial MSP compromise is usually through a spear phishing campaign.
(2) Once inside, APT10 silently but rapidly deploys malware to establish a foothold and sustained access to a victim's network.
(3) APT10 uses credential (user ID and password) theft tools such as mimikatz or PWDump against the MSP's authentication servers.
(4) APT10 also installs malware on low-profile systems to avoid the attention of system administrators to ensure persistent remote access.
(5) This attack pattern can also lead to deployment of ransomware to all of the customers of the MSP.

The North Korean "Lazarus Group" is known to extort its victims by using ransomware to raise hard currency to fund its nuclear weapons program. They are the primary suspect behind the 2017 WannaCry ransomware attack, which caused billions of dollars in direct damage (U.S. Department of the Treasury, 2020).

Beyond state-sponsored cyberattacks, the increase in MSP attacks is being driven in part by "affiliates" under the ransomware-as-a-service model. Here is how it works: sophisticated cyber criminals create an easy-to-use system where, if someone can sign up for Netflix, they can custom create and release their own ransomware, all for a 30% share of every ransomware payment collected to the service owners.

For example, on July 3, 2019, employees at Arbor Dental in Longview, Washington, could not view X-rays on their computers. Arbor was one of dozens of dental clinics in Oregon and Washington that was just hit by a ransomware attack that disrupted their business and blocked access to patients' records (Dudley, 2019). However, the cyberattackers did not target the clinics directly. Instead, they conducted a cyberattack on Portland-based PM Consultants, which handled the dentists' software updates, firewalls, and data backups. Arbor's frantic calls to their MSP went to voicemail, said Whitney Joy, the clinic's office coordinator.

> "The second it happened, they ghosted everybody," she said. "They didn't give us a heads up."

A week later, the MSP sent this email to its customers:

> Due to the size and scale of the attack, we are not optimistic about the chances for a full or timely recovery...

> At this time we must recommend you seek outside technical assistance with the recovery of your data...

Then, on July 22, the MSP notified customers by email that it was shutting down, "in part due to this devastating event." The contact phone number listed on the MSP website has been disconnected, and firm management did not respond to messages left on their cellphones (Dudley, 2019).

3.7. Compromising Legal Services

Conducting cyberattacks on law firms is conceptually identical to the attractiveness of the MSP as a target of cyberattack. As with the MSP, a law firm is seen as the weak link in a supply chain to get access to the sensitive data of their targets. The law firm is a single point of attack, and therefore a single point of failure, for all their clients. And, unlike the more technologically sophisticated MSP, law firms are generally laggards in the adoption and management of information technology.

According to the *Wall Street Journal*, in spring of 2016, a cyberattacker had successfully stolen the files of some of 48 of the most notable law firms in the US as part of an attempted insider-trading scheme (Hong and Sidel, 2016).

Further investigative reporting by other members of the media showed that two of the firms involved were Cravath, Swaine & Moore and Weil Gotshal & Manges. The cyberattackers used the information to make more than US$4 million of stock market profits (Raymond, 2016) based on confidential information on upcoming company mergers (Hong and Sidel, 2016).

3.8. Compromising Cloud Computing

People do not always recognize cloud computing in their lives, but there are many examples, such as these:

- Microsoft Office 365
- Google G-Suite
- Amazon Web Services (AWS)
- Slack
- Zoom
- WebEx
- ShareFile
- Dropbox
- Salesforce
- Tableau

Despite the well-designed marketing campaigns of cloud computing providers, the bottom line for buyers is that they are putting their sensitive data on someone else's computers. What most buyers fail to fully appreciate is the cloud providers are not obligated to do all the cybersecurity work required to keep the data safe. Worse still, many systems administrators lower the default permissions in order to ease the administrative burden of arranging initial and ongoing access for dozens or hundreds of co-workers.

Here is an example of the kind of failures that come from cloud customers who do not understand their responsibilities. Amazon has a cloud offering called S3: Simple Storage Service. S3 has more than 2 trillion objects stored inside and it is growing (Barr, 2013).

In June 2017, the personal data of 198 million American voters was publicly exposed. A firm called Deep Root Analytics stored voter personal information and voting pattern data on an S3 server but configured it with no access restrictions (O'Sullivan, 2017). In other words, anyone on the Internet who knew the data was there could look at any record. And, cyber criminals use automation to search 24/7 for unsecure data in the cloud.

In another case, on December 14, 2019, security researcher Bob Diachenko found over 267 million Facebook user records freely available to anyone on the Internet. The unprotected database, which had been created by an outside IT service provider hired by Facebook, was left open to the world for nearly two weeks. During that time, the names, phone numbers, and Facebook user IDs were exposed to anyone who thought to look for them (Webb, 2019).

Under one California Consumer Privacy Act (CCPA) formula for penalizing violators, that could be a US$200 billion fine. Here is how that might be calculated:

- A member of the California Plaintiffs Bar would bring a lawsuit against Facebook, as permitted by the CCPA.
- If they were successful, then the penalty applied could be US$750 for each of the breached PI records.
- The math looks like this: 267,000,000 × US$750 = US$200,250,000,000.

Effectively, a fine this large would be a corporate death sentence. That is probably not the fine that would be paid, of course, but it would give the regulators a powerful position over the future of the business.

3.9. Managing the Cybersecurity of a Supply Chain

Given the above common cyber risks in everyone's supply chains, what follows is a survey of the actions executives should take to reduce these risks down to an acceptable level.

3.9.1. *Cyber liability insurance policy*

In 2017, the Erie County Medical Center suffered a massive cyber-attack that took down more than 6,000 computers (Davis, 2017) and cost nearly US$10 million[1] to recover from. The attack forced the medical center back to the days of paper charts and face-to-face

---

[1] Source — https://buffalonews.com/business/local/ecmc-spent-nearly-10-million-recovering-from-massive-cyberattack/article_1786edc7-214e-5c48-84c5-8823a2a38e91.html

meetings for weeks. Luckily, they had increased their cyber insurance coverage the previous year from $2 million to $10 million, which saved their finances.

The financial impact of a cyberattack through an organization's supply chain could overwhelm it, so one should consider transferring some of the risk to an insurance company. According to a recent study of actual insurance claims, the overall average total breach cost was US$394,000 (NetDiligence, 2017, p. 2).

Of that total amount, Legal Defense averaged US$121,000 (NetDiligence, 2017, p. 46), and the payout for Crisis Management Services was US$249,000 (NetDiligence, 2017, p. 6). However, the average claim for a large company was US$3.2 million (NetDiligence, 2017, p. 22). Therefore, the larger an organization, the more a breach will probably cost.

There are currently two major strategies to use cyber insurance. The first one is to get just the financial coverage needed, at the least possible premium cost. This is ideal for companies who can and will handle cyber failures on their own.

The second strategy is to get the financial coverage and use advanced policy features to augment a cyber incident Respond and Recover capabilities. With this strategy, the insurance company will provide, typically on-demand, with pre-selected vendors, and at no additional charge, services such as:

- Digital forensics
- Crisis communications
- Legal defense
- Data breach notification

The organization can also get access to a data breach coach, usually a lawyer, who will expertly guide through the entire process.

So, how does one buy a cyber insurance policy? Today, the market is non-standard, which makes it difficult to understand the coverage being offered so one can compare quotes. It is important to find a good broker who has deep, current experience in cyber insurance. The broker will make sure the organization gets all the right coverages, while watching for exclusions.

The financial coverages fall into two major areas.

(1) First-party costs, which include items such as:
  • Digital forensics
  • Legal advice
  • Customer notification
  • Purchasing credit monitoring services
  • Public relations
  • Business interruption
(2) Third-party costs, which include items such as:
  • Settlements, damages, and judgments
  • Liability to banks for reissuing credit cards
  • Cost of responding to regulatory inquiries
  • Regulatory fines and penalties

Exclusions or missing coverages can be costly. For example, P.F. Chang's Chinese Bistro received a bill from Bank of America for the US$1.9 million in credit card reissuing costs from Chang's 2014 credit card breach. The restaurant had paid a US$134,052 premium for a Chubb cyber policy. So, Chang's filed a claim. However, the claim was denied because the costs fell outside the policy's coverage. In 2016, a lawsuit filed by the restaurant against Chubb failed and the denial was upheld (Greenwald, 2016).

3.9.2. *Implement NIST cybersecurity framework*

The above examples (along with coverage in the daily newspaper) have shown that cyberthreats have never been greater and will continue to increase for years to come. Recognizing this "new normal," the US government advised that putting the majority of our resources into prevention is no longer a viable strategy. Instead, we need to practice "reasonable cybersecurity."

The Federal Trade Commission (FTC, 2015) advises that an organization must practice "reasonable security measures" as compared to:

• An entity of similar size and sophistication and
• Given the type, amount, and methods of data collected.

Do otherwise and the FTC may charge the organization with unfair or deceptive acts. Now, following this definition, the FTC will compare the cybersecurity of a small pizza joint, not to that of a bank, but to other restaurants of its size.

To further define "reasonable," the FTC points to the NIST Cybersecurity Framework, which at a high level says an organization needs to:

- **Identify** its digital assets and cyber risks,
- **Protect** its digital assets from incidents,
- **Detect** incidents promptly,
- Quickly **Respond** to incidents,
- And, effectively **Recover** from incidents.

Now, let us look at two examples where the FTC charged organizations with having unreasonable cybersecurity. The first example relates to the Protect function:

> Twitter had given almost all of its employees administrative control over its core system. And, the FTC charged that by providing administrative access to so many employees, Twitter increased the risk that a compromise of any one of its employees' credentials could result in a serious breach (Arias, 2016).

The second example relates to the Respond function:

> In its case against Wyndham Worldwide Corporation, the FTC said the company failed to follow proper incident response procedures. As a result, intruders were able to gain access to the company's computer network on three separate occasions over a 21-month period. These cyber-attacks lead to the compromise of more than 619,000 payment card account numbers and $10.6 million in fraud (Arias, 2016).

By the way, typical FTC consequences for unreasonable cybersecurity includes:

- Orders to correct illegal practices,
- Plus 20 years of close oversight of their cybersecurity program,
- And, $40,000 fines for each new violation.

3.9.3. *Attorney–client privilege*

Before moving on, let us see how attorney–client privilege (ACP) can be useful when establishing a reasonable cybersecurity program. This is not legal advice, but rather the author's interpretation of how this works.

Let us say an organization actively manage its top five risks and accept the other risks for now. However, two months later, the sixth risk materializes and causes lots of damage. Without ACP, the organization's cyber risk records are subject to "discovery" in a lawsuit, and could be used to try and prove the organization was negligent.

However, with ACP, the cyber risk records are generally NOT subject to "discovery." However, if there is a great story to tell, some or all of the records may be revealed to strengthen the case. It is advised to consult a company attorney for specific guidance on establishing ACP for an organization's cyber risk management work.

3.9.4. Supply chain risk management (ID.SC) activity

Inside the NIST Cybersecurity Framework, one should pay particular attention to the Supply Chain Risk Management (ID.SC) activity, which asks:

How well has our organization established and implemented processes to identify, assess, and manage supply chain cybersecurity risks?

What this means is that all the vendors who play a large role delivering results to customers must be actively included in an organization's cyber risk management activities.

Here are the five detailed questions that make up this activity, which can be used as a guide for setting up an own program:

- ID.SC-1: How well does your organization identify, establish, assess, and manage cyber supply chain risk management processes?
- ID.SC-2: How well does your organization identify, prioritize, and assess suppliers of information systems, components, and services?
- ID.SC-3: How well does your organization implement contracts with suppliers and outside partners to meet the objectives of your organization's cybersecurity objectives?
- ID.SC-4: How well does your organization routinely assess suppliers and third-party partners to confirm they are meeting their contractual obligations?
- ID.SC-5: How well does your organization conduct response and recovery planning and testing with suppliers and third-party providers?

3.9.5. Implement third-party cyber risk management

When regularly transferring sensitive data to a service organization in a supply chain, the organization is relying on them to protect its data and prevent unauthorized access to its systems. This is similar to when a bank hires a company to print and mail account statements every month, or when a health insurance company hires an actuary to help determine how much money to charge for premiums next year.

In each case, the bank or insurer is trusting the outside company with highly sensitive data that must be well-protected. A data breach by the outside provider could cause severe financial and reputation damage to the bank or insurer. So, in addition to contractual firewalls covered in a section below, it would be wise to also use third-party cyber risk management with these kinds of service providers.

An organization needs to ensure the service provider can meet its particular requirements, such as:

• The corporate cybersecurity policy,
• Federal data protection regulations,
• State and regulatory data breach notifications,
• And the right to audit the service provider's cybersecurity controls.

Beyond the contractual warranties, one should also request a copy of the vendor's Service Organization Control (SOC) report. This report describes the effectiveness of the security controls that were selected by the service provider for testing and describes any deficiencies noted by the independent auditor during the control testing. One of the most important things one can do when evaluating the SOC report is to see if the controls that were assessed are the ones that the buyer needs. If not, ask the service provider for more details.

For a more in-depth cyber risk assessment with the service organization, one might use a tool like "The SIG Questionnaire." SIG stands for "Standardized Information Gathering." It was developed to document a service provider's complete profile across 18 risk domains. It is commonly sent by the buyer to the service provider, who then completes it and sends it back.

If one's organization is large, one should be careful about overwhelming small service organizations with dozens of detailed questions. They often do not have enough resources to respond to the questions with the quality and thoroughness needed. Service providers who rely on cloud services should also provide the organization with the SOC reports for Rack Space, AWS, or whoever they use.

Remember: The security of cloud services operate on a shared responsibility model (see 3.10 below), so ask the vendor how they perform their part.

No matter how one chooses to manage third-party cyber risk, encourage transparency and offer to work with them. Otherwise, one may simply be told what the service organization thinks one wants to hear. This is a problem because it is very difficult to manage cyber risk without reliable information.

3.10. Cyber Risk Management of Cloud Computing

How does cybersecurity really work in the cloud? Here is how Amazon Web Services describes it:

> While AWS manages security of the cloud, security in the cloud is the responsibility of the customer (Amazon, 2020).

So, the cloud works on a "Shared Responsibility Model." This means when one uses AWS, they "inherit" the AWS' controls, which is great, and then build controls on top of that of the AWS.

So, security "of the cloud" means one automatically get helpful services such as:

- Data center access control,
- Cooling and humidity control for hardware,
- All-around protection from threats, vulnerabilities, abuse, and fraud for the infrastructure of the service that is bought.

In contrast, security "in the cloud" means one is responsible for turning on, properly configuring, and then managing the security functions one needs to achieve "reasonable cybersecurity." This includes:

- Access controls
- Data encryption
- Identity management

In reality, this part is no different than what an organization did in their own datacenter before availing the services of the cloud. This is why, according to Gartner Research, through 2025, at least 99% of cloud security failures will be the customer's fault (Panetta, 2019). So, in order for an organization to answer the question, "How do I secure my data on someone else's computers?" it needs to know which cloud services it is using and how the controls are configured. The specific steps will be different for each cloud provider that is being used.

Heavy users of cloud services should consider adding a Cloud Access Security Broker (CASB). A CASB will extend the enforcement of an organization's security policy into all its cloud vendors simultaneously. In addition, it can provide productivity enhancements like single sign-on. Also, it provides centralized account management across nearly all its cloud applications.

3.11. Contractual Firewalls

If a vendor in an organization's supply chain causes a large cyber failure, such as a long outage or a breach of sensitive information, its reputation and its customers will suffer.

So, both the vendors and customers should be told what one expects them to do to protect against, and ultimately deal with, cyber failures. Setting these expectations using carefully written contract language indemnifies an organization against excessive financial losses, which creates a contractual firewall for the organization. (By the way, the word "indemnify" means "to compensate someone for harm or loss.")

Expectations are set with vendors in a Master Services Agreement or similar contract. There are two primary points required: first, both parties will share responsibility for data security. Second, include an indemnification provision that describes who is financially responsible in the case of cyber failure along with the limits of that responsibility. If the vendor is responsible for a cyber failure, require them to cover the costs of liability, legal defense, and crisis management for both first-party and third-party costs.

To set expectations with customers, limit the organization's liability in the case of cybersecurity failure. Make sure the organization's service offerings are "as is" and its liability is limited to the amount customers actually paid.

3.12. Implement Strong Measures Against Malicious Code

Because malicious code is such a common tool for a cyberattacker, either inside or outside an organization's supply chain, one of the most important goals for managing the supply chain cyber risk is to protect it from falling for malicious code attacks.

Start by setting expectations in the form of a concise, easy-to-read policy. Use language that can be understood by anyone who works for the organization. A ninth-grade reading level is a good target. Keep the policy to one page, if possible. Publish it to everyone, and support the management team's effort to implement it. Be sure to fully answer any questions that may arise.

Next, conduct regular training to explain how people can follow the organization's policy. Short, online training sessions are a good way to go and it creates an automatic completion record. To make sure the messages get through, have all direct supervisors give regular, face-to-face reminders to their people.

Here are some essential outcomes the IT department must deliver on to implement an organization's policy; however, note that cyberattackers change their tactics often, so this is not a "set it and forget it" list so be sure to revisit it at least every year:

(1) Require everyone in the organization to use only non-administrator accounts for routine work like email and web browsing
(2) Perform centralized device management, both desktop and mobile, to provide such tasks as:
    (i) Automatic software updates,
    (ii) Data encryption,
    (iii) Advanced anti-malware protection,
    (iv) Software installation from clean, internal sources.
    (v) And, putting an "ad blocker" in the web browsers on all computers and mobile devices.
(3) Perform comprehensive data backups with proven restoration ability.
(4) Provide a corporate VPN or other alternatives to using public Wi-Fi.
(5) Finally, have ability to lock and wipe data from a lost or stolen mobile device.

To reduce the risk of a major attack, have staff report all malicious code incidents so others can be warned and tune the systems to block further attempts using that method.

Do not pay ransom to get back control of the data or systems. One may never know if attackers will follow-through on their promises. Most payments probably support terrorist organizations or terrorist-sponsoring nations like North Korea or Iran. Ultimately, ransom payments are votes for more cyberattacks, which is bad for our online community.

A final word on security updates: It is very difficult for most organizations to consistently get them out on time, but one needs to keep trying! However they need to be installed quickly because the amount of time between patch release and exploitation is gradually shrinking. It is critical to include all software publishers in the scope of the work. The 2017 NotPetya cyberattack, the 2017 Equifax data breach, and the 2016 Panama Papers data breach were all caused by a failure to quickly patch systems.

3.13. Takeaways

An organization must accept that it cannot prevent all supply chain cyberattacks and cyber failures and realize that good cyber risk management can provide a competitive advantage. Norsk Hydro is an excellent example of how to expertly handle the public relations aspect of a major cyberattack. Immediately after their 2019 cyberattack, their stock went up!

It is also an opportunity to thrive when one's competitors are struggling with the economic and legal fallout of cyberattacks. For example, consider the contrasting effect that NotPetya had on FedEx and DHL in 2017. FedEx (called TNT in Europe) immediately closed its doors for days (Greenberg, 2018). DHL did not. On seeing the published financial results of each company in the months following the cyberattack, we can clearly see that shipping volumes, revenue, and profit soared for DHL and, at the same time, they cratered for FedEx (US$300 million loss, no cyber insurance). DHL did not have to run any special marketing campaigns or put any service on sale. All they did was stay in business when its competitor called in sick. Once a shipper switches brands, they tend to stay. What a coup for DHL!

A well-prepared organization should expect more cyber supply chain attacks in the future, because such attacks work very well for patient, well-funded adversaries, and be ready to respond and recover from such an attack in a moment's notice.

References

ASUS (2019). About ASUS history. Available at: https://www.asus.com/About-ASUS-History/. Accessed July 20, 2020.

Amazon (2020). Shared responsibility model. Available at: https://aws.amazon.com/compliance/shared-responsibility-model/. Accessed July 20, 2020.

Arias, A. (2016). The NIST Cybersecurity Framework and the FTC. Available at: https://www.ftc.gov/news-events/blogs/business-blog/2016/08/nist-cybersecurity-framework-ftc. Accessed July 20, 2020.

Barr, J. (2013). Amazon S3 — Two trillion objects, 1.1 million requests/second. April 18. Available at: https://aws.amazon.com/blogs/aws/amazon-s3-two-trillion-objects-11-million-requests-second/. Accessed July 20, 2020.

Crawford, E. (2019). Made in China 2025: The industrial plan that China doesn't want anyone talking about. May 07, PBS. Available at: https://www.pbs.org/wgbh/frontline/article/made-in-china-2025-the-industrial-plan-that-china-doesnt-want-anyone-talking-about/. Accessed July 20, 2020.

Davis, H. (2017). How ECMC got hacked by cyber extortionists — and how it's recovering. May 20, *Buffalo News*. Available at: https://buffalonews.com/business/local/how-ecmc-got-hacked-by-cyber-extortionists-and-how-its-recovering/article_bfdd8b2e-d3e3-5750-9329-2c20e8634a70.html. Accessed July 20, 2020.

Dudley, R. (2019). The new target that enables ransomware hackers to paralyze dozens of towns and businesses at once. September 12, *ProPublica*. Available at: https://www.propublica.org/article/the-new-target-that-enables-ransomware-hackers-to-paralyze-dozens-of-towns-and-businesses-at-once. Accessed July 20, 2020.

Federal Bureau of Investigation (2018). APT 10 GROUP., December 07. Available at: https://www.fbi.gov/wanted/cyber/apt-10-group. Accessed July 20, 2020.

Federal Trade Commission (2015). Start with security: A guide for business. June. Available at: https://www.ftc.gov/tips-advice/business-center/guidance/start-security-guide-business. Accessed July 20, 2020.

Gartner (2018). Gartner says worldwide PC shipments declined 2 percent in 4q17 and 2.8 percent for the year. January 11. Available at: https://www.gartner.com/en/newsroom/press-releases/2018-01-11-gartner-says-worldwide-pc-shipments-declined-2-percent-in-4q17-and-28-percent-for-the-year. Accessed July 20, 2020.

Greenberg, A. (2018). The untold story of NotPetya, the most devastating cyber-attack in history. August 22. Available at: https://www.wired.com/story/notpetya-cyberattack-ukraine-russia-code-crashed-the-world/. Accessed July 20, 2020.

Greenwald, J. (2016). Chubb scores victory in key cyber ruling. June 2. Available at: https://www.businessinsurance.com/article/00010101/NEWS06/160609935/Chubb-scores-victory-in-key-cyber-ruling-. Accessed July 20, 2020.

Hong, N. & Sidel, R. (2016). Hackers breach law firms, including Cravath and Weil Gotshal. March 30. Available at: https://www.wsj.com/articles/hackers-breach-cravath-swaine-other-big-law-firms-1459293504. Accessed July 20, 2020.

Marke, J. (2016). McVirus — Attack on McDonald's cyber supply chain. January 27. Available at: https://jmarke.wordpress.com/2016/01/26/mcvirus-attack-on-mcdonalds-cyber-supply-chain/. Accessed July 20, 2020.

Nash, K., Castellanos, S. & Janofsky, A. (2018). One year after NotPetya cyberattack, firms wrestle with recovery costs. June 27. Available at: https://www.wsj.com/articles/one-year-after-notpetya-companies-still-wrestle-with-financial-impacts-1530095906. Accessed July 20, 2020.

NetDiligence (2017). *2017 Cyber Claims Study* (Gladwyne, PA: NetDiligence).

Kaspersky (2019). Operation ShadowHammer: New supply chain attack threatens hundreds of thousands of users worldwide. March 25. Available at: https://www.kaspersky.com/about/press-releases/2019_operation-shadowhammer-new-supply-chain-attack. Accessed July 20, 2020.

O'Sullivan, D. (2017). The RNC files: Inside the largest US voter data leak. UpGuard, June 19. Available at: https://www.upguard.com/breaches/the-rnc-files. Accessed July 20, 2020.

Panetta, K. (2019). Is the cloud secure? Gartner, October 10. Available at: https://www.gartner.com/smarterwithgartner/is-the-cloud-secure/. Accessed July 20, 2020.

Raymond, N. (2016). U.S. accuses Chinese citizens of hacking law firms, insider trading. *Reuters*, December 28. Available at: https://www.reuters.com/article/us-cyber-insidertrading-idUSKBN14G1D5. Accessed July 20, 2020.

Reuters (2017). Deutsche post DHL sees volume gains in Q3 after cyber attack hurts rivals. August 8. Available at: https://www.reuters.com/article/deutsche-post-results-cyber/deutsche-post-dhl-sees-volume-gains-in-q3-after-cyber-attack-hurts-rivals-idUSL5N1KU0S5. Accessed July 20, 2020.

Securelist (2019). Operation ShadowHammer: A high profile supply chain attack. March 25. Available at: https://securelist.com/operation-shadowhammer-a-high-profile-supply-chain-attack/90380/. Accessed July 20, 2020.

U.S. Department of the Treasury (2020). Available at: https://home.treasury.gov/news/press-releases/sm774. Accessed July 20, 2020.

Webb, K. (2019). Over 267 million Facebook users had their names, phone numbers, and profiles exposed thanks to a public database, researcher says. *Business Insider*, December 19. Available at: https://www.businessinsider.com/facebook-profile-267-million-users-exposed-names-phone-numbers-2019-12. Accessed July 20, 2020.

CHAPTER 4

Humans of the Supply Chain: The First Frontier in the Battle Against Cyber Vulnerabilities

Esen Andiç-Mortan

North Central College, Naperville, Illinois, USA

4.1. Introduction

Humans have become the latest target of cyberattacks, as targeting cyber systems became less fruitful due to their increased protection. Raising awareness regarding this issue and training people has become instrumental so that they do not fall victim to these attacks. Most people, through their multiple roles in the society, have access to an array of sensitive information as a user of personal and/or professional systems that are frequently brought together due to the syncing capabilities of cyber systems. The access to all of this information can be compromised, even if parts of systems may be defended very well, since weaker parts of the systems make the whole system susceptible to cyber vulnerabilities. Therefore, the human factor's capability to help fight against cybersecurity issues is crucial for supply chains. This chapter proposes to look at these issues through a social sustainability lens in order to: (1) make sense of the context through a look at literature and detailed discussions, and (2) to provide some insights regarding how these issues can be managed better to create solutions for supply chains.

Cyberattacks and cyber defense have been embroiled a vicious cycle for a while now, with each side upping their game at each step to gain the upper hand. In time, this has meant that cyber systems are now being defended much better than ever, which has lead cyberattacks to change their main target: from systems to humans (Abawajy, 2014). What is especially being targeted are the habits of people that lead them to be less careful than necessary when using cyber systems, including various types of technology such as information systems, social networking platforms, and cloud services, which allow them to access often-times confidential and critical data. Some examples of human behavior that makes systems more vulnerable include sharing passwords, clicking on unknown links, opening untrusted email attachments, and skipping virus scanning (Abawajy, 2014; Aytes and Connolly, 2004; Cone *et al.*, 2007; Evans *et al.*, 2016). Another example stems from how employees might be interacting other systems, rather than the targeted system, as those systems may appear from the employees' perspective to be completely separate from the targeted system. Shaw *et al.* (2009) point these kinds of occurrences out and provide examples of how employees engage in online activities without realizing the added security risks they themselves and their organizations are becoming exposed to.

Regardless of systems or humans beings targeted, usually what the attackers are after is the capability of behavior control via exploiting the accessed information within cyber systems (Zegzhda, 2016). It has been shown in the literature that, especially when organizations fail to upkeep their systems secure from cybersecurity issues, their reputation is impacted (Gal-Or and Ghose, 2004; Piggin, 2016; Wilding, 2016). Considering the fact that their reputation is on the line, organizations are recognizing the need to be much better at securing their cyber systems and identify better ways of managing cybersecurity issues throughout their supply chains.

In any given context, when improvements are sought, understanding the current challenges and identifying weaknesses in systems are crucial in order to achieve any kind of better results. In the context of cybersecurity, the weakness is recently identified as the human elements of supply chains (Abawajy, 2014), which includes any person that interfaces with cyber systems.

The first necessary step in cybersecurity improvement is to recognize that humans are being targeted and to develop ways to raise awareness of the ways in which human behavior is engaging with cyber systems create vulnerabilities in the face of these types of attacks. In their study, von Solms and van Niekerk (2013) draw attention to the fact that, despite growing use of cybersecurity terminology, how it differs from information security is not addressed most often times. When making the distinction between information security and cybersecurity, the authors make note that cybersecurity not only regards "protection of information sources but also that of other assets, including the person." This purview of cybersecurity signifies the involvement of the human factor, which signifies societal impacts due to humans being targeted.

The effect goes beyond than that, creating ripple effects in the society and thus affecting the social well-being. It is possible to view these targets as having negative impacts on humans, with the amount of worry and anxiety created even when they themselves have not experienced an attack but their fellow humans have (Cheung-Blunden and Ju, 2016; Pink *et al.*, 2018). And for the victims, these worries are sometimes actualized, as their privacy is shattered, identities are stolen, and important information they are privy to are exposed or locked away, depending on the type of attack (Maillart and Sornette, 2010; Roberds and Schreft, 2009; Wheatley *et al.*, 2016). It is important to note that these types of effects fall in the purview of social sustainability (Mnguni, 2010), as the topics start revolving around social well-being (Danna and Griffin, 1999; Di Fabio, 2017; Magee *et al.*, 2012; Michalos, 1997; Rogers *et al.*, 2012).

Identifying the fit of these issues within the purview of social sustainability is helpful in the exploration of management strategies and to provide any hope for the improvement of conditions, as without proper definition of areas, it is not quite possible to manage and rather extremely difficult to identify and maintain a consistent direction of efforts.

Speaking of social sustainability, it is first necessary to frame what is meant by it in the particular context of the human factor in cybersecurity issues. Weingaertner and Moberg (2014) examine a wide variety of definitions of social sustainability and arrive at the conclusion that context-dependent definitions are needed as otherwise definitions can end up being too vague (Woodcraft, 2012), which gets in the way of it being explored or applied to specific contexts. In the current literature, although there is work that sheds light on what can be some important elements of the effects of cybersecurity issues on social sustainability (e.g. Liu *et al.*, 2012), to the best of the author's knowledge, there is no work that brings together all these elements to create a holistic definition. Therefore, in this chapter, it is first sought to describe and detail a frame for defining social sustainability within the context of cybersecurity. Following this definition, this context is further examined through the diverse literature background in order to explore the dynamics of how social sustainability is impacted by cybersecurity issues. Finally drawing upon this exploration, strategies for managing various aspects of cybersecurity in order to have a more positive impact on social sustainability are discussed in detail.

4.2. Defining Social Sustainability Within the Cybersecurity Context

Since its conception, social sustainability has been largely unexplored relative to its two other counterparts (Marshall *et al.*, 2015; Murphy, 2012; Rasouli and Kumarasuriyar, 2016; Vallance *et al.*, 2011; Wątróbski *et al.*, 2018) in the Triple Bottom Line (Elkington, 1997): environmental and economic sustainability. While it is largely unexplored, it has been attracting increasing attention in the last decade or so, including efforts by many scholars working on its definitions, including notions of social capital, human capital, social equity, human rights, and social well-being (Colantonio, 2009; Dempsey *et al.*, 2011; Murphy, 2012; Sachs, 1999; Weingaertner and Moberg, 2014). As mentioned earlier, the general definition of social sustainability does not solve the problem with its lack of specificity, rather it actually adds to it (Weingaertner and Moberg, 2014; Woodcraft, 2012). Therefore, there is a need to define it within the specific contexts in which it is being studied. When looking at literature regarding cybersecurity, there is currently no existing definition of the term "social sustainability."

However, when working to define this in the cybersecurity context, there is one comparable construct which is a bit more mature in the literature that can help guide the endeavor: Corporate Social Responsibility (CSR). Despite being around for a considerable amount of time, CSR still does not have a definition that is agreed upon by everyone (Taneja *et al.*, 2011), quite similar to social sustainability (Carter and Rogers, 2008). The reason for the symmetry in their levels of development can be due to the fact that the borders of either concept have not been discovered and that there is a general lack of understanding regarding how far these areas should extend (Kuhlman and Farrington, 2010). Additionally, CSR is seen by some scholars as embodying social sustainability as it looks at the interplay between environmental and social sustainability (Awaysheh and Klassen, 2010; Carter and Rogers, 2008; Huq *et al.*, 2014; Tate *et al.*, 2010).

However, in general terms, CSR can be seen as the "a company's obligations to consumers" (Smith, 1995). And when these obligations regard "ethical, environmental, and social contexts," and there is a violation in these areas, this is called corporate wrongdoing (Romani *et al.*, 2013). Seeing how people expect organizations to take responsibility for the social and environmental issues that stem from their operations (Detomasi, 2008; Russell *et al.*, 2016), it can be thought that users' expectations regarding safety and privacy in light of cybersecurity issues can be considered part of their social obligations and thus can be expected to be having similar dynamics seen with corporate wrongdoing. What is known regarding organizations failures of these responsibilities, promises, and obligations is that people react in different ways toward them (Russell *et al.*, 2016).

Romani *et al.* (2013) categorize these reactions into two groups: "constructive punitive actions" and "destructive punitive actions." The former aims getting businesses to correct their behavior and continue their relationship with the business while the latter aims to harm the business and eventually to no longer have the relationship (Romani *et al.*, 2013; Russell *et al.*, 2016). Whichever might be the case, once those reactions, or lack of them, are observed, in a way this determines what organizations can *get away with* (Aßländer, 2011). However, it is also been seen that if such situations regarding CSR initiatives are handled well, they often lead to improved business reputation (Bhattacharya *et al.*, 2009; Sen and Bhattacharya, 2001).

Seeing how an organization's promises and obligations have such a crucial role in business reputation, it should be part of the framework while defining social sustainability in the context of cybersecurity. Therefore, the expectations as set forth by organizations should be part of the social sustainability premise, and these should not set out to harm individuals, the environment, and the society, while upholding ethical principles and human rights.

Another related element that comes from a slightly different standpoint, i.e. from the view of the user (or the consumer), is one where Mohr *et al.* (2001) define socially responsible consumer behavior (SRCB) as "a person basing his or her acquisition, usage, and disposition of products on a desire to minimize or eliminate any harmful effects and maximize the long-run beneficial impact on society." The definition provides a strong understanding of what it means to be a socially responsible consumer and provides an opportunity to be adapted into the cybersecurity context, as similar behavior can be thought to be applicable to users of systems as well, as that is in fact another type of consumption. The biggest challenge regarding the conceptualization is the inherent ability (or inability) of consumers/users to see the social impact of their choice (Annunziata *et al.*, 2019; Goworek, 2011). It can be seen from various streams of literature that when people's expectations are not matched with reality, such as them finding out their information are being sold to third parties by the companies they have trusted their business with, they often feel cheated and betrayed (Castelluccia *et al.*, 2012; Meng *et al.*, 2016; Vohs *et al.*, 2007). It is then possible to make the connection that when users are not able to see or understand the social impact of their choice — especially in terms of complex products, such as the cyber systems that either they directly use or are used by organizations they purchase products and services from — they can feel cheated. Depending on the level of effort put forth by the organizations prior to incidents regarding cybersecurity, cybersecurity incidents can spark different emotions and reactions from the users, as discussed before (Aßländer, 2011; Russell *et al.*, 2016). Therefore, the transparency of expectations and impact of decisions should be seen as another crucial element when defining social sustainability in this context.

When observing the transparency element, it is possible to see that the trust users/consumers have on systems and the organizations these systems belong to is necessary but not always supplied. Wilkowska and Ziefle (2012) show that, in adopting new technology, privacy and security aspects are important for users. However, when potential issues and risks with these are not known to the users at the time of adoption due to lack of transparency or the use of complicated language when relaying this information, it can be quite problematic (Akkermans *et al.*, 2004; Torous and Roberts, 2017). Studies in this area specifically address technology-based products, which fall in the purview of cybersecurity. Thus, the key takeaway from this discussion is the need for meaningful transparency and an accessible awareness level to help remedy the asymmetry between user expectations and the reality of risks. The sought symmetry should be allowing users/consumers to achieve an awareness level to empower them to make decisions that help to "minimize or eliminate" negative social impacts (Mohr *et al.*, 2001).

One last element that would be instrumental to be included in this framing is the ever-changing realities of what cyber vulnerabilities look like due to the ongoing innovation from both sides of the battle, as put forth earlier, i.e. the attackers and the defenders (Abraham *et al.*, 2005; Hatfield, 2018). Therefore, there is no one maxim that can be reached in terms of awareness. The awareness level is more of a moving target, and the responsibility falls on the organizations to have strategic and rigorous efforts in place to build and keep up the awareness of all users — internally and externally (Aloul, 2012; Bada *et al.*, 2019). Thus, this element can be summarized as the need for the awareness efforts to be continuous.

Bringing all these elements together, the framing for social sustainability within the context of cybersecurity can be summarized as follows:

Socially responsible management of cybersecurity issues achievements are twofold: (1) setting and maintaining clear expectations and awareness of societal impacts that users/consumers can objectively understand, and (2) empowering them with the capability of practicing this understanding through their consumption choices and decisions regarding their use of cyber systems.

4.3. Dynamics and Complicating Factors

In order to supplement the framing of social sustainability within the cybersecurity context, it is helpful to examine and identify dynamics and complicating factors that may be unique to this context and therefore that may require further consideration.

To cope with the increasing complexity of modern life, people are seeking more ways to manage the various aspects of their life with technologies that provide them with conveniences (Weinberg *et al.*, 2015). Thus, people are subjected to an increasing number of ways in which their personal and private information is compromised. One area in which the convenience is increasingly sought specifically is home automation (Jiménez *et al.*, 2014) and, more generally, the convenience offered by devices enabled by the Internet of Things (IoT) (Cone *et al.*, 2007). It is often true that people use multiple platforms, such as voice-controlled systems (intelligent virtual assistants), sensing systems that can be controlled via the Internet (e.g. temperature, movement), and cloud systems (backup, passwords, cross-device syncing). Thus, people are connected to the cloud in their homes and as part of their jobs as well. Sometimes each platform people use are offered by different providers, seeking to answer the call for convenience in different areas consumers are usually happy to *try out*. The main feature that gives such devices and platforms their operating power is constant connectivity and data collection and sharing (Thomas *et al.*, 2015). Once these platforms are able to *talk to each other*, the convenience level is upgraded for users, as they are able to cross-sync their systems together to create a more *seamless* experience (Cassandras, 2016; Liu *et al.*, 2012). The complicating factor here is the unique combination of platforms and systems used by each person. These newly added connections of systems/platforms/devices sometimes create entirely new and largely unmanaged links in the supply chain that is normally not seen and sometimes not even anticipated by the organizations of the systems (von Solms and van Niekerk, 2013). The ethical implications of these unmanaged links create unprecedented harm to individuals and all others that are connected with them while there is either no or relatively little harm to the providers of these systems. As evidenced by von Solms and van Niekerk (2013) these harms can include direct harm to persons through the exploitation of their information accessible via the weaknesses of some of these providers, which is a critical damage to social well-being. Managing this issue is not a straightforward process however, since the syncing and monitoring abilities of these systems are often presented to users with inaccessible language and/or not in an effective manner (Marshall and Tang, 2012; Stuart, 2016). Therefore, most often times, users might not be truly aware just how connected the systems they are using are, or what security issues they are becoming vulnerable to because of them. The existence of potential threats regarding their information may be something they realize; however, that does not necessarily equate to them being cognizant of just how much of those threats are real for their case. For instance, a user forwarding their business email to their personal account for a particular reason, then with the same personal account, allowing access to a different app, perhaps a parcel tracking app, may end up compromising their business account in case there was a data breach with the tracking app's providers. In other words, people's lack of awareness on which systems are having access to which parts of their lives — and which systems might be sharing these, often personal and/or sensitive information, with others either knowingly or unknowingly — are abused by businesses, which again is a form of corporate wrongdoing. The interconnectedness of systems, and therefore, the additional threats to which people and their information become vulnerable to, needs to be better understood by *everyone*.

The previous point is not to say that there is a complete lack of information provided to people regarding the systems they use. Most systems, platforms, and apps have terms of use that are presented to the user as they first begin their use. However, there is an oversaturation of people's exposure to these terms of use, mirroring the proliferation of apps or app/Internet-enabled interfaces, usually devices powered by IoT, and other types of systems people use and sign up for on a daily basis, that leads them to become blind to these terms (Cone *et al.*, 2007). Complicating matters even further is the dynamics that is created by the combinations of these systems and devices being used at the same time by each person, as noted earlier as well. For instance, the use of OAuth, which enables signing up for new apps/systems with already existing accounts elsewhere (e.g. Facebook, Google), have even added to that issue (Ferry *et al.*, 2015). Staying on top of the information being collected by the systems being used, and how and to whom these information are shared with and/or sold to, becomes almost impossible (Cassandras, 2016; Liu *et al.*, 2012). Top this off with the fact that not all providers are as transparent with their practices, and not all providers have the most up-to-date and effective countermeasures for staying on top of cyber vulnerabilities, the classic metaphor of "a chain is only as strong as its weakest link" fits here. Therefore, systems affecting each other's security capabilities is a crucial dynamic belonging to this context.

Another dynamic branching from this last one, is people's exposure to poor versus good practices, with each of them having some consequences. If people are always exposed to poor practices, they may never become aware of a better option, and their view of the nature of these contexts can be based off only these poor practices. This, coupled with the finding discussed earlier that people's reactions determine what practices organizations can get away with (Aßländer, 2011), can prove to be a dangerous dynamic. On the opposite end of the spectrum of possibilities, if users are always exposed to good practices, or at least are — or believe that they are — aware of vulnerabilities, and generally are untouched by cybersecurity threats, they may still face threats that they have not seen before, but due to the confidence they have based on previous experiences, could have more confidence in their ability to handle situations than they actually should have (Aytes and Connolly, 2004). Therefore, they may still fall prey to the threats. Abawajy (2014) provide an excellent example of this when they bring up when Google was hacked back in 2010, when an employee fell victim to a phishing email attack. Thus, the proximity of people to the contexts might not be lowering their chance of becoming a victim of cyberattacks.

All the complicating factors boil down to one main component: the human factor. As discussed throughout this section, humans being targeted opens up the scope of the issues around cybersecurity even further. On the other hand, it also creates better visibility of just how vast the impact of cyberattacks can extend. When the target is companies' systems, it is possible or easier for other components of supply chains — i.e. partners that are not directly linked with the attacked system, including end-consumers — to distance themselves from the attack and think "this won't happen to me," even though they might not be completely in the clear (Ciolan, 2014; Scully, 2014). In contrast, when it is the humans being targeted, a straightforward logic can help highlight how much bigger the issue becomes, along with an opportunity to see if it can be seen and managed that way: organizations, businesses, and therefore supply chains are made up of humans (Gowen and Tallon, 2003; Shub and Stonebraker, 2009). Most humans have multiple roles in their lives with two of them being work and family. In this context, being a consumer can be thought of as part of the family role, and being a professional, part of the work role. It is perhaps intuitive to think that the behaviors and awareness in one role can affect the other one, but as Greenhaus and Beutell (1985) discuss, the awareness of that may not be present within individuals, or difficulties with keeping a balance between them may mean that behaviors seen in one role may be missing from the other. Despite the challenges, the potential of cross-learning and cross-application between these roles perhaps holds the key to *upping the game* of the defense. If effective, consistent, and continuous training can be delivered to more humans, either through their consumer or employee identities, the effectiveness of these attacks might be decreased.

4.4. Discussion of Management Strategies Within the Supply Chain

The existence and the increase of the unmanaged links in the supply chain borne out of the integrations of systems due to consumer choices, and the unique set of applications used, in their personal and professional lives is problematic to say the least, as detailed in Section 4.3. One of the ways this can be managed is through standardization of protocols and principles used for syncing capabilities and seeking ways to increase visibility and the saliency of actively, and sometimes unintendedly, integrated systems from the users' point of view, and thus allowing them access to and management of this information with better quality, so that opting out of systems or ceasing relationship (Romani *et al.*, 2013) with organizations is less painful, and thus accessible to more people.

Along a similar theme, government regulations also play a role in determining how much awareness can be created and what types of actions and practices will draw reaction from users/consumers. Russell *et al.* (2016) find that highly conscious consumers were not the only ones to react to failures of CSR promises and also that self-mandated (as opposed to government regulated) promises were seen more negatively when they fail. They also find that even if regulations are not closely monitored, the existence of government regulation regarding issues lead consumers to react more harshly to these failures. Therefore, one of the ways to govern the following of better practices is surely through government regulations; however, especially in the areas of technological contexts, regulations are usually slow to catch up with the latest advancement (Hildner, 2006; Satchell *et al.*, 2011), and thus the self-mandated promises have a bigger presence. Connecting back to the previous point regarding standardization, the self-mandated promises again would be better handled if these were a collective effort within the supply chain so as to create a healthier frame of mind for users and consumers.

In terms of providing internal and external training by organizations, the most effective ways for increasing cybersecurity awareness have been found to be multi-method approaches that are engaging, relatable, and easy to partake in (Abawajy, 2014). Cone *et al.* (2007) posit that cybersecurity trainings often fail as people are just "used to these things" and the level of attention paid and lack of thinking from the user's end do not enable true learning to take place. Therefore, it can be thought that the method of conveying important security and privacy information should be designed to be interactive, allowing for better learning to take place. In terms of seeking interactivity, one of the methods Abawajy (2014) looks at is online delivery methods, including written materials, which have been shown to have effectiveness when users have actually read the contents (Kumaraguru *et al.*, 2007). However, with more interactivity (Schaffer and Hannafin, 1986; Zhang *et al.*, 2006), people learn and retain information much better. Abawajy (2014) finds that interactive online video training is the most effective method, and they theorize that this may be due to the ease of taking part in the activity, and the clarity of the information due to the visual and auditory delivery method, which helps with understanding the materials. When interactivity is mentioned, teaching through video games is a good option as well (Prensky, 2001). However, research also shows that the video game delivery method may be less effective, especially when the people involved may not be used to playing games, and the particulars of the game(s), such as how steep the learning curve is, affects the effectiveness of the method (Abawajy, 2014; Cone *et al.*, 2007). Additionally, even if playability is not in question, language and cultural differences may create some barriers (Abawajy, 2014; Fung *et al.*, 2008). The main takeaway from these considerations is the need to address the different learning styles and provide a chance for interactivity when possible.

In conclusion, the way to create a more sustainable approach to managing cyber vulnerabilities is to actually take strides in integrating these kinds of awareness and capability building along with ethical considerations, start early, and seek to integrate these into curriculum. As the ideas are being phased in, surely the awareness building and training would ideally be happening at every level and throughout supply chains. However, with the passage of time, the goal should be to have these components as standard portions of learning new technology. Just by doing a simple thought experiment on the rapid development of technology and the human capability of keeping up with these advancements, it is clear that technological advancements need to be rolled out with more understanding and transparency regarding not only the benefits of the advancement but also identifying areas that make the new development vulnerable and the threats that exist and practicing greater caution while in cyberspace.

4.5. Closing Thoughts and Future Research Areas

The main connection sought to be made in this chapter has been to build a logic chain starting from how humans are the main unit of analysis of supply chains, and then drawing attention to the fact that humans have recently become the target of cyberattacks. Therefore, the need for organizations to consider the human factor in the supply chain in regard to how humans interact with personal and professional systems and how they impact the cyber vulnerabilities of supply chains has become undeniable.

As pointed out in the discussion regarding how to manage these dynamics, setting transparent expectations toward users/consumers and providing engaging training that allows for real learning to take place are instrumental. Examples of human errors that give way to vulnerabilities to be exploited are noteworthy. The fact that even people who are working in close proximity to cybersecurity issues can fall victim to certain types of cyberattacks can be seen as an alarming issue. The reason for this should be looked at further: what is causing people to be susceptible to cyberattacks, particularly those experienced in their employee roles, and specifically in the modality of phishing attacks? Surely, one reason is lack of awareness of the particular method of attack; however, is there also a counterweight, such as the anxiety of keeping up with emails, which leads to carelessness? When looking at cybersecurity issues in terms of its impact on social sustainability, it would be instrumental to understand dynamics such as these to not only offer increased training but also create more lasting changes through understanding the mechanisms and dynamics that lead people to be careless, which in turn creates vulnerabilities in systems due to human actions in the first place.

With increased empowerment of users with regard to their information and technology use, the mental taxation caused by these issues in people can be alleviated, thereby creating a positive impact on social well-being, and thus, social sustainability. With humans, as the main unit of analysis of supply chains, more in control over these dynamics, having greater awareness of issues, and able to proactively manage their activities in cyber systems, the seemingly *weaker* chain in the supply chains will be fortified.

References

Abawajy, J. (2014). User preference of cyber security awareness delivery methods. *Behaviour & Information Technology*, **33**(3), 237–248. https://doi.org/10.1080/0144929X.2012.708787

Abraham, A., Grosan, C. & Chen, Y. (2005). Cyber security and the evolution of intrusion detection systems. *I-Manager's Journal on Future Engineering and Technology*, **1**(1), 74–82. https://doi.org/10.26634/jfet.1.1.968

Akkermans, H., Bogerd, P. & van Doremalen, J. (2004). Travail, transparency and trust: A case study of computer-supported collaborative supply chain planning in high-tech electronics. *European Journal of Operational Research*, **153**(2), 445–456. https://doi.org/10.1016/S0377-2217(03)00164-4

Aloul, F. A. (2012). The need for effective information security awareness. *Journal of Advances in Information Technology*, **3**(3), 176–183. https://doi.org/10.4304/jait.3.3.176-183

Annunziata, A., Mariani, A. & Vecchio, R. (2019). Effectiveness of sustainability labels in guiding food choices: Analysis of visibility and understanding among young adults. *Sustainable Production and Consumption*, **17**, 108–115. https://doi.org/10.1016/j.spc.2018.09.005

Aßländer, M. S. (2011). Corporate social responsibility as subsidiary co-responsibility: A macroeconomic perspective. *Journal of Business Ethics*, **99**(1), 115–128. https://doi.org/10.1007/s10551-011-0744-x

Awaysheh, A. & Klassen, R. D. (2010). The impact of supply chain structure on the use of supplier socially responsible practices. *International Journal of Operations & Production Management,* **30**(12), 1246–1268. https://doi.org/info:doi/10.1108/01443571011094253

Aytes, K. & Connolly, T. (2004). Computer security and risky computing practices: A rational choice perspective. *Journal of Organizational and End User Computing (JOEUC)*, **16**(3), 22–40. https://doi.org/10.4018/joeuc.2004070102

Bada, M., Sasse, A. M. & Nurse, J. R. C. (2019). Cyber security awareness campaigns: Why do they fail to change behaviour? *International Conference on Cyber Security for Sustainable Society, 2015*, 11.

Bhattacharya, C. B., Korschun, D. & Sen, S. (2009). Strengthening stakeholder–company relationships through mutually beneficial corporate social responsibility initiatives. *Journal of Business Ethics*, **85**(2), 257–272. https://doi.org/10.1007/s10551-008-9730-3

Carter, C. R. & Rogers, D. S. (2008). A framework of sustainable supply chain management: Moving toward new theory. *International Journal of Physical Distribution and Logistics Management*, **38**(5), 360–387.

Cassandras, C. G. (2016). Smart cities as cyber-physical social systems. *Engineering*, **2**(2), 156–158. https://doi.org/10.1016/J.ENG.2016.02.012

Castelluccia C., Kaafar, M. A. & Tran, M. D. (2012) Betrayed by Your Ads! In S. Fischer-Hübner & M. Wright (eds.) *Privacy Enhancing Technologies. PETS 2012. Lecture Notes in Computer Science*, Vol. 7384 (Berlin, Heidelberg: Springer), https://doi.org/10.1007/978-3-642-31680-7_1.

Cheung-Blunden, V. & Ju, J. (2016). Anxiety as a barrier to information processing in the event of a cyberattack. *Political Psychology*, **37**(3), 387–400. https://doi.org/10.1111/pops.12264

Ciolan, I. M. (2014). Defining cybersecurity as the security issue of the twenty first century. A constructivist approach. *Revista de Administratie Publica Si Politici Sociale*. Available at: https://search.proquest.com/openview/dbcb9167972ccf85a9782076dcd2aaa8/1?pq-origsite=gscholar&cbl=816332

Colantonio, A. (2009). Social sustainability: A review and critique of traditional versus emerging themes and assessment methods. *Second International Conference on Whole Life Urban Sustainability and its Assessment.* Available at: http://eprints. lse.ac.uk/35867/1/Colantonio_Social_sustainability_review_2009.pdf

Cone, B. D., Irvine, C. E., Thompson, M. F. & Nguyen, T. D. (2007). A video game for cyber security training and awareness. *Computers & Security,* **26**(1), 63–72. https://doi.org/10.1016/j.cose.2006.10.005

Danna, K. & Griffin, R. W. (1999). Health and well-being in the workplace: A review and synthesis of the literature. *Journal of Management,* **25**(3), 357–384. https://doi.org/10.1016/S0149-2063(99)00006-9

Dempsey, N., Bramley, G., Power, S. & Brown, C. (2011). The social dimension of sustainable development: Defining urban social sustainability. *Sustainable Development,* **19**(5), 289–300. https://doi.org/10.1002/sd.417

Detomasi, D. A. (2008). The political roots of corporate social responsibility. *Journal of Business Ethics,* **82**(4), 807–819. https://doi.org/10.1007/s10551-007-9594-y

Di Fabio, A. (2017). The psychology of sustainability and sustainable development for well-being in organizations. *Frontiers in Psychology,* **8**. https://doi. org/10.3389/fpsyg.2017.01534

Elkington, J. (1997). *Cannibals with Forks: Triple Bottom Line of 21st Century Business* (Oxford, UK: Capstone Publishing Ltd).

Evans, M., Maglaras, L. A., He, Y. & Janicke, H. (2016). Human behaviour as an aspect of cybersecurity assurance. *Security and Communication Networks,* **9**(17), 4667–4679. https://doi.org/10.1002/sec.1657

Ferry, E., O Raw, J. & Curran, K. (2015). Security evaluation of the OAuth 2.0 framework. *Information & Computer Security,* **23**(1), 73–101. https://doi. org/10.1108/ICS-12-2013-0089

Fung, C. C., Khera, V., Depickere, A., Tantatsanawong, P. & Boonbrahm, P. (2008). Raising information security awareness in digital ecosystem with games — A pilot study in Thailand. *2008 2nd IEEE International Conference on Digital Ecosystems and Technologies,* 375–380. https://doi.org/10.1109/ DEST.2008.4635145

Gal-Or, E. & Ghose, A. (2004). The economic consequences of sharing security information. In L. J. Camp & S. Lewis (eds.), *Economics of Information Security* (USA: Springer), pp. 95–104. https://doi.org/10.1007/1-4020-8090-5_8

Gowen, C. R. & Tallon, W. J. (2003). Enhancing supply chain practices through human resource management. *Journal of Management Development,* **22**(1), 32–44. https://doi.org/10.1108/02621710310454842

Goworek, H. (2011). Social and environmental sustainability in the clothing industry: A case study of a fair trade retailer. *Social Responsibility Journal,* **7**(1), 74–86. https://doi.org/10.1108/17471111111114558

Greenhaus, J. H. & Beutell, N. J. (1985). Sources of conflict between work and family roles. *The Academy of Management Review*, **10**(1), 76. https://doi.org/10.2307/258214

Hatfield, J. M. (2018). Social engineering in cybersecurity: The evolution of a concept. *Computers & Security*, **73**, 102–113. https://doi.org/10.1016/j.cose.2017.10.008

Hildner, L. (2006). Defusing the threat of RFID: Protecting consumer privacy through technology-specific legislation at the state level. *Harvard Civil Rights-Civil Liberties Law Review*, **41**, 133.

Huq, F., Stevenson, M. & Zorzini Bell, M. (2014). Social sustainability in developing country suppliers: An exploratory study in the ready made garments industry of Bangladesh. *International Journal of Operations & Production Management*, **34**, 610–638. https://doi.org/10.1108/IJOPM-10-2012-0467

Jiménez, M., Sánchez, P., Rosique, F., Álvarez, B. & Iborra, A. (2014). A tool for facilitating the teaching of smart home applications. *Computer Applications in Engineering Education*, **22**(1), 178–186. https://doi.org/10.1002/cae.20521

Kuhlman, T. & Farrington, J. (2010). What is sustainability? *Sustainability*, **2**(11), 3436–3448. https://doi.org/10.3390/su2113436

Kumaraguru, P., Rhee, Y., Acquisti, A., Cranor, L. F., Hong, J. & Nunge, E. (2007). Protecting people from phishing: The design and evaluation of an embedded training email system. *Proceedings of the SIGCHI Conference on Human Factors in Computing Systems*, 905–914. https://doi.org/10.1145/1240624.1240760

Liu, J., Xiao, Y., Li, S., Liang, W. & Chen, C. L. P. (2012). Cyber security and privacy issues in smart grids. *IEEE Communications Surveys Tutorials*, **14**(4), 981–997. https://doi.org/10.1109/SURV.2011.122111.00145

Magee, L., Scerri, A. & James, P. (2012). Measuring social sustainability: A community-centred approach. *Applied Research in Quality of Life*, **7**(3), 239–261. https://doi.org/10.1007/s11482-012-9166-x

Maillart, T. & Sornette, D. (2010). Heavy-tailed distribution of cyber-risks. *The European Physical Journal B*, **75**(3), 357–364. https://doi.org/10.1140/epjb/e2010-00120-8

Marshall, C. & Tang, J. C. (2012). That syncing feeling: Early user experiences with the cloud. *Proceedings of the Designing Interactive Systems Conference*, pp. 544–553. https://doi.org/10.1145/2317956.2318038

Marshall, D., McCarthy, L., McGrath, P. & Claudy, M. (2015). Going above and beyond: How sustainability culture and entrepreneurial orientation drive social sustainability supply chain practice adoption. *Supply Chain Management: An International Journal*, **20**(4), 434–454. https://doi.org/10.1108/SCM-08-2014-0267

Meng, W., Ding, R., Chung, S. P., Han, S. & Lee, W. (2016). The price of free: Privacy leakage in personalized mobile in-app ads. *Proceedings 2016 Network and Distributed System Security Symposium*. Network and Distributed System Security Symposium, San Diego, CA, USA. https://doi.org/10.14722/ndss.2016.23353

Michalos, A. C. (1997). Combining social, economic and environmental indicators to measure sustainable human well-being. *Social Indicators Research*, **40**(1), 221–258. https://doi.org/10.1023/A:1006815729503

Mnguni, P. P. (2010). Anxiety and defense in sustainability. *Psychoanalysis, Culture & Society*, **15**(2), 117–135. https://doi.org/10.1057/pcs.2009.33

Mohr, L. A., Webb, D. J. & Harris, K. E. (2001). Do consumers expect companies to be socially responsible? The impact of corporate social responsibility on buying behavior. *Journal of Consumer Affairs*, **35**(1), 45–72. https://doi.org/10.1111/j.1745-6606.2001.tb00102.x

Murphy, K. (2012). The social pillar of sustainable development: A literature review and framework for policy analysis. *Sustainability: Science, Practice and Policy*, **8**(1), 15–29. https://doi.org/10.1080/15487733.2012.11908081

Piggin, R. (2016). Cyber security trends: What should keep CEOs awake at night. *International Journal of Critical Infrastructure Protection*, **C**(13), 36–38. https://doi.org/10.1016/j.ijcip.2016.02.001

Pink, S., Lanzeni, D. & Horst, H. (2018). Data anxieties: Finding trust in everyday digital mess. *Big Data & Society*, **5**(1), 2053951718756685. https://doi.org/10.1177/2053951718756685

Prensky, M. (2001). *Digital Game-based Learning* (New York, USA: McGraw-Hill).

Rasouli, A. H. & Kumarasuriyar, A. (2016). The social dimensions of sustainability: Towards some definitions and analysis. *Journal of Social Science for Policy Implications*, **4**(2), 23–34.

Roberds, W. & Schreft, S. L. (2009). Data breaches and identity theft. *Journal of Monetary Economics*, **56**(7), 918–929. https://doi.org/10.1016/j.jmoneco.2009.09.003

Rogers, D. S., Duraiappah, A. K., Antons, D. C., Munoz, P., Bai, X., Fragkias, M. & Gutscher, H. (2012). A vision for human well-being: Transition to social sustainability. *Current Opinion in Environmental Sustainability*, **4**(1), 61–73. https://doi.org/10.1016/j.cosust.2012.01.013

Romani, S., Grappi, S. & Bagozzi, R. P. (2013). My anger is your gain, my contempt your loss: Explaining consumer responses to corporate wrongdoing. *Psychology & Marketing*, **30**(12), 1029–1042. https://doi.org/10.1002/mar.20664

Russell, C., Russell, D. & Honea, H. (2016). Corporate social responsibility failures: How do consumers respond to corporate violations of implied social contracts? *Journal of Business Ethics*, **136**(4), 759–773. https://doi.org/10.1007/s10551-015-2868-x

Sachs, I. (1999). Social sustainability and whole development: Exploring the dimensions of sustainable development. In E. Becker & T. Jahn (eds.), *Sustainability and the Social Sciences: A Cross-disciplinary Approach to Integrating Environmental Considerations into Theoretical Reorientation* (London, UK and New York, NY, USA: Zed Books Ltd.), pp. 25–36.

Satchell, C., Shanks, G., Howard, S. & Murphy, J. (2011). Identity crisis: User perspectives on multiplicity and control in federated identity management. *Behaviour & Information Technology*, **30**(1), 51–62. https://doi.org/10.1080/01449290801987292

Schaffer, L. C. & Hannafin, M. J. (1986). The effects of progressive interactivity on learning from interactive video. *ECTJ*, **34**(2), 89–96. https://doi.org/10.1007/BF02802581

Scully, T. (2014). The cyber security threat stops in the boardroom. *Journal of Business Continuity & Emergency Planning*, **7**(2), 138–148. https://www.ingentaconnect.com/content/hsp/jbcep/2014/00000007/00000002/art00006

Sen, S. & Bhattacharya, C. B. (2001). Does doing good always lead to doing better? Consumer reactions to corporate social responsibility. *Journal of Marketing Research*, **38**(2), 225–243. https://doi.org/10.1509/jmkr.38.2.225.18838

Shaw, R. S., Chen, C. C., Harris, A. L. & Huang, H.-J. (2009). The impact of information richness on information security awareness training effectiveness. *Computers & Education*, **52**(1), 92–100. https://doi.org/10.1016/j.compedu.2008.06.011

Shub, A. N. & Stonebraker, P. W. (2009). The human impact on supply chains: Evaluating the importance of "soft" areas on integration and performance. *Supply Chain Management: An International Journal*, **14**(1), 31–40. https://doi.org/10.1108/13598540910927287

Smith, N. C. (1995). Marketing strategies for the ethics era. *Sloan Management Review*. Available at: https://sloanreview.mit.edu/article/marketing-strategies-for-the-ethics-era/

Stuart, A. (2016). The dangers of file sync and sharing services. *Computer Fraud & Security*, **2016**(11), 10–12. https://doi.org/10.1016/S1361-3723(16)30090-2

Taneja, S. S., Taneja, P. K. & Gupta, R. K. (2011). Researches in corporate social responsibility: A review of shifting focus, paradigms, and methodologies. *Journal of Business Ethics*, **101**(3), 343–364. https://doi.org/10.1007/s10551-010-0732-6

Tate, W. L., Ellram, L. M. & Kirchoff, J. F. (2010). Corporate social responsibility reports: A thematic analysis related to supply chain management. *Journal of Supply Chain Management*, **46**(1), 19–44. https://doi.org/10.1111/j.1745-493X.2009.03184.x

Thomas, D., Paul, G. & Irvine, J. (2015). Going beyond the user — The challenges of universal connectivity in IoT, *Wireless World Research Forum Meeting*

35 (WWRF35), Aalborg University, Copenhagen Campus, Copenhagen, Denmark, 4 pp.

Torous, J. & Roberts, L. W. (2017). Needed innovation in digital health and smart-phone applications for mental health: Transparency and trust. *JAMA Psychiatry*, **74**(5), 437–438. https://doi.org/10.1001/jamapsychiatry.2017.0262

Vallance, S., Perkins, H. C. & Dixon, J. E. (2011). What is social sustainability? A clarification of concepts. *Geoforum*, **42**(3), 342–348. https://doi.org/10.1016/j.geoforum.2011.01.002

Vohs, K. D., Baumeister, R. F. & Chin, J. (2007). Feeling duped: Emotional, moti-vational, and cognitive aspects of being exploited by others. *Review of General Psychology*, **11**(2), 127–141. https://doi.org/10.1037/1089-2680.11.2.127

von Solms, R. & van Niekerk, J. (2013). From information security to cyber security. *Computers & Security*, **38**, 97–102. https://doi.org/10.1016/j.cose.2013.04.004

Wątróbski, J., Ziemba, E., Karczmarczyk, A. & Jankowski, J. (2018). An index to measure the sustainable information society: The Polish households case. *Sustainability*, **10**(9), 3223. https://doi.org/10.3390/su10093223

Weinberg, B. D., Milne, G. R., Andonova, Y. G. & Hajjat, F. M. (2015). Internet of Things: Convenience vs. privacy and secrecy. *Business Horizons*, **58**(6), 615–624. https://doi.org/10.1016/j.bushor.2015.06.005

Weingaertner, C. & Moberg, Å. (2014). Exploring social sustainability: Learning from perspectives on urban development and companies and products. *Sustainable Development*, **22**(2), 122–133. https://doi.org/10.1002/sd.536

Wheatley, S., Maillart, T. & Sornette, D. (2016). The extreme risk of personal data breaches and the erosion of privacy. *The European Physical Journal B*, **89**(1), 7. https://doi.org/10.1140/epjb/e2015-60754-4

Wilding, N. (2016). Cyber resilience: How important is your reputation? How effec-tive are your people? *Business Information Review*, **33**(2), 94–99. https://doi.org/10.1177/0266382116650299

Wilkowska, W. & Ziefle, M. (2012). Privacy and data security in E-health: Requirements from the user's perspective. *Health Informatics Journal*, **18**(3), 191–201. https://doi.org/10.1177/1460458212442933

Woodcraft, S. (2012). Social sustainability and new communities: Moving from concept to practice in the UK. *Procedia — Social and Behavioral Sciences*, **68**, 29–42. https://doi.org/10.1016/j.sbspro.2012.12.204

Zegzhda, D. P. (2016). Sustainability as a criterion for information security in cyber-physical systems. *Automatic Control and Computer Sciences*, **50**(8), 813–819. https://doi.org/10.3103/S0146411616080253

Zhang, D., Zhou, L., Briggs, R. O. & Nunamaker, J. F. (2006). Instructional video in e-learning: Assessing the impact of interactive video on learning effective-ness. *Information & Management*, **43**(1), 15–27. https://doi.org/10.1016/j.im.2005.01.004

CHAPTER 5

An Ontology of Supply Chain Cybersecurity

Myles D. Garvey[1], Jim Samuel[2] and Andrey Kretinin[3]

[1]*D'Amore-Mckim School of Business, Northeastern University*
360 Huntington Ave, Boston, MA 02151, USA
[2]*School of Business, University of Charleston, Charleston, WV 25304, USA*
[3]*Department of Marketing, Management, and Professional Sales Costakos*
College of Business William Paterson University, 1600 Valley Road,
Wayne, NJ 07470, USA

5.1. Introduction

Supply chains are not only the backbone of our modern economy but also essential to ensure the adequate delivery of supply to match demand. One does not need to look any further than the recent COVID-19 crisis to understand the often invisible, yet salient role supply chains play not only to our national security but also to our way of life. If our nations' supply chains fail, this endangers our nations' food, water, and health supplies. However, despite the level of importance of our nations' supply chains in our daily lives, they continue to be susceptible to the risk of disruption. As part of the transcendence from the Internet Revolution to Industry 4.0, opportunities have led to technological opportunism. Just as our nations' supply chains are at risk from more traditional sources of disruption, the continual integration of artificial intelligence, technology, and science into operations and strategies of these supply chains lead to a new frontier that managers must take into account: cyberspace.

No longer are we in the days where economic and political battles are strictly fought on physical battlegrounds; they now occur in *cyberspace*. While the transcendence toward Industry 4.0 has led to great technological innovations in just the short period of time during this new revolution, this has also led firms to operate and compete within cyberspace at an ever increasing rate of exposure. Yet, many firms have yet to adopt sound policies to handle the threats that exist in this technological Wild West, and many of them are not aware that "[E]very day, America's adversaries are testing our cyber defenses. They attempt to gain access to our critical infrastructure, exploit our great companies, and undermine our entire way of life" (Trump, 2018). Even more to the point, consumers and employees alike, in response to the recent COVID-19 pandemic, are now putting firms are even greater risk of being attacked in cyberspace due to more recent increased exposure to sensitive and privileged information (Stank, 2020). As of 2017, 64% of Americans own online accounts that store health, utility, financial, and other privileged and private information, yet 69% of Americans remain unconcerned with password security processes (Olmstead and Smith, 2017). Yet, there is a shocking 41% of Americans who have been subjected to credit card fraud (Olmstead and Smith, 2017). Between the nonchalant attitudes toward general cybersecurity and the increase in work- and school-at-home instances in response to the pandemic, supply chain organizations need to respond (Uberti, 2020; Stank, 2020) to ensure the security of not only physical but also the virtual supply chains.

In order to ensure that companies and corresponding supply chains remain accessible to American markets, firms along with their supply chains need to ensure that sound risk management practices are implemented to prevent these very same threats. Put simply, "[C]yber is, to a large extent, where it's at nowadays" (Trump, 2018). However, there still remains a problem in the academic literature when it comes to understanding how firms should characterize, measure, plan, understand, and implement their risk management policies and strategies to ensure that the virtual security of their supply chains remains strong. How can one know whether or not they have a "strong" supply chain cybersecurity if they have yet to define this concept? Put differently, "you cannot precisely measure what you cannot precisely define" (Wacker, 2008).

In fact, the concept of cybersecurity, irrespective of supply chain, is still being defined, with many different definitions offered and applied in varying contexts (Craigen *et al.*, 2014). This remains unsurprising, given the highly technical knowledge that is often required just to simply understand what "cyber" is, let alone "cybersecurity." Some view this as the more restrictive scope as measures that need to be taken to prevent attacks against information systems (BEISSEL, 2018), while other take the larger scope to include various types of actors, motives, processes, and devices (Craigen *et al.*, 2014). One thing is for sure, just as how the Internet is more than just a "series of tubes," cybersecurity is more than just security with computers involved (Singer and Friedman, 2014).

In response to the need to define these emerging fields, academics have advanced, in an ad hoc manner, various aspects and concepts that lie at the heart of the intersection of cybersecurity and supply chain management. For example, Johnson (2008) studied the concepts of inadvertent information disclosure on P2P networks, while Bartol (2014) designed a framework of best practices and standards that should be adopted by the industry to secure their supply chains. Boyson (2014) put forth a strategic conceptual model of supply chain cybersecurity while others studied the "IT supply chain" (Boyson, 2014, p. 346). Cohen (2018) advanced a collection of cyber-related risks related to a firm engaging in big data methodologies, while more recently, Ghadge *et al.* (2019) put forth a conceptual framework that suggests all threats to the firm originate from one of three areas: from IT, from within the organization, or from something physical within the supply chain. Others have focused their attention on classifying the types of cyber risks (Warren and Hutchinson, 2000; Pandey *et al.*, 2020), mitigation of these risks (Colicchia *et al.*, 2019), assessment (Akinrolabu *et al.*, 2018), as well as identification and prediction (Boiko *et al.*, 2019; Barron *et al.*, 2016; Urciuoli and Hintsa, 2017). Some authors have also studied corporate "cyber resilience" (Boyes, 2015; Urciuoli, 2015).

Despite the ad hoc progress in this body of literature, very few authors have organized, defined, and distinguished the various concepts that lie at the heart of "supply chain cybersecurity." Put simply, academics have been advancing the so-called tools of the trade without first defining the trade. We argue in this research that supply chain cybersecurity rests on two foundational pillars that have managed to find their way into cyberspace: supply chain risk management and supply chain security. Through a conceptual theory-building approach as well as a review of recent literature, this research addresses the following questions:

- What is the definition of "supply chain cybersecurity?" What is the collection of necessary concepts that constitute and require further investigation under the umbrella of "supply chain cybersecurity?"

5.2. Literature Review

In reviewing the literature, we began our search with two keywords: "Cybersecurity AND Supply Chain Risk" as well as "Cybersecurity AND Supply Chain Security" in the databases ABI/INFORM, EBSCOHost, Emerald Journals, JSTOR, ProQuest, Sage Journals, and Sprinker-Link. To cast a wider net to determine if any publications were missed, we also leveraged Google Scholar for additional keyword searches. The initial articles gathered allowed us to render the following related keywords: "Cyber Supply Chain," "Supply Chain Cyber," "Cyber Supply Resilience," "Supply Chain Cyber Risk," "Supply Chain Cyber Harm," "Supply Chain Cyber Threat," "Supply Chain Cyber Vulnerabilities," "Suppy Chain Cyber Disruption," and "Supply Chain Cyber Attack." We excluded any articles that were not related to supply chain management, or ones whose primary topic was more related to pure artificial intelligence, engineering, machine learning, or other non–supply-chain-related areas. After searching the databases and doing a first round of filtering, we "backtracked" and "forward tracked" through the literature, looking at the references of the references, etc., of each article in the initially filtered set of articles until we noticed that most of the articles appearing in searches have already been accounted or eliminated. The literature we obtained comprised a combination of technical papers, best practice documentation, academic research journal articles, dissertations and theses, and book chapters. Subsequently, for each paper, we organized the literature as falling under "supply chain security" or "supply chain risk," with some papers overlapping between the two fields. Our major criteria were based on the discussion of supply chain assets or disruptions. If the manuscript discussed in some manner the security of an asset, we categorized this under "security." If it discussed disruptions to the supply chain, we classified this as "risk." Under each folder, for each article, we then extracted the primary topical keywords for each article by hand. We last conducted a thematic analysis for the entire collection of articles and identified those that had common themes. We discuss the results of this review below.

5.2.1. *Supply chain cybersecurity*

Despite the need for supply chain managers to take into account the threats of cyberattacks and risks into their risk management and security planning, shockingly, there has been little academic work that specifically defines the area of supply chain cybersecurity. Our literature review began with a search of the phrase "supply chain cybersecurity." Doing so across multiple databases revealed that while some authors have put forth managerial frameworks to help mitigate against cyber risk, few have formally and theoretically defined and distinguished concepts within the area of "supply chain cybersecurity." As a starting point, our review focused on the few articles that did contain this exact phrase. While some articles we reviewed did advance an explicit definition, most actually used this phrase as a de facto meaning equivalent to a variety of other concepts.

For example, Agarwal (2019) used "supply chain cybersecurity" to refer to the various risks and classifications of risks that supply chains, specifically ICT supply chains, face as a result of incorporating Internet of Things (IoT) as well as more general information technologies into supply chains. She recommended using a probability-impact matrix to assess risks as well as following National Institute of Standards and Technology (NIST)-based mitigation best practices. Burnson (2013) also uses this phrase, but only in the title of his article. He does hint at its meaning, however. He puts forth a set of best practices to help enhance the cybersecurity efforts of organizations, namely through a framework of Discuss, Educate, Assess, and Adopt. He also advances the argument that cybersecurity in the supply chain needs a collaborative approach across firms so as to increase the levels of our national security. Others have assumed that this phrase is equivalent to an agent that intentionally installs specific types of malicious software on an organization's information technology pathway along the supply chain (Mansfield *et al.*, 2013; Mylrea and Gourisetti, 2018). Supply chain cybersecurity has also been indirectly characterized to be a set of tools to protect the three types of digital assets that the digital supply chain has created: information technology, intellectual property, and operational technology (Melnyk *et al.*, 2019). On the other hand, others have indirectly characterized supply chain cybersecurity to be the prevention of a cybercrime against the firm's information technology and other digital assets (Urciuoli *et al.*, 2013). Last, indirectly, Seckman *et al.* (2016) advanced the idea that supply chain cybersecurity comprises an understanding of how to reduce the possibility of security breaches in suppliers and contractors.

There have been some authors that have provided explicit definitions of this area of study. For example, Bartol (2014) uses the term "cyber supply chain security" as yet another synonym for ICT supply chain risk management, information and communication supply chain security, supply chain risk management, cyber supply chain, and cyber supply chain risk management. Others have taken a more refined scope in definition, namely that supply chain cybersecurity systems are the "integrated alignment of processes involving infrastructure network, IT system and organization" (Ghadge *et al.*, 2019, p. 227). Despite these definitions, we argue that the direct or de facto definitions are too arbitrary for serious academic inquiry. From the review of our literature on the matter, we have come to the observation that supply chain cybersecurity appears to have a few main themes, which we list below. Later in this chapter, we will advance a more refined and unambiguous definition of supply chain cybersecurity that will be more encompassing of recent research. The primary themes that will further guide our literature review and formalization of a definition are:

(1) There are digital assets, such as information, information technology, and new technologies such as the IoT and blockchain, which are now integrated into the physical infrastructure of supply chains.
(2) Supply chains are at risk of attack, breach, or disruption because they integrate their processes with IoT and information systems, both of which interact with "cyberspace."
(3) Not only should supply chain cybersecurity concern itself over the newer forms of assets, namely digital assets, but it should also attempt to understand how breaches or "cyberattacks" can disrupt the supply chain.

5.3. Major Themes Related to Supply Chain Risk Management

5.3.1. *Supply chain cyber disruptions and cyber harm*

Analogous to supply chain disruptions, the research that introduces the concept of "cyber" into this area is yet another major theme in the extant literature. A few authors have written on the matter. Siciliano and Gaudenzi (2018) consider "cyber risks" and information technology to be sources of disruption to supply chains operating in cyberspace. They argue that the disruption to a supply chain from a cyber risk or information technology (IT) may be accidental or malicious. More specifically, they suggest that cyber risk is more of a malicious attack that leads to an electronic event that will eventually cause a disruption to business or to money (Siciliano and Gaudenzi, 2018). They suggest that these risks could lead to what they refer to as "cyber disruption," which is characterized by a reduction in quality of service, business interruption, or loss of reputation or confidence in the firm. Others in the literature have opted for a more refined taxonomy of the more malicious type of cyber disruption, namely that of the subconcept "cyber-harm." Cyber harm can be thought of as the malicious intent to "harm" a firm along the dimensions of Physical/Digital, Economic, Psychological, Reputation, or Social/Societal (Agrafiotis *et al.*, 2018).

5.3.1.1. *Supply chain cyber risk and risk management*

Of all the literature surveyed, the discussion on supply chain cyber risk is by far the most researched topic. Researchers in this area have mainly addressed the ideas characterizing and defining cyber risk via the construction of taxonomies, proposing managerial processes for managing risks, identifying common mitigation policies and best practices, measuring risk within the context of cyberspace, understanding the drivers and consequences of cyber risk, characterizing the propagation of cyber risk, as well as understanding the challenges that firms face in addressing cyber risks. Primarily the literature has attempted to answer the questions of what is risk, and how should firms manage them in the scope of operating within cyberspace? We review through each of these areas below.

5.3.1.2. *Defining and characterizing cyber risk*

Cyber risk has been defined and characterized in many different ways in the extant literature. Estay (2017) argues that supply chain cyber risk is the phenomenon of disruptions in the physical world as a result of the digital connectivity of infrastructure. Put differently, it is considered to be the "risks associated with the use of IT" (Estay and Khan, 2016, p. 1). However, cyber risk is not only limited to just risks associated with the use of IT. Other definitions have focused strictly on the idea of risk to information. For example, Faisal *et al.* (2007) defines information risk as "the probability of loss arising because of incorrect, incomplete, or illegal access to information"(Faisal *et al.*, 2007, p. 679).

Meanwhile, some have suggested that cyber risk is the potential for a cyberattack to occur (Isbell *et al.*, 2019; Lamba *et al.*, 2017). Others have characterized this concept as the idea of having some agent act in a malicious manner toward the cyber supply chain (Mansfield *et al.*, 2013). Similar definitions have been provided, with an emphasis on the idea that the "risk" is an event that serves as a precursor to the disruption, with the added requirement that there must be malicious intent (Siciliano and Gaudenzi, 2018). Likewise, additional conditions have been suggested in other definitions of cyber risk, such as the requirement that actors intentionally focus on vulnerabilities within the supply chain so as to compromise confidentiality, integrity, and availability of the supply chain (Reuben and Ware, 2019). Other definitions have directed the definition of cyber risk to be more focused around the product or the service which the supply chain offers. For example, Pandey *et al.* (2020) suggests that cyber risk is defined as the supply chain members or products having malicious behavior which could lead to counterfeit services or components.

While some have provided direct or de facto definitions for cyber risks, many have also conflated this concept with cyberthreats and have used the two terms interchangeably (Urciuoli *et al.*, 2013; Zheng and Albert, 2019a; Wolden *et al.*, 2015). We also have seen the definition of cyber risk evolve from that of information security (IS) risk, which offers similar definitions as the ones provided above (Smith *et al.*, 2007). In summary, the concept of "supply chain cyber risk" is far from well-defined. While the current literature has attempted to offer various ad hoc and de facto definitions, there appears to be little conformity and agreement as to what constitutes a supply chain cyber risk. Questions remain, such as, is a cyberthreat different than a cyber risk? Is IS risk a subconcept of cyber risk? Or do all cyber risks necessitate information? Does a risk need to be malicious in nature? Could a cyber risk be without an actor and accidental? Unfortunately, the extant literature on the matter does not provide us much guidance on a well-grounded definition.

5.3.1.3. *Supply chain cyber risk taxonomies*

While the extant literature has not provided a clear and unambiguous definition of supply chain cyber risk, there is no shortage of taxonomies of cyber risk that have been suggested. Most of the taxonomies suggested appear to be based on whether or not the focus of the attack is on the physical IT hardware or on the software and/or virtual end of the supply chain system. For example, McFadden and Arnold (2010) suggest that there are three major types of physical hardware risks: hardware that can programmed (such as EPROM or EEPROM), firmware that can be modified, or the physical circuitry itself on the hardware itself. Agarwal (2019) suggests categorizing risk based on whether it is of low impact, such as outdated antivirus software or lack of backup of external hard drives, or high impact, such as introduction of malicious software through IoT or physical components. On the other hand, others have suggested categorizing risks based on the method of attack, such as through malicious code insertion, island hopping, or counterfeit parts (Boyd, 2020).

Cyber risks can also be classified as being internal or external to the focal firm, and as malicious or natural/non-intentional (Colicchia *et al.*, 2019). Other taxonomies have opted to have a strict focus on information-related risks, such as Faisal *et al.* (2007), who proposes that there are four major categories of risk: information security/breakdown, forecast, intellectual property rights, and IT/IS outsourcing risks. Gupta *et al.* (2020) suggest that supply chain cyber risks can be categorized into three major groups based on attacks to hardware, attacks to raw materials, and attacks to design files. More recently, it has been proposed that three major forms of risk exist in cyber environments: risk to DevOps (which are services such as MySQL, Docket, etc.), risk to IoT, and risk to cloud technologies (Lamba *et al.*, 2017). On the other hand, Mansfield *et al.* (2013) simplifies his risk taxonomy into three types: hardware, software, and network risk.

Some authors have provided a taxonomy of risk based on two major sources: vulnerabilities in the supply chain and the method of attack on the vulnerabilities. For example, Pandey *et al.* (2020) suggest that there are nine major sources of vulnerabilities in the cyber supply chain: partner trust, poor protection of cargo in transit, poor cryptographic decision, data manipulation, product specification fraud, failure of IT equipment, counterfeit products, plant malfunctioning, and information theft. They suggest six ways in which vulnerabilities can be taken for granted, namely through password sniffing/cracking; spoofing; denial of service; direct attack; malicious tampering; and via insiders (Pandey *et al.*, 2020). Others have classified cyber risks into five main areas, namely data storage, multi-tenancy, communication, outsourcing, and legal (Wulf *et al.*, 2019). More recently, Ghadge *et al.*

(2019) conducted a thorough review of this literature and proposed a conceptual framework for categorizing cyber risks. They suggested that all cyber risks fall within categories based on the impact of the risk, namely as the risks being physical, breakdown, indirect attack, direct attack, and insider threats.

5.3.1.4. *Cyber risk identification, measurement, and assessment*

Another theme in the literature related to supply chain cyber risk management is the identification, assessment, and measurement of cyber risk. The literature on cyber risk taxonomies aid managers and academics in constructing procedures and frameworks for identifying risks. In the case of hardware, it has been suggested that knowing the types of hardware risk aids the manager in designing methodologies in identifying and detecting cyber risk in hardware. For example, a power analysis on hardware can be conducted to detect any modifications that have been made to existing hardware. So too could time delay analysis as well as the use of IR thermography and X-rays (McFadden and Arnold, 2010). More generally, Agrafiotis *et al.* (2018) suggest the use of a cyber harm taxonomy to aid firms in identifying the possible targets within the supply chain for which it could be attacked. They argue that people are at the forefront of cyberspace, and hence they too must be taken into account in any risk identification and detection system. Likewise, it has been suggested that having a categorization of risk such as supply, operational, and demand risk with respect to cyberattacks would aid the firm in performing the first step in risk management: risk identification (Pandey *et al.*, 2020). More intricate approaches to identification and detection have also been proposed, such as gathering expert opinion of cyber risks and leveraging Bayesian Belief Networks to detect when it is likely that a risk will manifest into an attack or disruption (Yeboah-Ofori *et al.*, 2019).

The literature also suggests that cyber risk assessment is necessary once said risks have been identified and detected. In the cloud computing environment, it has been suggested that qualitative risk assessment by way of survey taking and statistical analysis can be conducted to gauge the extent to which events in the cloud pose a risk of manifestation (Akinrolabu *et al.*, 2017). Part of this assessment scheme involves understanding the various components of a cloud service as well as a supplier and subsequently visualizing this information with a diagram that depicts a supply chain flow of the cloud and its connected components (Akinrolabu *et al.*, 2018). Faisal *et al.* (2007)

suggest the use of interpretive structural modeling to assess the connection between various IS risks and mitigation policies. Likewise, other quantitative approaches have been suggested, such as measuring the likelihood, impact, and vulnerability of a specific risk event and multiplying these measurements to obtain an index score for the risk (Schauer *et al.*, 2017).

Generally speaking, it has been proposed that cyber risk assessment follow in the same path as traditional risk assessment. That is, the goal should be to estimate the impact of loss as well as the probability of loss and leverage a probability-loss matrix to compute risk scores for each risk (Pandey *et al.*, 2020). Others have suggested adopting existing standards such as ISO/IEC 27005:2011 for cyber risk assessment, which involves a two-step process of risk analysis and evaluation (Akinrolabu *et al.*, 2019). Last, others have put forth assessment methodologies which include involving propagation effects of risk and attack (Schauer *et al.*, 2019), leveraging sensing technology from IoT (Yang *et al.*, 2019), and focusing on the likely occurrences of events (Yeboah-Ofori and Islam, 2019). In summary, "the main result of a risk assessment exercise is the quantitative or qualitative evaluation of the possible impact of threat sources on a given system and its vulnerability, while considering the context of such risk scenarios" (Akinrolabu *et al.*, 2019, p. 3).

However, in order to ensure that a thorough risk assessment procedure is undertaken, part of assessment is having a toolbox of measures that can adequately reflect the true underlying risk of a particular event. Because risk is often thought to be a subjective construct generally speaking (Garvey *et al.*, 2015), this means that a variety of risk measures is needed to actually conduct the risk assessment. In the scope of cyber risk, some measures have been proposed for usage in assessment processes. For example, risk can be measured by first understanding the objectives of the decision-maker, which translate into being able to measure the impact. Such objectives could include security, authenticity, confidentiality, exclusivity, integrity, reliability, availability, dependability, resiliency, robustness, maintainability, survivability, safety, quality, and trustworthiness (Windelberg, 2016). Other measures involve more complex formulations, such as the forming risk indices based on mathematical graph theory (Faisal *et al.*, 2007); computing coverage of vulnerability metrics (Zheng and Albert, 2019b); focusing on the measurement of mitigation through pre-attack, trans-attack, and post-attack phases (Ghadge *et al.*, 2019); designing psychological-based malicious index scores

(Clim, 2019); and qualitatively measuring individual, cumulative, and propagated risk levels (Schauer *et al.*, 2019).

5.3.1.5. *Drivers and consequences of cyber risk*

The ability of managers to engage in risk identification, measurement, and assessment rests upon knowing where the vulnerabilities within the cyber supply chain lie as well as the drivers of other cyber risks, which may be salient in the supply chain. Hence, it comes as no surprise that the extant literature has demonstrated devotion to the topic of why and from where risks emanate, as well as factors the heighten risks. Some work has been conducted on identifying common drivers of cyber risk. For example, Clim (2019) suggests that firms should take into account the common psychological reasons as to why attackers engage in malicious acts against the supply chain. Having such an understanding would enable the firm to identify the various vulnerabilities within the supply chain, especially those where human interaction is highly involved in cyber supply chains. Other drivers of cyber risk rest within the products and components sourced within the supply chain. Such concerns stem from products that come from distrusted countries, companies, products, or processes (Charney *et al.*, 2011). Others have suggested that the main source of cyber risk stem from employees and their behaviors, which is what makes supply chain cyber risk different than traditional supply chain risk (Colicchia *et al.*, 2019). Ghadge *et al.* (2019) suggest that cyber risks stem not only from humans but also technical and physical points of penetration such as IT systems abruptly failing or manufacturing facilities failing to mitigate against attacks.

While understanding the drivers of risk will aid the firm in setting proper investments into mitigating the cyber risks, an equal level of understanding of the consequences of each risk is also necessary. Short of the statistical and anecdotal evidence presented earlier regarding the potential negative consequences that firms face, the consequences of cyber risk can best be understood through the framework of cyber harm as discussed earlier. Indeed, as Agrafiotis *et al.* (2018) argue, cyber harm comes in many forms. When firms ignore the possible consequences of each cyber risk, and fail to understand the possible harms (i.e. consequences) of the manifestation of those risks, the firm and entire supply chain becomes more susceptible to loss in economic, reputation, and societal objectives. We have seen many examples of the consequences of cyber risks manifesting, such as Ashley Madison becoming liable to lawsuits as a result of violation of their members privacy, JP Morgan having their customers names and other private information hacked into (Agrafiotis *et al.*, 2018), as well as the entire manufacturing sector at risk due to phishing attacks (Pandey *et al.*, 2020).

5.3.1.6. *Cyber risk management frameworks and best practices*

In addition to the identification, assessment, and measurement of cyber risk, we also found in our review the theme of various risk management frameworks and sets of best practices proposed to handle such risks. These greatly vary in approach from using established risk management practices from the supply chain management literature to resting on various standards set by organizations and government. The set of best practices that have been proposed in the literature to specifically handle cyber risk greatly vary. Schauer *et al.* (2017) designed the MITIGATE system, which comprises supply chain security analysis, cyberthreat analysis, vulnerability analysis, impact analysis, risk assessment, and subsequently risk mitigation. This framework offers managers a set of best practices in each area to accomplish the goals of cybersecurity in the supply chain (Schauer *et al.*, 2017). Others have suggested using frameworks proposed by NIST; the Open Trusted Technology Provider Standard (O-TTPS); the Center for the Protection of National Infrastructure (CPNI); the approach designed by Huawei to adopt ISO 28000; as well as other existing standards to identify, assess, and map risks to standards (Agarwal, 2019; Pal and Alam, 2017).

Boyd (2020) suggests an eight-step list of key practices to manage cyber risks, which involve integrating cyber supply chain risk management across the organization; establishing a formal program; knowing and managing critical suppliers; understanding the firm's supply chain; collaborating with key suppliers, including key suppliers in resilience and improvement activities; assessing and monitoring risk throughout supplier relationships; and planning the full lifecycle of risk management. Others have argued that efforts to reduce cyber risk in the supply chain must involve various organizations and governments adopting practices that are risk-based and standards that are collaboratively developed, transparent, flexible, and reciprocal, all at the tactical level of organizations (Charney *et al.*, 2011). Others have suggested a frame, assess, respond, monitor approach, and offered more granular standards for 18 control areas that mitigate risk, including but not limited to controlling access, awareness, accountability, security assessment, media protection, and risk assessment (Boyens *et al.*, 2015). Reuben and Ware (2019) summarize various standards that firms and governments have set, such as initiatives set by the US Department of Defense, adopting blockchain technology, compliance with cybersecurity regulations, effective vendor management, blackbox testing to check for unusual processes and connections, and the physical inspection of hardware.

While some in the practitioner literature have recommended or reported on best practices for cyber risk management, others in the academic literature have put forth various management frameworks. Boyson (2014, p. 344) suggests the use of a two-dimensional management framework, where risk management activities related to cyber should seek to "harden both defense in depth, which covers the entire system life cycle starting with design, and defense in breadth, which spans the focal organizations extended supply chain from suppliers to customers." Colicchia *et al.* (2019) designed a framework to classify not only the types of cyber risks but also the types of initiatives that can be undertaken to mitigate them. They argued that initiatives fall under organizational, training, and internal awareness; compliance and external awareness; event management; data management; IT security tools; and IT operational resilience (Colicchia *et al.*, 2019). Gaudenzi and Siciliano (2018) also propose a cyber risk management framework but suggested that its core focus should be on IT and Cyber Risk Assessment, Prevention, and Mitigation, each supported by compliance and risk governance. More specifically, they argued that risk governance should comprise defining the appetite and tolerance for risk while investing in security training programs and human resources, but at the same time ensuring risk compliance by selecting a set of standards that address risk and security (Gaudenzi and Siciliano, 2018, p. 88).

Others have suggested more parsimonious approaches, such as the plan, do, check, and act model. This framework comprises first determining and following various compliance requirements and implementing new technologies (plan), then engaging with vendors to ensure accountability via a chain of custody accounting (do), followed by conducting audits to detect for the manifestation of risks and various vulnerabilities (check), and last modifying the plan to reduce vulnerabilities (act) (Reuben and Ware, 2019). Yeboah-Ofori and Islam (2019) suggest a five-phase process for cyberthreat modeling, which entails determining organization objectives, understanding various attack processes, modeling the attack probability and cascading effects of cyberattacks, modeling the threats by specifying the form of the attack process, and, lastly, understanding control mechanisms to handle and mitigate the attacks. Other approaches to risk management have focused more on identification and measurement in frameworks, such as the ability to understand the identification of drivers of risk and their connections to mitigation policies (Faisal *et al.*, 2007). On the other hand, some scholars have refined the scope of cyber risk management specifically to projects, such as proposing a six-step process of risk identification, response and security plan, implementation, assessment, authorization, and monitoring (Presley and Landry, 2016). More general approaches to cyber risk management frameworks have followed in the footsteps of best-practice frameworks. More specifically, the MITIGATE framework suggests general processes that comprise supply chain service analysis, cyberthreat analysis, vulnerability analysis, impact analysis, risk assessment, and risk mitigation (Schauer *et al.*, 2017). More objective- and goal-based frameworks have also been proposed, where managers should focus on various objectives related to cyber risk mitigation and understand the various types of trade-offs firms face, such as addition, omission, and suboptimization (Windelberg, 2016).

5.3.1.7. *Cyber risk mitigation*

As one may expect, just as some in the literature have proposed risk classifications and management frameworks, some have also proposed mitigation strategies, policies, and processes. Generally, the research falls into one of two areas: proactive and reactive mitigation. Proactive mitigation is the collection of policies, strategies, or processes that are established prior to a cyberattack in the hopes of reducing the probability of the attack in the first place, or by reducing the number of vulnerabilities. A few papers have addressed the types of strategies that can be taken to reduce the number of vulnerabilities and/or probability of attack. Colicchia *et al.* (2019) recommend that firms should align their IS strategy with the more general firm strategy and its mission; mandate security training and awareness programs to all employees throughout the firm so as to ensure good "cyber hygiene"; enforce compliance of suppliers and customers with their established security policies; implement data management practices to know who, when, and where data within the firm is being accessed; as well as implement IT security tools.

Others have suggested that a firm needs to have a comprehensive mapping of the entire supply chain to implement sound mitigation policies, such as the assurance of suppliers, due diligence, accreditation, audit arrangements, and security compliance (Agarwal, 2019). Pandey *et al.* (2020) also echo the mitigation strategy of having sound data management practices as well as ensuring that vulnerabilities in software are reduced or eliminated. Some scholars have suggested removing or securing vulnerabilities by preemptively running game-theory models to identify where within the supply chain mitigation should be focused (Schauer *et al.*, 2017; 2019). The sentiment of software security also intersects with user behavior, and it has been suggested that firms should enforce more protective security policies, such as requiring passwords, encryption, authorization and authentication of users, as well as accreditation of security standards and training staff in sound security practices (Warren and Hutchinson, 2000).

Risk mitigation policies have also be proposed to reduce cyber risk that is salient in more specialized areas of the supply chain, such as in additive manufacturing, government-dependent supply chains and products, the cloud, and in physical hardware devices. In the case of additive manufacturing, Gupta *et al.* (2020) recommend implementing a robust information infrastructure so as to keep track of knowledge of the materials and entities within the supply chain. They further recommend the implementation of anti-reverse engineering technologies as well as policies that secure CAD files. In the case of the international space station, Falco (2019) proposes various mitigation strategies to reduce the risk that is salient in the dependent supply chain. They suggest that implementing access control management, specialized security workforce and appropriate security tools, the fostering of a security culture, the engagement with the security research community, as well as the development of custom security tools can be leveraged to mitigate cyber risk.

They also highly recommend that sound proactive, rather than reactive, policies be put into place, since the consequences of cyberattacks have grave implications (Falco, 2019). The strategies of hardware security and software security have also been echoed by Mansfield *et al.* (2013). They further suggest that network security policies such as bandwidth allocation, encryption, and authorization and authentication can improve the proactive mitigation of cyber risk. It has even been suggested that having a more modular design of the cyber supply chain, moderated by the decision rights of the IT unit in the organization, can reduce perceived cyber risk (Xue *et al.*, 2013). Last, implementing mitigation policies through contract design, governance, third-party integration, protection of stored data, and the authentication and communication of secured data can also alleviate the concerns of cyber risk (Wulf *et al.*, 2019).

A less discussed area in the literature is the idea of reactive mitigation policies. While it has been suggested that reactive policy with respect to cyber risk can have devastating outcomes (Falco, 2019), some scholars in the literature have suggested the reactive policies are necessary in the event that a risk manifests despite the implementation of proactive mitigation strategy. For example, Colicchia *et al.* (2019) suggest implementing an event management system to increase situational awareness. This involves identifying dependencies between agents within the supply chain and the various external and internal systems present throughout the supply chain. Likewise, it has been suggested that the use of advanced analytical models and information systems can aid managers in cyberattack scenarios in the event of a cyber risk event manifesting so as to aid reactive mitigation at the time of, rather than preemptive of, the attack (Zheng and Albert, 2019b).

5.3.1.8. *Cyber risk, harm, and attack propagation*

Interestingly enough, while the concept of more general supply chain risk propagation is still in its infancy in the supply chain academic literature (Garvey and Carnovale, 2020), some have actually identified and taken into account this concept with respect to cyber supply chain risk management. For example, Agrafiotis *et al.* (2018) suggest that when a cyber risk has manifested into tangible harm, this may lead to a propagation of the harm itself downward to customers and upward to the organization. In their case on the propagation of cyber harm in Sony, they found that the organization having exposed or leaking their data led to a disruption in operations, which led to a cost in the appropriate public relations (PR) response, subsequently followed by a loss in revenue, damaged relationship with customers, punitive damages, and reduced profits. Likewise, on the customer end, the exposure of the data led to confusion, a loss of service, the feeling of being upset, having their identity stolen, leading to a loss of money and subsequently frustration (Agrafiotis *et al.*, 2018).

Others have suggested that when a business partner in the supply chain has cyber vulnerabilities, they are not just isolated to that one firm, but rather the exploitation of the vulnerability may "propagate in the overall network of interconnected ICT assets" (Schauer *et al.*, 2019, p. 2). Hence, it has been suggested that there are two views that "need to be considered in the analysis of a specific vulnerability: on the one hand, what are the possible ways (paths in the asset network) to reach that vulnerability instead of attacking it directly (if that is possible at all). On the other hand, after exploiting one vulnerability, what are the other possible vulnerabilities an adversary is able to reach (e.g. due to additional privileges or access to other assets)" (Schauer *et al.*, 2017, pp. 417–418). In order to model these effects of propagation, Ghadge *et al.* (2019) suggest a parsimonious model of tripropagation zones. They argue that risk propagation affects three major zones: within the firm (primary propagation), within the supply chain of the firm (secondary propagation), and outward to the society in general (tertiary propagation) (Ghadge *et al.*, 2019). More analytical approaches that take into account the probability of attacks and the various attack scenarios related to propagation have also been proposed in this literature (Yeboah-Ofori and Islam, 2019).

5.3.1.9. *Challenges faced by firms*

Firms not only face cyber risk and need to implement mitigation strategies to prevent them from manifesting and spreading but also need to be aware of the various challenges that exist within and outside of the organization in implementing the said strategies. Another theme that is present in the cyber supply chain literature is the set of challenges firms face in not only preventing risk but also detecting and measuring it. For example, Urciuoli (2015) argues that firms will face challenges in implementing polices due to differing regulations in the context of cross-border trade. The various companies within such a supply chain "need to deal with different cultures, geopolitical and organizational issues, regulatory compliance frameworks, and ultimately with different ICT systems, standards, and technologies operated by different actors and under different business logics" (Urciuoli, 2015, p. 14). Essentially, trying to treat the virtual supply chain as a single entity to manage necessitates doing so over multiple companies in multiple organizations across multiple countries with differing regulations.

This poses a challenge to instating and ensuring compliance with cyber risk mitigation strategies. This sentiment is echoed by Ghadge *et al.* (2019), who further add that supply chain cybersecurity can be difficult to accomplish due to employees being considered the first line of defense in the cybersecurity world. Training employees to keep up to date with new forms of attacks, as well as the technical knowledge that is often needed to understand the attacks, poses an additional burden on firms looking to obtain a security culture around those in the firm. It it further compounded when such employees feel a wearing down of commitment as a result of not witnessing a cyberattack. A question remains for firms: how can they ensure not only commitment but also continuous commitment toward a secure supply chain (Ghadge *et al.*, 2019)?

5.3.2. *Supply chain cyber resilience*

The literature also conveyed the theme of resilience in cyber supply chains, a concept that many refer to as "supply chain cyber resilience," for which a few different definitions have been proposed. For example, some have adopted the definition of cyber resilience as "the ability of systems and organizations to withstand cyber events, measured by the combination of mean time to failure and mean time to recovery" (Boyes, 2015, pp. 28–29) while others have taken a wider perspective, arguing that it is "a business issue and should be woven into business or enterprise risk management, it should be considered across all business operations, and it has special relevance to an acquirer's supply chains" (Davis, 2015, p. 24). Others have chosen to take into account the idea of robustness into the definition of resilience, such as it being "the evolving characteristic of an organization to withstand disruptions to the information systems essential for supply chain operations, through capabilities that allow it to react with adaptability (agility, flexibility, and learning), limiting the disruption effect on customers" (Estay and Khan, 2015, p. 6), as well as it being "the capability of a supply chain to maintain its operational performance when faced with cyber-risk" (Khan and Estay, 2015, p. 2).

To date, a variety of cyber resilience frameworks have been proposed within the context of supply chain management. Urciuoli (2015, p. 15) suggests that "by smartly combining technologies and services that exist today on the marketplace or that are being developed in RD projects," cyber resilience can be achieved. In addition, models have been proposed that put people, process, physical assets, and technological assets at the forefront of the variety of sources of vulnerability, as well as the variety of threats such as hacktivism, corporate espionage, etc. These vulnerabilities as well as threats have been argued to directly affect a supply chain's cyber resilience (Boyens *et al.*, 2015). In addition to managerial frameworks, others in this literature have repurposed the term "resilience" and have conflated it with "risk" (Urciuoli *et al.*, 2014; Hannan, 2018). Some have proposed analytical models to study supply chain cyber resilience from the perspective of response, restoration, and recovery (Heath *et al.*, 2020; Sepulveda and Khan, 2017; Heath *et al.*, 2017).

5.3.3. *National security and supply chain cyber risk*

A theme that was very prevalent in the literature at the intersection of cybersecurity and supply chain management was the idea that various governments around the world hold an interest in understanding, characterizing, managing, and regulating supply chain cyber risk and resilience. Countries have major and complex supply chains that are not only responsible for satisfying market demands and needs within these various countries but also supply governments' needs worldwide. As such, various countries have responded and set official policies to address the cyberthreats and risks faced by many supply chains. For example, the US' Initiative 11 of the Comprehensive National Cybersecurity Initiative, India's National Cyber Security Policy, China's Administrative Measures for the Multi-level Protection of Information Security, as well as Russia's plans to scrap all US-made software and switch to Linux-based operating systems have all been proposed as policy initiatives to not only protect the assets of each of these countries but also to help mitigate the risks of their national supply chains and the supply chains from which these governments source (Charney *et al.*, 2011). Supply chain cyber risk management and resilience management have been studied and proposed for use in the International Space Station (Hannan, 2018). Furthermore, NIST has set forth a list of standards for managing such risks in the US Federal Government (Boyens *et al.*, 2015). Frameworks have also been proposed for handling cyberthreats and risks at the project level within the Department of Defense (Presley and Landry, 2016) as well as understanding the risks and mitigation policies for IT equipment on the battlefield (Mansfield *et al.*, 2013).

5.4. Major Themes Related to Supply Chain Security

Separate from risk management and cyber disruption, another set of themes we uncovered in our review of the literature were those related to the ideas of security. Security, while related to risk and resiliency, is a different concept, one that tends to concern itself over the various policies, processes, and strategies for the protection of assets. This is yet another field that has not found an unambiguous definition upon which to settle. Yet, some have offered insights and hints of what this area could comprise. For example, Linton *et al.* (2014, p. 340) suggest that security in the cyber supply chain "relate to protection of valuable information, assets, and funds." Similar definitions have been hinted at, but with a more refined scope on the various physical assets within the supply chain for which are connected to, physically or virtually, an information system or other forms of IT (Urciuoli and Hintsa, 2017). On the other hand, Safa (2017) provides a more refined definition, precisely that of the protection of information assets within the supply chain. Despite some progress in this stream of literature, few have offered a definition of "security in the supply chain."

5.4.1. *Information flow between firms and actors*

Another theme we uncovered was that of the protection of information and information assets that are involved in the flow of information between two or more firms. Research in this area has primarily been conducted on the operational level by constructing specific security protocols in the communication of sensitive information (Chiu and Chen, 2005) or in the transfer of IT itself (da Silva *et al.*, 2019). Karlsson *et al.* (2016) put forth a framework that suggests IS between firms involves people, organization design and strategy, technology, and process. Other frameworks have been proposed for the purpose of securing useful data sharing by way of understanding how models can be used with tools and techniques on various types of abstracted data in varying contexts, such as government or general data providers (Sarathy and Muralidhar, 2006).

System designs have also been proposed, such as the one that Chiu and Chen (2005) suggested, which involves implementing multiple service layers such as the integrated intermediary level, the database storage and retrieval level, the XML document conversion level, and the message transmission level, to ensure secure interchange of data between systems across firms.

Another topic lightly discussed in this body of literature also involves the security of digital confidentiality, which is the "property of proprietary assets kept private to their owner(s)" (Massimino *et al.*, 2018, p. 1493). However, not all assets related to cyber supply chain security relate to information transfer. Indeed, da Silva *et al.* (2019) offer a taxonomy of different types of technological assets that may transfer between firms and necessitates protection, such as tangible assets (machines and equipment, products, hardware, etc.), tangible and/or intangible assets (results of scientific research), and intangible assets (logical software, experiences, knowledge, and technical support).

5.4.2. *Digital and physical asset security*

The literature pertaining to cybersecurity concepts in the supply chain appear to create a distinction between physical assets and digital assets, both of which are called for protection via strategy and policy formation. For example, software is often considered a digital asset that is vulnerable to illegal distribution (Lahiri, 2012). However, restricting focus to merely digital assets in the scope of cybersecurity, despite popular opinion, is misleading. Indeed, "one of the common mistakes about cybersecurity is restricting the phenomenon to technology" (Mayounga, 2017, p. 20). The literature appears to support the broad idea that there are different types of assets for which cybersecurity within the supply chain should protect. For example, Melnyk *et al.* (2019, pp. 34–35) suggest three majors types of assets that should be protected: IT (digital assets), intellectual property (intangible assets), and operational technology (computer-controlled processes that drive operations). A similar taxonomy of assets has also been suggested by Rodger and George (2017). Essentially, the assets for which cybersecurity in the supply chain should protect are those digital/intangible as well as tangible assets that interact with cyberspace.

5.4.3. *Cyber crime and cyber harm*

While cyber harm is not well defined in the literature, as we have illustrated earlier, it appears to be an intersecting theme with security. What distinguishes security from risk is that of protection of assets versus protection from disruption. Thus, cyber harm also happens to make its way in the discussion of security, since part of the harms are not only to intentionally or unintentionally disrupt various processes within the supply chain but also to cause harm to digital or physical assets within the parts of the supply chain exposed to cyberspace. Take for example the taxonomy of cyber harm proposed by Agrafiotis *et al.* (2018), who suggest that physical or digital harm can occur as a result of an attack, such as the corruption of a computer file or the description of a computer itself. Clim (2019), in his description of Industry 5.0 being the next revolution, which is Industry 4.0 with the added feature of cognition, explains that industry is headed toward full digitalization, and many of the physical assets that are at risk could result from various types of cyber-related attacks. However, a distinction appears to be implicitly emphasized in various papers with the idea of "cyber crime." If there is intentional cyber harm by an individual, the implication is that the individual perpetrating the harm is thus potentially committing a crime (Agrafiotis *et al.*, 2018). While this concept has been used interchangeably with cyber harm, risk, and security in the literature (Melnyk *et al.*, 2019; Simon and Omar, 2020; Wolden *et al.*, 2015), it is worth noting that the literature appears to correlate it with the intent of an individual to damage an asset of some form for some form of social or economic benefit (Agrafiotis *et al.*, 2018). Put differently, the literature seems to portend that the behavior of individuals is necessary to understand since such behaviors may be drivers of cyber harm. Indeed, "those committing such crimes are getting bolder, more creative and more unpredictable" (Melnyk *et al.*, 2019, p. 35).

5.4.4. *Supply chain design and visibility FE*

In the scope of security, the literature also discusses ways in which security could and should be an objective in the design of supply chains as well as take into account the visibility of those supply chains. Visibility refers to not only the ability of the supply chain to "see" its own structure but also the ability and willingness to share information about infrastructure, policies, strategies, and processes across the various members (Mayounga, 2017). Such visibility is important and can be achieved through collaborative security practices (Urciuoli, 2010). Such visibility allows firms the ability to understand which assets need protecting, as well as who is responsible for the protection. Put simply, visibility in the supply chain aids its cybersecurity. The design itself of the supply chain thus enhances this visibility. The literature suggests that the integration of blockchain technology in the design of the supply chain not only helps secure transactions and increases accountability but also aids in increasing the visibility throughout the supply chain (Yang *et al.*, 2015; Lu *et al.*, 2013; Smith and Dhillon, 2019). However, some have suggested that cyberharm and risk can impede on the design of the supply chain itself. It has been suggested that such harms may disrupt electric grids or infect autonomous vehicles (Fawcett and Waller, 2014). Put simply, the literature suggests that a major concern of supply chain cybersecurity is not just restricted to process but also the design of the entire supply chain itself.

5.5. Major Themes Related to IT and Systems

On the third major area of the literature review, we identified that the extant research related to supply chain management and cybersecurity discussed matters related to the digital infrastructure of the supply chain. As we will explain soon, some in the literature have mentioned a concept known as the "cyber supply chain," with varying conceptualizations and definitions. In addition, some have suggested the role that information systems play in not only serving as a bedrock for information management within the firm and the supply chain but also as an enabling force to aid firms in the risk, resilience, and security processes of the firm. We will conduct a review of this literature as well. Lastly, the literature discusses a relatively new set of ideas in the scope of supply chain management: Industry 4.0. This is the integration of various technologies that are not information systems, but rather newer forms of IT that aid in the execution and planning of the various supply chain processes. Such an introduction of technology has put firms at greater risk of cyberattacks and harm, and some in the literature are now questioning if the purported benefits of these technologies in gaining efficiency have been gained at the cost of compromised security and increased risk.

5.5.1. *The "cyber" supply chain*

The advancement of information systems and technology, as well as the introduction of Industry 4.0–related concepts such as additive manufacturing, radio frequency identification devices (RFIDs), IoT, and blockchain, have led to new concept in supply chain design and management known as the "cyber supply chain." This stream of literature is still in its infancy.

Some, however, have spent time to define this new concept in supply chain management. One of the earlier definitions of the cyber supply chain is the "entire set of key actors involved with/using cyber infrastructure: system end-users, policymakers, acquisition specialists, system integrators, network providers, and software/hardware suppliers. These users/providers' organizational and process-level interactions to plan, build, manage, maintain, and defend cyber infrastructure" (Boyson *et al.*, 2009, p. 5). Kim and Im (2014, p. 387) define it as "a supply chain enhanced by cyber-based technologies to establish an effective value chain." On the other hand, Melnyk *et al.* (2019) define the cyber supply chain as the collection of technologies such as Industry 4.0, the IoT, cloud computing, machine-to-machine communication, 3D printing, social media, and various other forms of digital communication and technology integrated into supply chain processes. Other authors, while not explicitly using the phrase "cyber supply chain," appear to refer to this same concept in other ways. However, what adds confusion to this term is that some in the literature refer to a type of supply chain based on the *product* being manufactured (i.e. hardware, software, etc.), while others refer to the concept of the *integration* of the product itself into a supply chain.

For example, Zheng and Albert (2019b) refer to the "IT supply chain" as being synonymous with the "cyber supply chain," in that it is a supply chain that is dependent on the integration of various IT assets into the various supply chain processes. On the other hand, Smith *et al.* (2007) refer to the "IT-enabled supply chain" as mainly being the medium through which information along the supply chain is communicated and stored. Other phrases have been used to describe a similar concept, such as the "digital supply chain," which is the "interorganizational systems (IOSs) that firms implement to digitize the processes of transaction and collaboration with their supply chain partners (i.e. upstream suppliers and downstream customers)" (Xue *et al.*, 2013, p. 326). While not explicitly defined, the "virtual supply chain" has been use to characterize the collection of "the formation of virtual trading communities, the emergence of virtual knowledge communities, and the relocation and integration of interorganizational business processes in the cyberspace" (Smith and Dhillon, 2019, p. 299). A more common phrase that the literature uses is the "Information and Telecommunications (ICT) supply chain." This is the specific type of supply chain that corresponds to the production and delivery of various types of information and telecommunications components (McDaniel, 2013; Urciuoli, 2015). Indeed, the

"ICT supply chain is the carrier of big data, as it is responsible for producing all the software and hardware related to the production, storage and application of big data" (Lu *et al.*, 2013, p. 1066). Others, however, have described such supply chains as a "cyber supply chain," which comprises the manufacturing and delivery of hardware, software, and firmware (Inserra and Bucci, 2014). Related terms that have been used to describe this type of supply chain also include the "software supply chain" (Ellison *et al.*, 2010) as well as the "electronic supply chain" (McFadden and Arnold, 2010). As such, the literature appears to have great conflation of these terms to refer to different concepts.

5.5.2. *IT and system designs*

While the concept of the "cyber supply chain" remains to be clarified, one set of topics that the extant literature has discussed is the various types of information systems that have been integrated within the supply chain and its corresponding processes. It further has been discussed how various types of information systems can be used to aid the supply chain cybersecurity and risk management processes. For example, Mamun *et al.* (2018) propose a method for secured path authentication in RFID-enabled supply chains. Xue *et al.* (2013) propose that various information technologies used in the supply chain should be designed in a modular structure so as to increase the cybersecurity across the supply chain. Others have advanced specific cybersecurity analysis methods, such as the attack graph analysis, to embed in risk management information systems (Polatidis *et al.*, 2018). Boiko *et al.* (2019) suggest that information systems are designed for the purpose of managing the supply maintance as well as the distribution of the product throughout the entire organization. Braund (2016) put forth a set of requirements for a platform that would aid firms in being able to carry out the various mitigation processes in supply chain cybersecurity. Last, it has been suggested that we have transcended from supply chains competing toward the information systems and analytics algorithms that support the competing cyber supply chains (Ivanov *et al.*, 2019).

5.5.3. *Information systems and human behavior*

An absence of integrated perspectives in other prominent disciplines such as information systems contributes to the ontological challenges of structuring cyber knowledge in supply chain and operations management; as aptly stated, there has been "…some scattered progress in developing disconnected pieces of knowledge associated with the potential weaknesses, flaws and intrinsic vulnerabilities… and have unwittingly failed to study the big picture" (Samuel, 2013). "Information systems" as the study of (and practice at) the intersection of information, technology, and human behavior, is an important aspect of supply chain cybersecurity as it provides insights into aspects of human contributions to both cyber harm and cyber defense. Extant research has demonstrated the vulnerability of human performance to information manipulation, and information format variation, which can be used to enhance, or inadvertently suppress human performance (Walsham, 2015; Samuel, 2017; Samuel *et al.*, 2017). While it is outside of the scope of the chapter to discuss the role of impact of human behavior, it is important to keep it in sight due to the pervasive influence of information, corresponding human behavior, and performance, upon supply chain cybersecurity.

5.5.4. *Industry 4.0/5.0, blockchain, and IoT*

Recently, the cyber supply chain literature pertaining to information technologies has transcended from discussions on the designs, implementations, and human behavior and interaction with various types of information systems to more advanced technologies that go beyond a simple computer system–hardware–database structure. Generally, Industry 4.0 refers to the digitalization of firm processes (Ardito *et al.*, 2019). Put simply, we are currently experiencing a shift from old pen-and-paper techniques of manufacturing, distribution, and other related supply chain processes to full integration with existing business intelligence and business analytics information systems. The purpose of Industry 4.0 is not only to digitalize any and all aspects of the supply chain but also aid in the integration of various processes across firms. The possibilities are essentially endless in what can be digitalized in the supply chain.

Ardito *et al.* (2019) provide a taxonomy of the current existing technologies that supply chains have already integrated into existing information systems and processes. They refer to these as the "enabling technologies," which comprise advanced manufacturing, additive manufacturing, augmented reality, simulation, cloud computing, industrial IoT, cybersecurity, and big data analytics and customer profiling. There is extensive literature on the topic of Industry 4.0 and its integration into supply chain processes, as well as the security and risks they pose due to such integration. Hiromoto *et al.* (2017) suggest that IoT faces many challenges, such as the infection of malicious malware. They suggest the design of an IoT-based supply chain necessitates securing networks as well as implementing machine learning models. The integration of RFID into supply chains have also shown to cause security vulnerabilities. Qi *et al.* (2016) suggest that firms that implement these technologies can freely share information with their vendors and other firms. The freedom to share this information, however, has led to security and privacy loopholes in the supply chain system. In addition, the devices themselves cause a problem from a physical perspective. RFIDs are susceptible to "ticket switching," which is the "illegitimate act of switching the price identifier on an item that results in the customer paying less than the item's retailer-set selling price" (Zhou and Piramuthu, 2013, p. 802). A related problem is the RFID tag separation, which is when a tag and its associated item is either intentionally or unintentionally separated. Indeed, tag separation effectively represents a "loss of item information and thus in turn incurs additional labor and other … costs for recovery…" (Tu *et al.*, 2018, p. 14).

Other issues arise in the area of the manufacturing of smart products. Analogous to how RFIDs are at risk for physical and virtual information breach, so too are the technologies that enable communication across states of manufacturing (Riel *et al.*, 2017).

More specifically, the properties of an IoT portend great security challenges. Yang *et al.* (2015) suggest that a common IoT has the properties of heterogeneity, specificity, resource constraint, wireless, infectivity, mobility, and scalability. While some of these are attractive properties to implement for the digitalization of a supply chain process, they lead to security issues, such as the trust of components, the need for device authentication, possible hardware theft, access control, data confidentiality, data integrity, service availability, finite lifetime, physical tampering, and user privacy. One technology that has been proposed as a means to further secure supply chains that is often associated with Industry 4.0 as well as IoT is blockchain. Blockchain is a "distributed ledger system that affords three primary benefits: decentralization, transparency, and anti-tampering" (White and Daniels, 2019, p. 1). Its use in supply chain management has been shown to reduce supply chain risk by providing speedy and simplified processes, reducing the risk and asymmetric information, identifying risk sources, mitigating the negative impact of disruptions, and eliminating fraud, among reducing other related risks that are salient throughout the supply chain (Alkhudary *et al.*, 2020).

Blockchain has also been suggested to be used as a method for authentication as well as understanding the authenticity of data (Fu and Zhu, 2019). In the energy sector, blockchain has also shown to provide accountability and smart contracting toward various supply chain processes (Liang *et al.*, 2018). On the IT end, it also has been used to aid software patching as well as configuration management in supply chain IT systems (Mylrea and Gourisetti, 2018). Furthermore, it has shown promise in maintaining trust among actors in supply chains and their relationship by providing additional transparency and authenticity (Smith and Dhillon, 2019). While it has been argued that blockchain is not the "end all, be all" of cybersecurity policy (Mylrea and Gourisetti, 2018), it has shown great promise in its ability to serve as a useful component of a larger cybersecurity strategy.

5.6. Supply Chain Security

After the events of 9/11, academics and practitioners alike came to the realization that the then recent globalized nature of business via the emergence of highly interconnected supply chains around the world necessitated a fresh look at security practices (Williams *et al.*, 2009). Since then, a large number of frameworks have been proposed to not only define and characterize the notion of *supply chain security* but also to develop strategies to handle this critically important factor (Lu *et al.*, 2019). Supply chain security is defined as the "prevention of contamination, damage, or destruction of any supply chain assets or products" (Autry and Sanders, 2009, p. 309). It can be envisioned to be a more general form of supply chain disruption and risk management, where managers attempt to mitigate not only the risk of disruption but also the more general possibility of damage to any assets within the supply chain (Autry and Griffis, 2008).

Many frameworks have been proposed as to how firms can measure and establish their supply chain security. Primarily, it has been suggested that firms can achieve security by increasing their dynamic capabilities (Autry and Griffis, 2008; Lu *et al.*, 2019). Through continuity planning, firms can identify their dynamic security management capabilities, which are defined as "resource bases that can be activated or deployed toward the goal of securing the firm's supply chain" (Autry and Sanders, 2009, p. 314).

These capabilities rest in one of three categories: processes, technology, and human resources (Autry and Griffis, 2008). Various supply chain security practices have also been suggested, such as establishing and ensuring security compliance policies as well as maintaining redundant supply of stock (Park *et al.*, 2016). Other approaches have suggested that security practices within firms can be categorized as being inter-organizational, intra-organizational, or a hybrid of the two (Williams *et al.*, 2009). This of course would necessitate a study of not only the types of relationships between firms that would enable such security practices to succeed but also a firm's culture toward security measures (Williams *et al.*, 2009). It has been suggested that the purpose of supply chain security is not only to protect the supply chain assets but also to ensure that the firm can achieve its objectives in a "safe" manner (Yang and Wei, 2013).

Various constructs have been proposed as a means to characterize supply chain security. One conceptualization is through the lens of supply chain security orientation (SCSO), which is defined as the "firm-level orientation representing the firm's collective attention to both supply chain security management and supply chain risk management principles" (Autry and Griffis, 2008, p. 44). The concept of SCSO is derived by observing the intersection of supply chain security and risk management. Its components consist of security planning and preparing, security-related partnerships, organizational adaptation, and security-dedicated communications and technology (Autry and Griffis, 2008). A related concept to supply chain security is that of supply chain visibility, which is defined as the ability to not only know who are members of the broader supply chain (Carter *et al.*, 2015) but also the current and near real-time inventories, stock in shipment, and other operational and strategic knowledge of the supply chain. It has been suggested that having such visibility of the supply chain enables firms to engage in continuity planning (Autry and Sanders, 2009).

In addition, specific applications of technology for the purpose of supply chain security have been suggested as a means to achieve performance. These include, but are not limited to, asset tracking, geofencing, on-board monitoring systems, entry-point passage facilitation, and shipment and network status information (Autry and Sanders, 2009). Previous studies have suggested that supply chain security culture, which is the set of shared values and beliefs of employees and upper management toward security initiatives and their willingness to "buy in," is a moderator of the implementation of supply chain security practices, which has also been shown to be related with supply chain security performance (Lu *et al.*, 2019). Supply chain security culture has also been shown to be an important construct in explaining, yet is distinct from supply chain resilience (Williams *et al.*, 2009). In addition, it has been suggested that decisions characterize supply chain security, namely those related to facility management, cargo management, inventory management, information management, personnel management and security training, business partner and company management, as well as crisis management and disaster recovery (Yang and Wei, 2013).

Supply chain security performance metrics have also been proposed in the extant literature as a way to determine the consequences of security practices. Supply chain security metrics, such as the ability to improve customer service, detect incidents, recover from incidents, and increase service levels and product quality, as well as the ability to reduce incidents, have been proposed as a means of measuring security performance (Whipple *et al.*, 2009). Likewise, so has cargo safety, supply chain visibility, supply chain efficiency, and supply chain resilience (Zailani *et al.*, 2015). In summary, the general concept of supply chain security is focused on the idea of protecting supply chain assets. While this concept is related to, and intersects with, supply chain risk management, it is distinct in that its focus is not so much process-based but rather resource-based (Autry and Sanders, 2009; Williams *et al.*, 2009).

5.7. Supply Chain Risk Management

In order to understand the nature of cybersecurity and cyberattacks in supply chains, one must first understand the nature of supply chain risk and disruption. Practitioners have come to realize that supply chain disruptions are an incredibly important concern to bear in mind throughout various supply chain planning processes (Craighead *et al.*, 2007). The consequences of not managing disruptions to supply chain processes has been shown to result in a reduction in firm performance (Hendricks and Singhal, 2005). As a result of this necessary focus, many scholars have shifted their attention to the study of characterizing, defining, theorizing, and analyzing the antecedents and consequences, as well as the possible mitigation strategies, of supply chain disruptions. The more recent literature on the matter define a supply chain disruption as "any event that prevents the supply chain from operating at an expected or planned state" (Garvey and Carnovale, 2020, p. 2). Most of the literature restrict their attention to the more refined scope of events that disrupt the flow of material itself (Bode and Macdonald, 2017; Craighead *et al.*, 2007).

Classifications and taxonomies of supply chain disruptions aid managers and academics in their ability to craft meaningful and impactful mitigation strategies (Jüttner *et al.*, 2003; Chopra and Sodhi, 2004). More recently, DuHadway *et al.* (2019) propose that supply chain disruptions should primarily be classified based on the type of events that led to the disruption itself. They propose that all supply chain disruptions can be categorized into one of two categories: endogenous and exogenous. Endogenous disruptions are those that occur within a firm's supply chain, but due to some event within the supply chain itself. On the other hand, exogenous disruptions are those that occur within a firm's supply chain but due to some event outside of the firm's supply chain itself (DuHadway *et al.*, 2019). It has more recently been suggested that firms should focus their disruption management strategies on endogenous and exogenous disruptions close to or within the control of the focal firm, rather than on exogenous events outside of the firm's visibility or control (Garvey and Carnovale, 2020).

Despite 20 years of academic research on the topic of supply chain disruption and risk (Ho *et al.*, 2015), some authors have noted that disruption and risk are often confounded yet distinct concepts (Park *et al.*, 2016; DuHadway and Carnovale, 2019). A supply chain disruption is the disturbance itself of a supply chain process (DuHadway *et al.*, 2019; Garvey and Carnovale, 2020), whereas a supply chain risk is any event that directly leads to a disruption (DuHadway *et al.*, 2018). Put differently, a supply chain disruption is the manifestation of a supply chain risk, and a supply chain risk is a manifestation of a firm's inability to control (Park *et al.*, 2016). The more recent literature on supply chain risk management has suggested that the study of these distinct concepts is of extreme importance to scholars and practitioners alike. Analogous to supply chain disruptions, academics have put forth various frameworks to not only measure supply chain risk (Ojha *et al.*, 2018; Qazi *et al.*, 2015; Lockamy III and McCormack, 2012) but also classify and categorize it (Bode and Wagner, 2015).

Despite the vast progress in the literature of understanding, modeling, and suggesting mitigation strategies of supply chain risk, many authors have restricted their attention to only a single firm with a handful of echelons, usually only two or three levels up or down from the focal firm (Ho *et al.*, 2015; Tomlin, 2009; Li, 2017). It was adequately and more recently pointed out that since supply networks are complex adaptive systems (Carter *et al.*, 2015), restricting the attention of study of supply chain risk management to only a single or handful of firms is highly unrealistic, and any results from such models may lack external validity (Garvey and Carnovale, 2020; Ivanov, 2018). As such, one should move to more of the "network level" to better understand supply chain dynamics such as risk (Borgatti and Li, 2009). Garvey *et al.* (2015, p. 619) were among the first in the literature to suggest that while supply chain risk aims to understand the *direct* causes of supply chain disruptions, many "current risk models are used on a smaller, more local level of analysis for very specific problems leading to locally optimal solutions…," and hence these "…models do not account for risk propagation."

A more recent observation has been the distinction between risk and disruption propagation (Dolgui *et al.*, 2018; Garvey and Carnovale, 2020), analogous to the distinction between disruption and risk (DuHadway *et al.*, 2019). Indeed, unlike "disruption propagation, where the potential sequence of disruption is solely dependent on the structure of the supply network, risk propagation is more general and describes non-structural as well as structural related events that can lead to disruptions, ripple effects, or other risk propagations" (Garvey and Carnovale, 2020, p. 3). Put differently, when we discuss supply chain disruption/risk propagation, the distinction is primarily due to which specific events manifested, and which events merely had a change in likelihood versus those that actually manifested. The so-called "ripple effect" is a specific term attributed to the concept of disruption propagation (Ivanov, 2018) and is defined as the collection of disruptions in the supply chain that have occurred specifically due to the occurrence of a dependent disruption. For example, if a product is moving from station 1 to station 2 in an assembly line with no buffer inventory, and station 1 is disrupted, then we know with certainty that station 2 will also be disrupted. This is an example of the disruption "propagating," and this specifically is referred to as the "ripple effect." On the other hand, if we add buffer inventory in between station 1 and station 2, now when station 1 is disrupted, we no longer have a ripple effect, but rather a *risk propagation*. This is due to the fact that we no longer have certainty on the disruption of station 2. Put differently, the shutdown of station 1 does not necessarily cause the shutdown of station 2, rather, it changes the *probability* that station 2 will shut down.

The change could occur due to a variety of explanations, such as an explosion that could have led to a fire that subsequently led to the disruption at station 1. The fire could, with a certain probability, spill over to the buffer inventory used by station 2, or the fire could directly damage station 2. In other words, it is not the outcome or manifestation of the outcome itself that is "trickling down", as it does in the case of disruption propagation, but rather, it is the probability of various interconnected events that is "trickling down" upon knowledge of the disruption or the manifestation of other non-disruption–related events (Pearl, 2014). Hence, the concepts of supply chain disruption, risk, disruption propagation, and risk propagation are all necessary to understand since they serve as a foundation of supply chain cybersecurity, as we will demonstrate in the later sections.

5.8. An Ontology of Supply Chain Cybersecurity

Now that we have reviewed the relevant literature in each body of knowledge related to security in the supply chain, we will use the themes to more formally define the various constructs within what many appear to be referring to as the "supply chain cybersecurity." That is, everyone has defined the tools of the trade, and in this section, we will provide an unambiguous definition of the trade itself. Our definition of "supply chain cybersecurity" rests upon the definition of the "cyber supply chain." Hence, we will first formally define this concept. Once we define it, we will leverage the themes and concepts reviewed in the literature to provide a formal definition for "supply chain cybersecurity." Last, we will propose various constructs that we argue constitute this body of knowledge.

5.8.1. *The cyber supply chain*

As we illustrated in Chapter 1, cyberspace has a mind and a body. If supply chains were to interact with cyberspace, then this would imply that it must do so in both of these spaces (i.e. the mind and the body). We can thus infer that in order for a supply chain to interact with "cyber space", it must do so by way of having various assets, be they tangible or intangible, in such respective spaces. We illustrated that supply chains further expand cyberspace by adding various forms of technologies to it and connecting them to the Internet, either directly or indirectly. The various physical components, such as network wires, fibre optic cables, "smart" devices, RFIDs, physical computer systems, and others help expand the "body" of cyberspace, albeit within the specific subspace of the supply chain. Likewise, the "mind" of cyberspace is further expanded by the addition of various forms of information artifacts ranging from knowledge bases, contracts, suppliers lists, performance metrics, and even specific products held in inventory. Put simply, when supply chains expand the body and mind of cyberspace by adding to it these various devices and information artifacts, they are doing so by appending assets to it. The assets themselves are used in various supply chain processes, such as the delivery and manufacturing of products, placing bids in auctions, as well as contracting with suppliers. Hence, we have the following definition:

Definition 1. A **supply chain cyber asset** is a tangible or intangible asset of the supply chain that is used to expand cyberspace either physically (i.e. the "body") or virtually (i.e. the "mind").

Essentially, when the supply chain is "connected" to cyberspace by way of physically expanding its body or mind via assets, the connected components, physical or digital, constitute a new layer of the supply chain not previously identified in the literature, yet hinted at. As the extant literature points out, various themes of the "cyber supply chain" include hardware, software, firmware, information, manufacturing, IoT, blockchain, etc. The supply chain under consideration can be viewed more expansively in scope as simply the original supply chain that has been appended with IT-enabling technologies, or more restrictive in scope as the supply chain that services the components of the IT-enabling technologies embedded in other supply chains. For the purpose of our field of study here, we argue that it is best to consider the "cyber supply chain" as a combination of both, along the two dimensions of the "mind" and "body" of cyberspace, each of which are appended by assets of the firm. While Carter *et al.* (2015) argue that supply chains consist of two layers: the product and support, we argue there is a third interwoven layer: the cyber layer. This layer may consist of physical devices used in any supply chain process (product) or firms that manufacture the physical devices (support). We suggest that two criteria need to hold true in order for an element to be considered to be part of the "cyber supply chain." First, the element must be clearly identified in the more traditional model of supply chain as being in the product or support supply chain (Carter *et al.*, 2015). The second condition is that the element needs to be connected in some fashion to cyberspace, be it physical or virtual. Therefore, we propose the following definition:

Definition 2. The **cyber supply chain** of a focal firm is the collection of nodes and linkages that compose of cyber assets, that are in either the product or support supply chain, that are directly or indirectly connected to cyberspace.

5.9. Supply Chain Cybersecurity

In order to motivate the definition of this new body of knowledge, we will reflect upon ideas from the areas of supply chain security and supply chain risk management. As we demonstrate in our literature review above, the current usage of the phrase "supply chain cybersecurity," and other related phrases, communicates the ideas that firms in a supply chain have a variety of assets that flow between firms via cyberspace. Those assets could be physical assets, such as IoT devices and computer systems, or they could be virtual (i.e. digital) assets such as blueprints, product orders, or inventory information. The extant definitions convey the ideas that these assets are either at risk of being destroyed, compromised, stolen, or altered, or that these assets are at risk of directly or indirectly causing a disruption. For sake of parsimony, when we say that the supply chain has suffered a "loss" of a cyber asset, we are referring to any form of damage, theft, manipulation, or any unintentional change in state of the asset itself. Put differently, the various definitions offered thus far are concerned primarily over the security and prevention of loss of the asset as well as the asset itself being the reason for a disruption in a supply chain process. With this in mind, we now offer the following definition of the body of knowledge that we refer to as "Supply Chain Cybersecurity":

Definition 3. Supply Chain Cybersecurity is the collection of strategies, policies, and processes that manage and mitigate against the possible loss of cyber assets and the possible subsequent disruption of any supply chain process that manifests as a result of the loss of a cyber asset.

5.10. Constructs of Supply Chain Cybersecurity

Now that we have defined the supply chain cybersecurity concept, we will propose related constructs for which we argue constitute this field. We have argued by way of our literature review that this field lies at the union of supply chain security and supply chain risk management, themselves supported by the field of IT and information systems as well as business analytics and intelligence. From these areas, we adapt older constructs to fit within the "cyberspace" framework. Before we borrow concepts from these respective fields and re-adapt them, we will borrow concepts that overlap both fields.

5.10.1. *Cyber capabilities*

Generally, the resource-based view (RBV) of the firm has suggested that firms achieve sustained competitive advantage by acquiring resources that are valuable, rare, inimitable, and non-substitutable (VRIN) (Barney *et al.*, 2001). In the supply chain context, a major drawback of the RBV is that it has failed to take into account the dynamic nature of markets. Thus, while a firm may be able to acquire resources that are VRIN, the question is what can it do with those resources to adapt to the radical and rapid changes within the market? The answer to this question lies in the firm's ability to develop dynamic capabilities, which are the "firm's processes that use resources- specifically the processes to integrate, reconfigure, gain and release resources-to match and even create market change. Dynamic capabilities thus are the organizational and strategic routines by which firms achieve new resource configurations as markets emerge, collide, split, evolve, and die" (Eisenhardt and Martin, 2000, p. 1107). The theory of dynamic capabilities is a response to critics that put forth the argument that the traditional RBV does not take into account the dynamic nature of markets (Reuter *et al.*, 2010). In other words, firms need to not only acquire resources that can lead them to a sustained competitive advantage but also develop the processes that can reconfigure these resources to adequately respond to the rapidly changing pace of markets.

Autry and Sanders (2009) suggest that a firm designs its set of security best practices and processes by way of building dynamic security management capabilities. They argue that these capabilities are "resource bases that can be activated or deployed toward the goal of securing the firm's supply chain" (Autry and Sanders, 2009, p. 314). They suggest that these capabilities rest in one of three categories: processes, technology, and human resources. Arguments have also been posed that a firm's supply chain risk management processes are developed by way of obtaining supply chain capabilities. For example, Teece *et al.* (2016) suggest that risk management processes can be designed by the firm acquiring the dynamic capabilities of knowledge assessment; supply chain partner development; co-evolving, reflexive supply chain control; and supply chain reconfiguration. On the other hand, Hong *et al.* (2018) suggest that a supply chain's set of sustainability practices, of which supply chain risk management is a component, will increase the overall supply chain's dynamic capabilities.

In the scope of IT and management, Fawcett *et al.* (2011) suggest that IT investment is an enabler of the dynamic capability of supply chain collaboration. Likewise, Cepeda and Vera (2007) argue that knowledge management infrastructure, which comprises people, processes, and technology, can impact a firm's available knowledge configuration, thus increasing the firm's operational capabilities. Given that our framework of constructs is dependent on these three major areas of study (security, risk, and IT/IS), we may suspect that firms have the opportunity to obtain sustained competitive advantages by not only creating dynamic capabilities related to supply chain security and supply chain risk management but also through the development, design, and management of the cyber supply chain itself. We thus define the following concept:

Definition 4. A **supply chain cyber capability** is a process that can be used to reconfigure the cyber supply chain and its cyber assets to achieve performance.

5.10.2. *Supply chain cyber visibility, distance, and cyber asset distance*

When discussing the structure of the cyber supply chain, other important constructs enter into the equation when carrying out the practices of design and management of said supply chain. As Carter *et al.* (2015) argue, the visibility of the focal firm's supply chain is the ability of the focal firm to "see" upstream and downstream. Put differently, focal firms have a limited view of not only the processes and products of members within the supply chain within which they operate but also the view of the members themselves. Since the firm's cyber supply chain itself is connected to cyberspace, we argue that the focal firm has a greater level of restriction in their view as to whom and to what they are exposed.

In supply chain management, what a firm could see under the assumption they could see everything is merely just the market, the entire downstream, and the entire upstream. However, cyberspace occupies a much more complex hyper-plane than just firms and consumers. It comprises everyday individuals who are unaffiliated with any form of production, delivery, or purchasing of the firm's product, such as governments, competitors, and everyday people. By merely expanding the space within which the firm's assets are exposed via integration into cyberspace, the ability to see into this "space" is much more restricted than just simply the space of the upstream and downstream supply chain. To describe the view of which the focal firm has of this new space within which it operates, we define:

Definition 5. Supply Chain Cyber Visibility is the amount of knowledge the firm possesses of not only the cyber assets of other firms within the cyber supply chain but also the cyber assets and the actors within cyberspace to which the firm's cyber supply chain is exposed.

Even though a firm must be aware of its visibility within cyberspace, knowing the level of visibility is in part dependent on the level of exposure to which the firm puts its cyber supply chain. By way of adding various cyber assets to the cyber supply chain, the firm further exposes itself to different elements of cyberspace. For example, if a fully vertically integrated firm only had a single connection to the Internet in one physical location, and the other locations, more local, were connected via local network wires that the firm owns, then the level of exposure to cyberspace that the firm puts its information and IoT-enabled systems is minimal. The only entry points into the cyber supply chain is (1) within the supply chain itself (internal actors), and the single entry point from the Internet. In a sense, this more hyperbolic example is "further away" from cyberspace. On the other hand, if the firm is more horizontally integrated, where it connects to other firms over the Internet, and the level of information artifacts, or other cyber assets, are more uniformly distributed across this cyber supply chain, it is in a sense "closer" to cyber space, and hence more exposed to it. Thus, this level of proximity can be adequately described as:

Definition 6. The **Supply Chain Cyber Distance** of a supply chain is the level of exposure it has to cyberspace. The more cyber assets within the cyber supply chain that are closer to actors or the internet, the "closer" it is to cyberspace. The fewer cyber assets it has within its cyber supply chain that are more "distant" from actors or the Internet, the more "distant" the supply chain is from cyberspace.

A point to consider here is that not all of the supply chain's cyber assets will be "close" to entry points within the Internet or to actors, be they internal or external. For example, a firm may have a single computer system that stores a database of its employees' private information. This system may only be accessed by a handful of actors within the firm, and, while it may be connected to the internal network of the firm, it may have various physical and virtual barriers, such as hardware and software firewalls, that make it more challenging for other unauthorized actors to access. This example and our above definition compels us to define a property of supply chain cyber assets, namely:

Definition 7. The **distance** of a supply chain cyber asset is the level of proximity to an internal or external actor or to the Internet.

5.10.3. *Supply chain attack, harm, and disruption*

Our literature review above demonstrates that some research offers varying definitions of cyberattacks, harm, and disruptions, while others consider these terms to be synonymous. In light of our review, we will disentangle these constructs, as we argue, based on the review of the literature, that these are actually distinct, yet, require discussion of each. Given our framework, we have specified that a cyber supply chain consist of supply chain cyber assets, each of which is integrated in some manner with a supply chain process. As we have pointed out in our review of the supply chain risk management literature, more recent definitions of a "supply chain disruption" have transcended from the more traditional view of it being a deviation from the firms ability to match demand (Kleindorfer and Saad, 2005) toward the more modern view of it being a deviation of any supply chain process from its expected operating state (Garvey and Carnovale, 2020). With this in mind, we can define a specific type of supply chain disruption in the scope of the cyber supply chain.

Definition 8. A **Supply Chain Cyber Disruption** is any unplanned deviation from a planned operating state of a supply chain process within the cyber supply chain.

As we have mentioned earlier, the "loss" of a supply chain cyber asset is essentially any unplanned change to the state of said asset. It could be damaged, deemed entirely null and void, or rendered non-existent by way of theft. This is different, as we have illustrated with our above definition, than a supply chain cyber disruption. While the loss of a cyber asset could indeed cause a supply chain cyber disruption, the two are distinct (in which case, the attack become a risk, more on this later). We hence need to distinguish between a few ideas. First, what can be "lost," what specific property of the "what" can be "lost," and by which mechanism can said property of the "what" can be "lost." For example, an inventory lot of cell phones can be tracked by an RFID. Suppose a malicious actor has a device that can remove the RFID, and the actor subsequently carries the lot to their vehicle. In this instance, what is being "attacked"? The "what" is the entire lot with the RFID on it. The property of the lot with the RFID is changed, in an unplanned and malicious manner. The way by which it is changed is through the action of RFID tag removal and the subsequent theft of the lot. Put differently, the lot with the RFID is a supply chain cyber asset, the harm that is being placed on the asset is a physical harm of removing the RFID tag, and the attack itself is "theft." From here, we can distinguish these two different concepts:

Definition 9. A **Supply Chain Cyber Harm** is the specific property of a supply chain cyber asset that can be destructively altered by intentional or unintentional action.

Definition 10. A **Supply Chain Cyber Attack** is the mechanism or strategy by which a malicious actor engages to cause cyber harm to a supply chain.

5.10.4. *Supply chain cyber vulnerability and cyber risk*

The set of themes we uncovered in our literature review were also those of risk and vulnerability. Again, many scholars in the literature appeared to use these synonymously; however, we argue that these are distinct. We do contend, after much theorizing, that the concept of cyber risk and cyberthreat are one in the same. In an attempt to try and find a situation where the two would differ in meaning, we have unfortunately failed in finding or designing such an example. Since many in the literature appear to use everyday language and do not rest on an ontology of well-defined constructs, we appeal to the standard dictionary for clarification. According to Merriam-Webster ("threat," 2020), a "threat" can be one of two related definitions: "an expression of intention to inflict evil, injury, or damage" or "an indication of something impending." Similar language is used in business models, such as the classic SWOT model. When we discuss the idea of "threat" in this model, it is something that *could* happen to the firm but has not yet materialized. This is why it is often distinguished in this model from "weakness." Analyzing the definitions, we see that the words "intent" and "impending" refer to something as well that *could* happen, but yet has possibly not materialized yet.

This is analogous to the concept of risk, which we defined earlier as any event that could lead to a supply chain disruption. It may not be the disruption itself, but rather, any event that may cause one. Since the event has yet to manifest, this is analogous to the ideas of "impending" or "intent," in that the event has yet to materialize. One does not say they "intend" to rob a bank if they already have. They would say they "intended," meaning the usage of the word is in its past tense, signaling that the use of the word "intend" or "intent" is a precursor to the action that is to be carried out or manifested. Hence, we consider the idea of "cyberthreat" and "cyber risk" to be one in the same. However, we would like to point out that in our framework, when we discuss the idea of "manifestation," we refer to one of two types of outcomes. Either a cyber asset is at a loss (cyber harm) or a supply chain process in the cyber supply chain has been disrupted (cyber disruption) as a result of the manifestation of an event (i.e. the "risk"). But what of the concept of "vulnerability"?

Again, the literature is not explicit or clear on this matter. Referring once again to Merriam-Webster ("vulnerable," 2020), a "vulnerability," or more specifically "vulnerable," is something that is "capable of being physically or emotionally wounded" or "open to attack or damage." While it is easy to see why many would confound this with risk, upon deeper inspection it is actually quite distinct. First, we need an entity to discuss what specifically is "vulnerable."

Such an entity is not needed for use of the language risk. While it is true we often speak of what is "at risk," this use of the word is different than just simply using the word "risk." We can think of the entity as being "at risk," and hence, this use of the word would thus be equivalent to "vulnerable."

However, when discussing the concepts of collections of "risks" and "vulnerabilities," we have distinction. "Risks" are events, as we had pointed out earlier. "Vulnerabilities" would be things that are "vulnerable" or open to attack. An event and a "thing" are not equivalent, since the former specifies a collection of things in a moment of time, while a thing is just, well, a thing. We can thus think of "vulnerabilities" as being "things" that can easily be attacked. Putting this within the scope of our framework, we argue that a vulnerability within the cyber supply chain would be anything that makes the supply chain "open to attack" (Merriam Webster, "vulnerable," 2020). As we have specified earlier, an attack is a strategy undertaken by an actor with the intent to cause cyber harm in the cyber supply chain. However, we also have the situation where specific "things" have properties which can deem the "thing" "vulnerable." But in our discussion, vulnerability is not just solely related to attack, despite the second definition. The first definition suggests that the "thing" could be physically or emotionally wounded. A disrupted process in the cyber supply chain is a form of harm, although we would like to keep the distinction between "disruption" and "harm" clean and separate for theoretical and practical reasons. Despite this, we can think of a "thing" as not only being vulnerable to harm, but also disruption, as harm could cause disruption and disruption could cause harm. Thus, when we speak of something in the cyber supply chain as being "vulnerable," it is something that is attractive for a malicious actor to cause harm, or it is something that is likely to disrupt. Thus we have:

Definition 11. A **Supply Chain Cyberthreat/Risk** is any event that could cause a supply chain cyber harm or supply chain cyber disruption to manifest.

Definition 12. A **Supply Chain Cyber Vulnerability** is any supply chain cyber asset that has attractive properties that make it susceptible to supply chain cyber harm or supply chain cyber disruption.

Definition 13. Supply Chain Cyberthreat/Risk is the extent to which the entire cyber supply chain is exposed to various supply chain cyber risks.

Definition 14. Supply Chain Cyber Vulnerability is the extent to which the entire cyber supply chain is exposed to various supply chain cyber vulnerabilities.

5.10.5. *Supply chain cyber propagation constructs*

As we have argued in the review of supply chain risk management, a recent advancement in the literature has been the transcendence from ordinary supply chain disruption and risk toward that of the propagation of disruption and risk. Traditional literature has only considered the events that directly or indirectly lead to a disruption (i.e. risk) as well as the disruption itself (Kleindorfer and Saad, 2005; Hendricks and Singhal, 2005; Jüttner and Ziegenbein, 2009). Recent advancements in this body of literature have suggested that when a risk manifests into a disruption, the disruption itself can change the probabilities of other events (i.e. risks) as well as the manifestation of other events or disruptions (Ivanov *et al.*, 2018a; Ojha *et al.*, 2018; Garvey *et al.*, 2015). This is referred to as disruption propagation, or more popularly known as the "ripple effect" (Ivanov *et al.*, 2018b). Distinct from this is the concept of the risk probabilities changing as well as other risk manifesting as a result of the risk events manifesting, a concept referred to as risk propagation (Garvey *et al.*, 2015; Garvey and Carnovale, 2020).

We have demonstrated in our literature review that some authors have actually discussed the concerns with similar dynamics in the case of cyberattacks and cyber risk management. When an event, or a supply chain cyber risk, manifests, it likely will cause a change in the probability of other related events in the cyber supply chain. It may even result in a cyber disruption or cyber harm. Hence, we have the idea of *cyber propagation*, where the manifestation of any event in the cyber supply chain can lead to a change in the probability of manifestation of other events, which themselves may eventually lead to a cyber harm or a cyber disruption. In light of the distinction between "disruption propagation" and "risk propagation," we offer analogous definitions for these constructs in the cyber context.

We would like to note that despite the popular literature on the matter, "propagation" implies that a linear sequence of events occur. However, the sequence is often mapped to a sequence of connected events or components. The manifestation of the sequence of events may not be a sequence at all, and it is best to generalize from "sequence" to "scenario." For example, it may be that we have a computer connected to a router, which itself is connected to the Internet, and a printer is connected to the computer. While the computer itself may not have exhibited any harm as the result of a cyberattack, the printer and the router may have, thus leading to the scenario, rather than sequence, of "Harmed," "Not Harmed," "Harmed." Hence, we have the following definitions of propagation-related constructs:

Definition 15. A **supply chain cyber disruption propagation** is a scenario where a disruption has manifested and has caused other supply chain cyber disruptions to manifest.

Definition 16. A **supply chain cyber harm propagation** is a scenario where a cyber harm has manifested and has caused other supply chain cyber harms or supply chain cyber disruptions to manifest.

Definition 17. A **supply chain cyber disruption risk propagation** is a scenario where a disruption has manifested and has caused other supply chain cyber disruptions to manifest or has caused a change in the probability of other supply chain cyber disruption risks to manifest.

Definition 18. A **supply chain cyber harm risk propagation** is a scenario where a risk event has manifested and has (1) caused other supply chain cyber risks to manifest, (2) has altered the probability of other supply chain cyber risks to manifest, (3) has caused a supply chain cyber disruption to manifest or disruption propagation, or (4) has caused a supply chain cyber harm to manifest or harm propagation.

5.10.6. *Supply chain cyber robustness and resilience*

Although it comprises only a small fraction of the literature we reviewed, the concept of "cyber resilience" was salient in the existing research on supply chain cybersecurity. However, many still confound the concepts of robustness, resilience, and risk. In an attempt to disentangle these constructs, Brandon-Jones *et al.* (2014) argue that these are all distinct. Similar concerns have been echoed by Garvey *et al.* (2015). Generally, resilience refers to the ability to "bounce back" after a disruption. Put simply, it is the ability of the system to overcome a displacement from its expected operating state and to return back to normal or an even better operating state. Robustness, on the other hand, refers to the ability to "withstand." That is, it is reflective of the property of "strength." For example, a paper clip is far from "robust." You can turn it, bend it, shape it in any way. However, it is resilient in that it can easily be bent back to its normal shape. Thus, while robustness may aid in resiliency, it is not a necessary condition for resiliency.

These concepts are unfortunately conflated in the existing literature on supply chain cyber risk and resiliency. Most authors use the three terms of robust, resilient, and risk to be synonymous. We argue they are not, and are all very distinct, yet highly related to each other. In the case of the cyber supply chain, firms can seek to build their corresponding chains to be "resilient" by leveraging existing risk management frameworks in the cyber literature. By identifying the threats/risks, harms, and vulnerabilities, while having a greater extent of visibility while tracking their distance to cyberspace, firm can plan pre-emptively for the types of harms and disruptions as well as attacks and various propagations through sound risk management processes. The same can be said of robustness, which often refers to the supply chain's ability to withstand a disruption (Brandon-Jones *et al.*, 2014). Borrowing these concepts from the extant literature in supply chain risk and resilience management and applying it to our framework, we thus have:

Definition 19. Supply Chain Cyber Robustness is the ability of the cyber supply chain to withstand the manifestation of a supply chain cyber harm, a supply chain cyber disruption, or the propagation of either.

Definition 20. Supply Chain Cyber Resilience is the ability of the cyber supply chain to either return back to normality or a more favorable state after the manifestation of a supply chain cyber harm, supply chain cyber disruption, or the propagation of either.

5.10.7. *Supply chain cybersecurity culture, orientation, and national security alignment*

The last set of concepts in our framework are more related to the security components of protecting the supply chain from harm. We adapt the concepts of orientation and culture from the supply chain security literature, since our review had identified that there is some research in understanding the general sentiment of organizations and their employees in adopting various security standards and processes. While having sound supply chain risk, resilience, and security management within the firm may indeed lead to the firm obtaining specific capabilities, prior research has shown that this is contingent on the organization fostering a security culture (Lu *et al.*, 2019). In addition, security and risk management need to be aligned, rather than conducted in isolation (Autry and Sanders, 2009).

By way of supply chain security orientation, firms can succeed in their strategies of mitigation and security by having a picture of not only how to secure but also what needs to be secured (Autry and Griffis, 2008). Another theme in our review of the cyber literature has seemed to be a reliance on the coordination with governments. As we argued earlier, supply chains have essentially become national security priorities since they have assumed the responsibility of servicing markets with necessary products, including governments themselves. A construct that is a natural consequence of this review would be the level of alignment that a cyber supply chain has with various national governments in not only complying with the various regulations that exist for cybersecurity-related issues but also in best practices and policy initiatives of those governments. Thus, we propose the following constructs for security-related concepts in the cyber supply chain:

Definition 21. Supply Chain Cybersecurity Culture is the collection of shared values and beliefs of actors within the cyber supply chain with respect to supply chain cybersecurity.

Definition 22. Supply Chain Cybersecurity Orientation is the extent to which the goals of supply chain risk and resilience management, supply chain security, and cybersecurity are aligned to effectively carry out the practices of supply chain cybersecurity management.

Definition 23. Supply Chain National Cybersecurity Alignment is the extent to which the management of the supply chain cybersecurity aligns with the regulations and policy recommendations of the national governments within where the supply chain operates.

5.11. Future Research Direction, Limitations, and Conclusions

We have reviewed much of the literature related to the intersection of supply chain management and cybersecurity. Upon our investigation, we discovered that the various themes present in the extant research relate to the already well-established literature of supply chain risk management and supply chain security. We argue that the key distinction between these fields and this new field for which we have taken great care to outline is the presence of the supply chain operating within cyberspace. It has been speculated that we are now in the Fourth Industrial Revolution, otherwise known as Industry 4.0 (Ardito *et al.*, 2019). This has been accelerated due to various enabling technologies such as IoT, blockchain, and the integration of RFID within supply chains (Yang *et al.*, 2015; Hiromoto *et al.*, 2017; Tu *et al.*, 2018). The key characteristic here that makes it an Industry 4.0 is that all of these devices are connected in some manner to cyberspace. Some have even argued that, with the integration of business analytics and artificial intelligence, we are slowly transcending toward Industry 5.0, which is when these devices and systems will obtain cognition (Clim, 2019).

Needless to say, there is a vast amount of literature on cybersecurity, but shockingly, unorganized into a cohesive framework that describes the field. As we have argued, many have been defining the tools of the trade without first defining the trade. In response, we have taken great care to propose the various constructs for which extant literature touches upon. Through our review, we found that a majority of the literature discussed the various cyber risks, harms, threats, and vulnerabilities, suggesting everything from managerial frameworks and processes (Boyson, 2014; Colicchia *et al.*, 2019; Gaudenzi and Siciliano, 2018), best practices (Schauer *et al.*, 2017; Agarwal, 2019; Pal and Alam, 2017), drivers and consequences of cyber risk (Charney *et al.*, 2011; Ghadge *et al.*, 2019), the challenges that firms face (Urciuoli, 2015; Ghadge *et al.*, 2019), and even touching upon a bit of risk propagation (Ghadge *et al.*, 2019; Agrafiotis *et al.*, 2018). The most dense part of this literature has been the proposal of cyber harm and cyber risk taxonomies (McFadden and Arnold, 2010; Boyd, 2020; Colicchia *et al.*, 2019; Gupta *et al.*, 2020). Through the design of our model, this literature can now be reflective of a field of study which we have formalized and defined as the Supply Chain Cybersecurity.

Despite the progress some researchers have made, there are still a large number of gaps which remain to be filled. First, most of the research that has been conducted on cybersecurity and the supply chain has occured at the tactical and operational levels of the firm. Few studies have observed how integration of the supply chain into cyberspace impacts the firms' strategy and its ability to compete. Likewise, dynamics of competition within cyber supply chains remains to be studied. We argue that as supply chains continue to transcend toward digital supply chains, the traditional mechanisms of contracting, coordinating, risk pooling, and even buyer–supplier relationships could radically change. This is due to the various risks of harm and threats that we have demonstrated are salient in cyber supply chains.

Another understudied area within this body of knowledge is in the design of the supply chain itself. Just as we had seen in the late 1990s, cyber supply chains are emerging, and soon, we argue, they will grapple with control (Carter *et al.*, 2015). Integrating various cyber assets into the supply chain to slowly expand the size and complexity of the cyber supply chain will only further expose the supply chain to additional externalities. At the operations level of the firm, academics will need to study the impact of not only inventory, production, transportation, and distribution policies but also how all of these traditional areas and theory holds when the supply chain is further exposed to cyberspace and the various risks within it.

This chapter maintains its core focus on supply chain cybersecurity and is purposefully limited in its discussion on big data analytics and artificial intelligence technologies that are becoming more pervasive in all information systems, including those of the supply chain. Extant research has addressed the challenges and benefits of big data analytics, and their specialized capabilities, such as those for identifying and classifying human sentiment for crisis events (Chen *et al.*, 2012; Samuel *et al.*, 2020a). Human interaction with big data and technologies are nuanced and can impact soft informational areas of the supply chain, such as human communications, which can be influenced both by human traits as well as technology (McKinney Jr and Yoos, 2010; Samuel *et al.*, 2014).Similarly, social media analytics can also play a role in affecting human behavior, with more relevance to downstream supply chain interfaces, through platforms such as Twitter (Samuel *et al.*, 2020b). While ample research exists in these areas, future research could address supply chain cybersecurity risks relevant issues of informational influences on human behavior in an integrated manner to provide further insights for making supply chains safer.

Another important and extremely understudied area is in the alignment of national security priorities and supply chain strategies and objectives. As we have witnesses over the prior 30 years, supply chains have grown larger in size, become more complex, and span over numerous economic, social, political, and geographic areas. Now, the supply chain is expanding into cyberspace, a space wherein governments not only actively source within and regulate but also conduct modern warfare. Just as firms needs to be cognizant of the various geopolitical risks of operating supply chains in other countries, they also need to be aware of any "active battles," so to speak, occurring between countries, not on the physical battlefield, but that in cyberspace. Research is needed to clarify how supply chains can not only align their mission and strategies with various government regulations regarding cybersecurity but also avoid national cybersecurity risks "trickling down" to their own cyber supply chains.

Last, while we have taken great care to define an ontology of concepts that constitute the area of Supply Chain Cybersecurity, we have intentionally held off on theorizing the relationships between these constructs, as well as the various measures, subconstructs, and operationalizations. Our goal was to summarize the literature and propose unambiguous definitions, rather than to speculate on the relationships between the concepts within the body of knowledge itself. Future research is needed to further refine these constructs by understanding how they impact the various strategies and policies of firms at the strategic, tactical, and operational levels of the supply chain. For example, how can firms go about crafting supply chain cyber capabilities? What resources are needed to enable the creation of said capabilities? What are the tradeoffs involved between supply chain cyber distance, risk, harm, disruption, and general performance? What set of processes are within each of these areas, and how do they differ from more traditional risk and security management processes? What is the nature of risk, disruption, and harm propagation? How can the tools of business analytics and data science be leveraged to aid managers in their supply chain cybersecurity goals? Many questions still remain to be answered.

While we argue that our framework encompasses a large portion of the intersection of the supply chain management and cybersecurity literature, it is not without its limitations. First, we have not proposed measures or operationalizations on these constructs. Empirical validations for their formative and reflective determination will be needed for more thorough internal and external validation. As for our review, most of our literature was found to be in non-supply-chain management journals. Despite our best efforts to project much of this literature within the theory of supply chain management, we may have overlooked other important constructs that should be necessary to exist within this ontology. Future theorizing is needed to further expand this body of knowledge. Last, much of our review excluded engineering-based journals, yet there is much research on the methodologies of cyber-security. Integration of this body of literature into the supply chain context is needed.

As we continue to transcend into the abyss of cyberspace, we are expect-ing to act the same as in ordinary space, yet finding new challenges everyday. Industry 4.0 is ever expanding with every smart thermostat connected to the firms' manufacturing facility to live GPS trackers on trucks. From machines in distribution centers that aid the worker in their productivity and general quality of life, to the large cloud computing services that crunch the numbers and run the complicated set of data analytics on all the data gathered. We are all connected, and this trend of Industry 4.0 will only continue until we have the first fully cognitive machine thrusting us into Industry 5.0. Until that time comes, we need to address the major chal-lenges ahead in securing our assets as we continue this transition deeper into cyberspace. Only sound and theoretically grounded frameworks will help securely guide us in our journey through the virtual world. Our framework is the first step in a journey of the supply chain moving a thousand miles into cyberspace.

References

Agarwal, N. (2019). Cyber security threats in supply chain and its solutions. *Cybernomics*, **1**, 18–20.

Agrafiotis, I., Nurse, J. R., Goldsmith, M., Creese, S. & Upton, D. (2018). A tax-onomy of cyber-harms: Defining the impacts of cyber-attacks and understand-ing how they propagate. *Journal of Cybersecurity*, **4**, tyy006.

Akinrolabu, O., Martin, A. & New, S. (2018). Assessing cloud risk: The supply chain perspective. Available at: <https://www.bcs.org/content-hub/assessing-cloud-risk-the-supply-chain-perspective/>, Accessed 10 February 2021.

Akinrolabu, O., New, S. & Martin, A. (2017). Cyber supply chain risks in cloud computing–bridging the risk assessment gap. *Open Journal of Cloud Computing*, **5**, 1–19.

Akinrolabu, O., Nurse, J. R., Martin, A. & New, S. (2019). Cyber risk assessment in cloud provider environments: Current models and future needs. *Computers & Security*, **87**, 101600.

Alkhudary, R., Brusset, X. & Fenies, P. (2020). Blockchain and risk in supply chain management, *International Conference on Dynamics in Logistics* (Springer International Publishing, Cham), pp. 159–165.

Ardito, L., Petruzzelli, A. M., Panniello, U. & Garavelli, A. C. (2019). Towards industry 4.0. *Business Process Management Journal*, **25**(2), 323–346.

Autry, C. & Sanders, N. (2009). Supply chain security: A dynamic capabilities approach. In G. A. Zsidisin & B. Ritchie (eds.), *Supply Chain Risk. International Series in Operations Research & Management Science*, Vol. 124 (Boston, MA: Springer), pp. 307–329, https://doi.org/10.1007/978-0-387-79934-6_19.

Autry, C. W. & Griffis, S. E. (2008). Supply chain capital: The impact of structural and relational linkages on firm execution and innovation. *Journal of Business Logistics*, **29**, 157–173.

Barney, J., Wright, M. & Ketchen Jr, D. J. (2001). The resource-based view of the firm: Ten years after 1991. *Journal of Management*, **27**, 625–641.

Barron, S., Cho, Y. M., Hua, A., Norcross, W., Voigt, J. & Haimes, Y. (2016). Systems-based cyber security in the supply chain, *2016 IEEE Systems and Information Engineering Design Symposium (SIEDS)*, pp. 20–25.

Bartol, N. (2014). Cyber supply chain security practices DNA–filling in the puzzle using a diverse set of disciplines. *Technovation*, **34**, 354–361.

BEISSEL, S. (2018). *Cybersecurity Investments: Decision Support Under Economic Aspects* (Switzerland: Springer International Publishing).

Bode, C. & Macdonald, J. R. (2017). Stages of supply chain disruption response: Direct, constraining, and mediating factors for impact mitigation. *Decision Sciences*, **48**, 836–874.

Bode, C. & Wagner, S. M. (2015). Structural drivers of upstream supply chain complexity and the frequency of supply chain disruptions. *Journal of Operations Management*, **36**, 215–228.

Boiko, A., Shendryk, V. & Boiko, O. (2019). Information systems for supply chain management: uncertainties, risks and cyber security. *Procedia Computer Science*, **149**, 65–70.

Borgatti, S. P. & Li, X. (2009). On social network analysis in a supply chain context. *Journal of Supply Chain Management*, **45**, 5–22.

Boyd, F. C. (2020). The effectiveness of federal policy in the identification and mitigation of cybersecurity supply chain threats. Ph.D. Thesis. Utica College, NY, USA.

Boyens, J., Paulsen, C., Moorthy, R., Bartol, N. & Shankles, S. A. (2015). Supply chain risk management practices for federal information systems and organizations. NIST Special Publication, 800, 1.

Boyes, H. (2015). Cybersecurity and cyber-resilient supply chains. *Technology Innovation Management Review*, **5**, 28.

Boyson, S. (2014). Cyber supply chain risk management: Revolutionizing the strategic control of critical it systems. *Technovation*, **34**, 342–353.

Boyson, S., Corsi, T. & Rossman, H. (2009). Building a cyber supply chain assurance reference model. Science Applications International Corporation (SAIC).

Brandon-Jones, E., Squire, B., Autry, C. W. & Petersen, K. J. (2014). A contingent resource-based perspective of supply chain resilience and robustness. *Journal of Supply Chain Management*, **50**, 55–73.

Braund, P. (2016). Platform requirements to support cyber supply chain risk management (CSCRM) an up-stream approach. Masters Thesis, Luleå University of Technology.

Burnson, P. (2013). Supply chain cybersecurity: A team effort. *Supply Chain Management Review*, **17**(3), 6–7.

Carter, C. R., Rogers, D. S. & Choi, T. Y. (2015). Toward the theory of the supply chain. *Journal of Supply Chain Management*, **51**, 89–97.

Cepeda, G. & Vera, D. (2007). Dynamic capabilities and operational capabilities: A knowledge management perspective. *Journal of Business Research*, **60**, 426–437.

Charney, S., Computing, T. & Werner, E. T. (2011). Cyber supply chain risk management: Toward a global vision of transparency and trust. Microsoft Corporation Paper, pp. 6–8.

Chen, H., Chiang, R. H. & Storey, V. C. (2012). Business intelligence and analytics: From big data to big impact. *MIS Quarterly*, **36**(4), 1165–1188.

Chiu, R. K. & Chen, J. C. (2005). A generic service model for secure data interchange. *Industrial Management & Data Systems*, **105**(5), 662–681.

Chopra, S. & Sodhi, M. (2004). Supply-chain breakdown. *MIT Sloan Management Review*, **46**, 53–61.

Clim, A. (2019). Cyber security beyond the industry 4.0 era. A short review on a few technological promises. *Informatica Economica*, **23**, 34–44.

Cohen, M. C. (2018). Big data and service operations. *Production and Operations Management*, **27**, 1709–1723.

Colicchia, C., Creazza, A. & Menachof, D. A. (2019). Managing cyber and information risks in supply chains: insights from an exploratory analysis. *Supply Chain Management: An International Journal*, **24**(2), 215–240.

Craigen, D., Diakun-Thibault, N. & Purse, R. (2014). Defining cybersecurity. *Technology Innovation Management Review*, **4**.

Craighead, C. W., Blackhurst, J., Rungtusanatham, M. J. & Handfield, R. B. (2007). The severity of supply chain disruptions: Design characteristics and mitigation capabilities. *Decision Sciences*, **38**, 131–156.

da Silva, V. L., Kovaleski, J. L. & Pagani, R. N. (2019). Technology transfer in the supply chain oriented to industry 4.0: A literature review. *Technology Analysis & Strategic Management*, **31**, 546–562.

Davis, A. (2015). Building cyber-resilience into supply chains. *Technology Innovation Management Review*, **5**.

Dolgui, A., Ivanov, D. & Sokolov, B. (2018). Ripple effect in the supply chain: An analysis and recent literature. *International Journal of Production Research*, **56**, 414–430.

DuHadway, S. & Carnovale, S. (2019). Malicious supply chain risk: A literature review and future directions. In G. Zsidisin & M. Henke (eds.), *Revisiting Supply Chain Risk* (Springer, Cham: Springer Series in Supply Chain Management), Vol. 7, https://doi.org/10.1007/978-3-030-03813-7_13.

DuHadway, S., Carnovale, S. & Hazen, B. (2019). Understanding risk management for intentional supply chain disruptions: Risk detection, risk mitigation, and risk recovery. *Annals of Operations Research*, **283**, 179–198.

DuHadway, S., Carnovale, S. & Kannan, V. R. (2018). Organizational communication and individual behavior: Implications for supply chain risk management. *Journal of Supply Chain Management*, **54**, 3–19.

Eisenhardt, K. M. & Martin, J. A. (2000). Dynamic capabilities: What are they? *Strategic Management Journal*, **21**, 1105–1121.

Ellison, R. J., Goodenough, J. B., Weinstock, C. B. & Woody, C. (2010). Evaluating and mitigating software supply chain security risks. Technical Report. Software Engineering Institute, Carnegie Mellon University, Pittsburgh, PA, USA.

Estay, D. A. S. (2017). Managing cyber-risk and security in the global supply chain: A systems analysis approach to risk, structure and behaviour, Ph.D Thesis, Technical University of Denmark.

Estay, D. A. S. & Khan, O. (2015). Towards a supply chain cyber-risk and resilience research agenda-a systematic literature review. *20th International Symposium on Logistics (ISL 2015)*, Bologna, Italy, July 5–8, 2015.

Estay, D. A. S. & Khan, O. (2016). Control structures in supply chains as a way to manage unpredictable cyber-risks. *Paper presented at 5th World Production and Operations Management Conference*, Havana, Cuba.

Faisal, M. N., Banwet, D. K. & Shankar, R. (2007). Information risks management in supply chains: An assessment and mitigation framework. *Journal of Enterprise Information Management*, **20**(6), 677–699.

Falco, G. (2019). Cybersecurity principles for space systems. *Journal of Aerospace Information Systems*, **16**, 61–70.

Fawcett, S. E. & Waller, M. A. (2014). Supply chain game changers — mega, nano, and virtual trends — and forces that impede supply chain design (ie, building a winning team). *Journal of Business Logistics*, **35**, 157–164.

Fawcett, S. E., Wallin, C., Allred, C., Fawcett, A. M. & Magnan, G. M. (2011). Information technology as an enabler of supply chain collaboration: A dynamic-capabilities perspective. *Journal of Supply Chain Management*, **47**, 38–59.

Fu, Y. & Zhu, J. (2019). Big production enterprise supply chain endogenous risk management based on blockchain. *IEEE Access*, 7, 15310–15319.

Garvey, M. D. & Carnovale, S. (2020). The rippled newsvendor: A new inventory framework for modelling supply chain risk severity in the presence of risk propagation. *International Journal of Production Economics*, 107752.

Garvey, M. D., Carnovale, S. & Yeniyurt, S. (2015). An analytical framework for supply network risk propagation: A Bayesian network approach. *European Journal of Operational Research*, **243**, 618–627.

Gaudenzi, B. & Siciliano, G. (2018). Managing IT and cyber risks in supply chains. In *Supply Chain Risk Management* (Singapore: Springer), pp. 85–96.

Ghadge, A., Weiß, M., Caldwell, N. D. & Wilding, R. (2019). Managing cyber risk in supply chains: A review and research agenda. *Supply Chain Management: An International Journal*, **25**(2), 223–240.

Gupta, N., Tiwari, A., Bukkapatnam, S. T. & Karri, R. (2020). Additive manufacturing cyber-physical system: Supply chain cybersecurity and risks. *IEEE Access*, 8, 47322–47333.

Hannan, N. (2018). An assessment of supply-chain cyber resilience for the international space station. *The RUSI Journal*, **163**, 28–32.

Heath, E. A., Mitchell, J. E. & Sharkey, T. C. (2017). Restoration decision making for a supply chain network under cyber attack, *Proceedings of the Summer Simulation Multi-Conference*, pp. 1–12.

Heath, E. A., Mitchell, J. E. & Sharkey, T. C. (2020). Models for restoration decision making for a supply chain network after a cyber attack. *The Journal of Defense Modeling and Simulation*, **17**, 5–19.

Hendricks, K. B. & Singhal, V. R. (2005). An empirical analysis of the effect of supply chain disruptions on long-run stock price performance and equity risk of the firm. *Production and Operations Management*, **14**, 35–52.

Hiromoto, R. E., Haney, M. & Vakanski, A. (2017). A secure architecture for IoT with supply chain risk management, *2017 9th IEEE International Conference on Intelligent Data Acquisition and Advanced Computing Systems: Technology and Applications (IDAACS)*, IEEE, pp. 431–435.

Ho, W., Zheng, T., Yildiz, H. & Talluri, S. (2015). Supply chain risk management: A literature review. *International Journal of Production Research*, **53**, 5031–5069.

Hong, J., Zhang, Y. & Ding, M. (2018). Sustainable supply chain management practices, supply chain dynamic capabilities, and enterprise performance. *Journal of Cleaner Production*, **172**, 3508–3519.

Inserra, D. & Bucci, S. P. (2014). Cyber supply chain security: A crucial step toward us security, prosperity, and freedom in cyberspace. The Heritage Foundation, pp. 273–284.

Isbell, R. A., Maple, C., Hallaq, B. & Boyes, H. (2019). Development of a capability maturity model for cyber security in IoT enabled supply chains.

Ivanov, D. (2018). Supply chain risk management: Bullwhip effect and ripple effect. In *Structural Dynamics and Resilience in Supply Chain Risk Management* (Springer, Cham), pp. 19–44.

Ivanov, D., Dolgui, A., Ivanova, M. & Sokolov, B. (2018a). Simulation vs. optimization approaches to ripple effect modelling in the supply chain, *International Conference on Dynamics in Logistics*, Springer, pp. 34–39.

Ivanov, D. *et al.* (2018b). *Structural Dynamics and Resilience in Supply Chain Risk Management* (Berlin, Germany: Springer).

Ivanov, D., Dolgui, A., Sokolov, B. & Ivanova, M. (2019). Intellectualization of control: Cyber-physical supply chain risk analytics. *IFAC-PapersOnLine*, **52**, 355–360.

Johnson, M. E. (2008). Information risk of inadvertent disclosure: An analysis of file-sharing risk in the financial supply chain. *Journal of Management Information Systems*, **25**, 97–124.

Jüttner, U., Peck, H. & Christopher, M. (2003). Supply chain risk management: Outlining an agenda for future research. *International Journal of Logistics: Research and Applications*, **6**, 197–210.

Jüttner, U. & Ziegenbein, A. (2009). Supply Chain Risk Management for Small and Medium-sized Businesses. In *Supply Chain Risk* (Boston, MA: Springer), pp. 199–217.

Karlsson, F., Kolkowska, E. & Prenkert, F. (2016). Inter-organisational information security: A systematic literature review. *Information & Computer Security*, **24**(5), 418–451.

Khan, O. & Estay, D. A. S. (2015). Supply chain cyber-resilience: Creating an agenda for future research. *Technology Innovation Management Review*, **5**.

Kim, K. C. & Im, I. (2014). Issues of cyber supply chain security in Korea. *Technovation*, **34**, 387–388.

Kleindorfer, P. R. & Saad, G. H. (2005). Managing disruption risks in supply chains. *Production and Operations Management*, **14**, 53–68.

Lahiri, A. (2012). Revisiting the incentive to tolerate illegal distribution of software products. *Decision Support Systems*, **53**, 357–367.

Lamba, A., Singh, S., Balvinder, S., Dutta, N. & Rela, S. (2017). Analyzing and fixing cyber security threats for supply chain management. *International Journal for Technological Research in Engineering*, **4**, 5678–5681.

Li, Y. (2017). Disruption information, network topology and supply chain resilience. Ph.D. Thesis. Virginia Tech, VA, USA.

Liang, X., Shetty, S., Tosh, D., Ji, Y. & Li, D. (2018). Towards a reliable and accountable cyber supply chain in energy delivery system using blockchain,

International Conference on Security and Privacy in Communication Systems, Springer. pp. 43–62.

Linton, J. D., Boyson, S. & Aje, J. (2014). The challenge of cyber supply chain security to research and practice–an introduction. *Technovation*, **34**(7), 339–341.

Lockamy III, A. & McCormack, K. (2012). Modeling supplier risks using Bayesian networks. *Industrial Management & Data Systems*, **112**, 313–333.

Lu, G., Koufteros, X., Talluri, S. & Hult, G. T. M. (2019). Deployment of supply chain security practices: Antecedents and consequences. *Decision Sciences*, **50**, 459–497.

Lu, T., Guo, X., Xu, B., Zhao, L., Peng, Y. & Yang, H. (2013). Next big thing in big data: the security of the ict supply chain, *2013 International Conference on Social Computing*, IEEE. pp. 1066–1073.

Mamun, M. S. I., Ghorbani, A. A., Miyaji, A. & Nguyen, U. T. (2018). Supauth: A new approach to supply chain authentication for the IoT. *Computational Intelligence*, **34**, 582–602.

Mansfield, K., Eveleigh, T., Holzer, T. H. & Sarkani, S. (2013). Unmanned aerial vehicle smart device ground control station cyber security threat model, *2013 IEEE International Conference on Technologies for Homeland Security (HST)*, IEEE. pp. 722–728.

Massimino, B., Gray, J. V. & Lan, Y. (2018). On the inattention to digital confidentiality in operations and supply chain research. *Production and Operations Management*, **27**, 1492–1515.

Mayounga, A. T. (2017). Cyber-supply chain visibility: A grounded theory of cybersecurity with supply chain management. Ph.D. Thesis. Northcentral University, San Diego, CA, USA.

McDaniel, E. (2013). Securing the information and communications technology global supply chain from exploitation: Developing a strategy for education, training, and awareness, *Proceedings of the Informing Science and Information Technology Education Conference*, Informing Science Institute, pp. 313–324.

McFadden, F. E. & Arnold, R. D. (2010). Supply chain risk mitigation for it electronics, *2010 IEEE International Conference on Technologies for Homeland Security (HST)*, IEEE, pp. 49–55.

McKinney Jr, E. H. & Yoos, C. J. (2010). Information about Information: A taxonomy of views. *MIS Quarterly*, **34**(2), 329–344.

Melnyk, S. A., Speier-Pero, C. & Connors, E. (2019). Blockchain is vastly overrated; supply chain cyber security is vastly underrated. *Supply Chain Management Review*, **23**(3), 32–39.

Merriam Webster (2020). "Threat." Available at: https://www.merriam-webster.com/dictionary/threat.

Merriam Webster (2020). "Vulnerable." Available at: https://www.merriam-webster.com/dictionary/vulnerable.

Mylrea, M. & Gourisetti, S. N. G. (2018). Blockchain for supply chain cybersecurity, optimization and compliance, *2018 Resilience Week (RWS)*, IEEE, pp. 70–76.

Ojha, R., Ghadge, A., Tiwari, M. K. & Bititci, U. S. (2018). Bayesian network modelling for supply chain risk propagation. *International Journal of Production Research*, **56**(7), 5795–5819.

Olmstead, K. & Smith, A. (2017). Americans and cybersecurity. *Pew Research Center*, **26**, 311–327.

Pal, O. & Alam, B. (2017). Cyber security risks and challenges in supply chain. *International Journal of Advanced Research in Computer Science*, **8**, 662–666.

Pandey, S., Singh, R. K., Gunasekaran, A. & Kaushik, A. (2020). Cyber security risks in globalized supply chains: Conceptual framework. *Journal of Global Operations and Strategic Sourcing*, **13**(1), 103–128.

Park, K., Min, H. & Min, S. (2016). Inter-relationship among risk taking propensity, supply chain security practices, and supply chain disruption occurrence. *Journal of Purchasing and Supply Management*, **22**, 120–130.

Pearl, J. (1988). *Probabilistic Reasoning in Intelligent Systems: Networks of Plausible Inference* (San Francisco, CA: Morgan Kaufmann Publishers).

Polatidis, N., Pavlidis, M. & Mouratidis, H. (2018). Cyber-attack path discovery in a dynamic supply chain maritime risk management system. *Computer Standards & Interfaces*, **56**, 74–82.

Presley, S. S. & Landry, J. P. (2016). A process framework for managing cybersecurity risks in projects, *Proceedings of the Southern Association for Information Systems Conference*, March 18–19, St. Augustine, FL, USA.

Qazi, A., Quigley, J., Dickson, A., Gaudenzi, B. & Ekici, Ş. Ö. (2015). Evaluation of control strategies for managing supply chain risks using bayesian belief networks, *2015 International Conference on Industrial Engineering and Systems Management (IESM)*, IEEE, pp. 1146–1154.

Qi, S., Zheng, Y., Li, M., Lu, L. & Liu, Y. (2016). Secure and private RFID-enabled third-party supply chain systems. *IEEE Transactions on Computers*, **65**, 3413–3426.

Reuben, J. & Ware, N. (2019). Approach to handling cyber security risks in supply chain of defence sector. *Industrial Engineering Journal*, **12**(7), 1–12.

Reuter, C., Foerstl, K., Hartmann, E. & Blome, C. (2010). Sustainable global supplier management: the role of dynamic capabilities in achieving competitive advantage. *Journal of Supply Chain Management*, **46**, 45–63.

Riel, A., Kreiner, C., Macher, G. & Messnarz, R. (2017). Integrated design for tackling safety and security challenges of smart products and digital manufacturing. *CIRP Annals*, **66**, 177–180.

Rodger, J. A. & George, J. A. (2017). Triple bottom line accounting for optimizing natural gas sustainability: A statistical linear programming fuzzy ilowa optimized sustainment model approach to reducing supply chain global cybersecurity vulnerability through information and communications technology. *Journal of Cleaner Production*, **142**, 1931–1949.

Safa, N. S. (2017). The information security landscape in the supply chain. *Computer Fraud & Security*, **2017**, 16–20.

Samuel, J. (2013). A conceptual investigation: Towards an integrative perspective of risks in information systems development & usage. *8th Annual Symposium on Information Assurance (ASIA'13)*, Citeseer. p. 83.

Samuel, J. (2017). Information token driven machine learning for electronic markets: Performance effects in behavioral financial big data analytics. *JISTEM-Journal of Information Systems and Technology Management*, **14**, 371–383.

Samuel, J., Ali, G., Rahman, M., Esawi, E., Samuel, Y., *et al.* (2020a). Covid-19 public sentiment insights and machine learning for tweets classification. *Information*, **11**, 314.

Samuel, J., Garvey, M. & Kashyap, R. (2020b). That message went viral?! Exploratory analytics and sentiment analysis into the propagation of tweets. arXiv preprint arXiv:2004.09718.

Samuel, J., Holowczak, R., Benbunan-Fich, R. & Levine, I. (2014). Automating discovery of dominance in synchronous computer-mediated communication, *2014 47th Hawaii International Conference on System Sciences*, IEEE, pp. 1804–1812.

Samuel, J., Holowczak, R. & Pelaez, A. (2017). The effects of technology driven information categories on performance in electronic trading markets. *Journal of Information Technology Management*, **28**(1–2), 1–14.

Sarathy, R. & Muralidhar, K. (2006). Secure and useful data sharing. *Decision Support Systems*, **42**, 204–220.

Schauer, S., Polemi, N. & Mouratidis, H. (2019). Mitigate: A dynamic supply chain cyber risk assessment methodology. *Journal of Transportation Security*, **12**, 1–35.

Schauer, S., Stamer, M., Bosse, C., Pavlidis, M., Mouratidis, H., König, S. & Papastergiou, S. (2017). An adaptive supply chain cyber risk management methodology. In *Digitalization in Supply Chain Management and Logistics: Smart and Digital Solutions for an Industry 4.0 Environment. Proceedings of the Hamburg International Conference of Logistics (HICL)*, Vol. 23 (Berlin: epubli GmbH), pp. 405–425.

Seckman, P., Sheppard, E. B. & McGuinn, M. J. (2016). Cybersecurity and your supply chain: What you don't know may hurt you. *Contract Management*, 14–21, February 2016.

Sepulveda, D. & Khan, O. (2017). A system dynamics case study of resilient response to IP theft from a cyber-attack, *2017 IEEE International Conference on Industrial Engineering and Engineering Management (IEEM)*, IEEE, pp. 1291–1295.

Siciliano, G. G. & Gaudenzi, B. (2018). The role of supply chain resilience on it and cyber disruptions. In *Network, Smart and Open* (Springer), pp. 57–69.

Simon, J. & Omar, A. (2020). Cybersecurity investments in the supply chain: Coordination and a strategic attacker. *European Journal of Operational Research*, **282**, 161–171.

Singer, P. W. & Friedman, A. (2014). *Cybersecurity: What Everyone Needs to Know* (USA: OUP).

Smith, G. E., Watson, K. J., Baker, W. H. & Pokorski I. J. (2007). A critical balance: Collaboration and security in the IT-enabled supply chain. *International Journal of Production Research*, **45**, 2595–2613.

Smith, K. J. & Dhillon, G. (2019). Supply chain virtualization: Facilitating agent trust utilizing blockchain technology. In *Revisiting Supply Chain Risk* (Springer, Cham), pp. 299–311.

Stank, D. (2020). Commentary: Cybersecurity safeguards should extend to supply-chain partners. Available at: https://www.wsj.com/articles/cybersecurity-safeguards-should-extend-to-supply-chain-par.

Teece, D., Peteraf, M. & Leih, S. (2016). Dynamic capabilities and organizational agility: Risk, uncertainty, and strategy in the innovation economy. *California Management Review*, **58**, 13–35.

Tomlin, B. (2009). Impact of supply learning when suppliers are unreliable. *Manufacturing & Service Operations Management*, **11**, 192–209.

Trump, D. (2018). Remarks by President Trump at signing of H.R.3359, Cybersecurity and Infrastructure Security Agency Act. Available at: https://www.whitehouse.gov/briefings-statements/remarks-president-trump-signing-h-r-3359-cyb. Accessed 30 July 2020.

Tu, Y.J., Zhou, W. & Piramuthu, S. (2018). A novel means to address RFID tag/item separation in supply chains. *Decision Support Systems*, **115**, 13–23.

Uberti, D. (2020). Utilities team up to face growing cybersecurity risks to supply chains. Available at: https://www.wsj.com/articles/utilities-team-up-to-face-growing-cybersecurity-risks-to-supply-chains-11593077401. Accessed Feb 10th, 2021.

Urciuoli, L. (2010). Supply chain security — mitigation measures and a logistics multi-layered frame- work. *Journal of Transportation Security*, **3**, 1–28.

Urciuoli, L. (2015). Cyber-resilience: A strategic approach for supply chain management. *Technology Innovation Management Review*, **5**.

Urciuoli, L. & Hintsa, J. (2017). Adapting supply chain management strategies to security–an analysis of existing gaps and recommendations for improvement. *International Journal of Logistics Research and Applications*, **20**, 276–295.

Urciuoli, L., Männistö, T., Hintsa, J. & Khan, T. (2013). Supply chain cyber security–potential threats. *Information & Security: An International Journal*, **29**, 51–68.

Urciuoli, L., Mohanty, S., Hintsa, J. & Boekesteijn, E. G. (2014). The resilience of energy supply chains: A multiple case study approach on oil and gas supply chains to Europe. *Supply Chain Management: An International Journal*, **19**(1), 46–63.

Wacker, J. G. (2008). A conceptual understanding of requirements for theory-building research: Guidelines for scientific theory building. *Journal of Supply Chain Management*, **44**, 5–15.

Walsham, G. (2015). Interpreting information systems in organizations.

Warren, M. & Hutchinson, W. (2000). Cyber attacks against supply chain management systems: A short note. *International Journal of Physical Distribution & Logistics Management*, **30**(7/8), 710–716.

Whipple, J. M., Voss, M. D. & Closs, D. J. (2009). Supply chain security practices in the food industry. *International Journal of Physical Distribution & Logistics Management*, **39**, 574.

White, J. & Daniels, C. (2019). Continuous cybersecurity management through blockchain technology, *2019 IEEE Technology & Engineering Management Conference (TEMSCON)*, IEEE, pp. 1–5.

Williams, Z., Ponder, N. & Autry, C. W. (2009). Supply chain security culture: Measure development and validation. *The International Journal of Logistics Management*, **20**, 243–260.

Windelberg, M. (2016). Objectives for managing cyber supply chain risk. *International Journal of Critical Infrastructure Protection*, **12**, 4–11.

Wolden, M., Valverde, R. & Talla, M. (2015). The effectiveness of Cobit 5 information security frame — work for reducing cyber attacks on supply chain management system. *IFAC-PapersOnLine*, **48**, 1846–1852.

Wulf, F., Strahringer, S. & Westner, M. (2019). Information security risks, benefits, and mitigation measures in cloud sourcing, *2019 IEEE 21st Conference on Business Informatics (CBI)*, IEEE, pp. 258–267.

Xue, L., Zhang, C., Ling, H. & Zhao, X. (2013). Risk mitigation in supply chain digitization: System modularity and information technology governance. *Journal of Management Information Systems*, **30**, 325–352.

Yang, C. C. & Wei, H. H. (2013). The effect of supply chain security management on security performance in container shipping operations. *Supply Chain Management: An International Journal*, **18**(1), 74–85.

Yang, H., Kumara, S., Bukkapatnam, S. T. & Tsung, F. (2019). The Internet of Things for smart manufacturing: A review. *IISE Transactions*, **51**, 1190–1216.

Yang, K., Forte, D. & Tehranipoor, M. M. (2015). Protecting endpoint devices in IoT supply chain, *2015 IEEE/ACM International Conference on Computer-Aided Design (ICCAD)*, IEEE, pp. 351–356.

Yeboah-Ofori, A. & Islam, S. (2019). Cyber security threat modeling for supply chain organizational environments. *Future Internet*, **11**, 63.

Yeboah-Ofori, A., Islam, S. & Brimicombe, A. (2019). Detecting cyber supply chain attacks on cyber physical systems using Bayesian belief network, *2019 International Conference on Cyber Security and Internet of Things (ICSIoT)*, IEEE. pp. 37–42.

Zailani, S. H., Subaramaniam, K. S., Iranmanesh, M. & Shaharudin, M. R. (2015). The impact of supply chain security practices on security operational performance among logistics service providers in an emerging economy. *International Journal of Physical Distribution & Logistics Management*, **45**(7), 652–673.

Zheng, K. & Albert, L. A. (2019a). Interdiction models for delaying adversarial attacks against critical information technology infrastructure. *Naval Research Logistics (NRL)*, **66**, 411–429.

Zheng, K. & Albert, L.A. (2019b). A robust approach for mitigating risks in cyber supply chains. *Risk Analysis*, **39**, 2076–2092.

Zhou, W. & Piramuthu, S. (2013). Preventing ticket-switching of RFID-tagged items in apparel retail stores. *Decision Support Systems*, **55**, 802–810.

CHAPTER 6

Surviving NotPetya: Global Supply Chains in the Era of the Cyber Weapon

Andy Jones* and Omera Khan†

*Distinguished Analyst. Information Security Forum Ltd
†Professor Royal Holloway University of London

6.1. Introduction

In 2017, on a warm sunny day in June, Mærsk Line, the world's biggest container shipping business, was about to be visited by an unwelcomed guest — NotPetya. In this chapter, we get up close and personal with the former Chief Information Security Officer (CISO) of Mærsk — Andy Jones. An in-depth interview reveals the crisis at key stages and the critical quick response of key personnel to the attack that infiltrated and brought down the entire network within minutes. The chapter begins with a short introduction describing the importance of maritime in global supply chains and how it has seen an increase in cyber vulnerabilities. Then the interview is documented, revealing the crisis first-hand and gaining intimate insights into the actual events preceding and following the crisis. This case, described by industry commentators as "the single most expensive computer security incident in history" (Hyppönen, 2018), has huge implications, and the lessons learned and key takeaways act as an *aide memoire* to ALL managers on how to prepare for the inevitable and be more resilient when the next crisis hits.

6.2. The Importance of Maritime in Global Supply Chains

Over 90% of world trade is moved by sea, and container ports and container terminals play a critical role in global logistics and transportation, since their seamless operations ensure orderly flows of standardized, multi-modal containers between cargo vessels and landside transportation (Bichou *et al.*, 2007; Russell and Waters, 2009). The world has become a complex and fragile system of maritime pathways in which ports are linked and interdependent. Furthermore, end-to-end shipping networks and linkages reflect trade dependencies among regions (Bichou *et al.*, 2007). It is extremely important that all the actors in a given supply chain understand the need for realizing, analyzing, and tracking different risk elements throughout the whole chain of operations. In maritime supply chains, ports act as nodes, while shipping lanes act as links (Talley and Ng, 2013). Today, approximately 70% of global trade by value, and more than 90% by volume, is transported on cargo ships, and most supply chains use the maritime industry to transport products as it is one of the most cost-efficient ways of moving goods through long distances (Russell and Waters, 2009; Rodrigue, 2013; UNCTAD, 2016).

Maritime logistics operations are not only sequences of complex cargo handling and administrative operations (such as contracting, warehousing, loading, shipping, offloading, inventory management, customs clearance, assembly, and product configuration) but also bring together many supply chain actors and activities. Thus, these operations have to be carried out with high accuracy and precision in order to ensure the seamless and disruption-free flow of materials and information, especially in today's global supply chains with a fragile and complex system of maritime pathways and ports acting as an interface between sea and land and with nations being dependent on foreign trade (Bichou *et al.*, 2007; Stopford, 2009).

6.3. Cyber Vulnerabilities of the Maritime Supply Chain

The maritime industry is undergoing an intensive period of digitization (Digitisation in the Maritime Industry, 2019) as it moves from a paper-based, offline industry to a digital, always-connected modern business. This is apparent in not only IT initiatives such as TradeLens (applying blockchain to cargo manifests) but also the connectivity of industrial control systems (ICS), such as ship propulsion and container tracking, enabled by the

Internet of Things (IoT) devices. In essence, these initiatives bring ships into the always-connected world of the Internet, through maritime satellite and ship-to-shore connections.

Digital initiatives often expose ICS to previously unexpected cyber risks and is a growing concern within the maritime community manifest by mandatory regulations related to cybersecurity onboard ships, namely the International Maritime Organisation Resolution MSC.428(98) — *Maritime Cyber Risk Management in Safety Management Systems*. Examples of maritime ICS and IoT components being compromised are most evident in GPS navigation systems and evidenced by incidents in the Black Sea area (Grant *et al.*, 2009).

Whilst port and terminal infrastructure is often classified as critical national infrastructure through legal or regulatory instruments such as the EU NIS Directive — *Directive on Security of Network and Information Systems* and the US *National Infrastructure Protection Plan Transportation Systems Sector-Specific Plan for 2015*, they differentiate between shipping transport and port infrastructure on the premise that shipping operations are globally dispersed whereas port infrastructure is relatively concentrated and localized. In reality, however, an incident at a shipping company may well have a knock-on effect on critical port infrastructure.

Analysis of data from Lloyd's List (Lloyd's List, 2020) shows that, of the top ten global port terminal operators, four are also significant shipping operators, and that a cyberattack on these operators may well impact both global shipping and global port terminal operations simultaneously, compounding the effect on the maritime supply chain. The implication of interconnected maritime infrastructures is further supported by König (2019), who concludes that there is a "strong mutual dependence of infrastructures on one another." Damage one and you damage the other.

Cyber risk and resilience are undoubtedly key issues in the maritime industry, since supply chains, and in particular just-in-time supply chains, can be severely hit by any related disruption, such as GPS signal spoofing and the hijacking of vessels. (Mikkelsen and Khan, 2015). Therefore, better alignment between ICT or IT security and supply chain management, as well as the synchronization of supply chain resilience and cyber resilience processes are greatly desirable (Mikkelsen and Khan, 2015).

Having established the importance of maritime in the global supply chain and cyber vulnerabilities within that sector, a question remains — what if it all stops?

6.4. Interview with Andy Jones, former Mærsk CISO

Q1: Can you describe the situation before the NotPetya attack?

In 2017, A. P. Moller-Mærsk powered the global supply chain. From Mærsk Line, with a fleet of nearly 800 bulk and containerized ships, to Damco, with its freight-forwarding operations, to APM Terminals operating 76 key port terminals across the globe, Mærsk played a critical role in many organizations' and governments' supply chain.

Like many large multinationals Mærsk took cybersecurity seriously. But, like many organizations with a 100-year proud history and an acquisitional strategy, it had a complicated IT setup spread across the globe, with multiple systems of various ages interconnected and dependent on each other. The risk of a cyberattack to the company was known and managed, being specifically recorded as a business risk in the 2016 Annual Accounts, published prior to the attack.

In terms of cybersecurity, 2017 had started as a turbulent year. The most prominent incident was the WannaCry attack, subsequently attributed by the US Department of Homeland Security (Whitehouse, 2017) to the North Korean state, which targeted Microsoft's vulnerabilities across the globe and compromised the UK's National Health Service. Hospitals were disabled and key healthcare equipment failed, leading to estimated losses in excess of £50M GBP (Ghafur, 2019). Companies across the globe — Mærsk amongst them — rushed to patch their IT estate against this vulnerability and were largely successful in ensuring that the damage from this attack was relatively bounded.

An analysis of WannaCry revealed that a core component of the attack was a piece of code originally developed by the US National Security Agency and subsequently acquired by a hacking group. This piece of code was known as Eternal Blue. Within six weeks, Eternal Blue would return in a different guise.

Q2: Can you describe the immediate business impact and how you responded to the cyberattack?

Around late morning on June 27, 2017, in Mærsk's UK IT global hub, some initial reports were received of PCs failing. Within the next quarter of an hour, all the IT at the hub had failed, a situation replicated in offices in over 60 countries. Within the hour, all Mærsk offices globally had been taken down.

Mærsk had been visited by what became known as NotPetya: a destructive cyber weapon, subsequently attributed by the US Government (Whitehouse, 2018) to the Russian state.

Not only were over 45,000 PCs rendered into bricks, but IT infrastructure services were brought down by the attack. The effect of this was to disable all business systems, network access, and telephone capability; to reduce the company to pen and paper. Mærsk would spend several weeks battling to recover.

The direct impact to the operational business became clearer over time. One consequence of a complete infrastructure failure for any large company is that basic communication is very difficult. Without email, messaging, or a phone system and, in the absence of any online directories, communication channels had to be rebuilt manually. More imaginative solutions emerged over time, such as the use of WhatsApp, but these also proved to have considerable limitations, as they are designed for consumer, rather than corporate, use.

For the shipping line, the immediate concern was safety and to understand the operational capability of its vessels. Ships are highly computerized, from propulsion systems up to administration systems, and would be expected to be adversely affected by the NotPetya attack. It became apparent that, as the ships were on a separated part of the IT infrastructure, they had not experienced the attack and were operational and safe. Throughout the incident, ships remained operational and were able to dock and offload cargo using a combination of manual and local systems, but at a reduced rate of efficiency. Forward bookings were severely impacted by the incident and, in many cases, the status of cargo was simply unknown.

For the port terminal operations, the situation was more complicated, in that the computerized handling systems (Terminal Operating System) had been affected in around 17 of the terminals, effectively disabling the operation. In addition, the complexity of the terminal operations, with some of the operations being joint ventures, led to a disparity in the system type used in the terminal. Terminals in Rotterdam, New York, New Jersey, Mumbai, and Los Angeles were among those closed for a period, causing significant disruption to cargo travelling through those ports. In some cases, alternate terminals within the port were used, causing some disruption to reliability and availability.

Q3: Can you describe the impact to the wider supply network, your customers, their customers, and what were the implications of this cascading effect?

Closing terminals at busy ports, such as Mumbai or Rotterdam, quickly led to port congestion. Land-side, fleets of lorries were unable to deliver or receive their loads, leading to road congestion. Shipments were delayed or diverted with short- or medium-term impact on just-in-time supply chains or perishable loads. Sea-side, ships of many different operators, booked for the closed terminals, were diverted to other terminals or ports, causing open terminals to become congested and less efficient. Although Mærsk ships were able to operate, the loss of centralized planning systems meant that their loading efficiency was reduced, increasing the time spent docked and causing further congestion at busy ports.

For the customer this situation can create a number of costs such as:

- *Increased labor costs* — slower turnaround and traffic congestion at ports results in drivers sitting idle.
- *Additional logistics costs* — ship diversions to other ports may result in additional transport costs to retrieve goods from a different port, possibly in a different city or country.
- *Compliance costs* — importing a diverted cargo from a different country may have significant additional costs associated with customs.
- *Adjacent costs* — late goods can mean spoilt goods or can disrupt the supply chain, causing downstream problems and additional costs.

In 2017, Mærsk handled about 15% of world trade. Whilst the impact of the attack was felt most acutely at the corporate level rather than the operational level, that should not lessen the importance of the attack. For the briefest moment, approximately 15% of world trade stopped in its tracks and it was not clear that it would restart.

Q4: Can you describe the lessons learned and Mærsk's approach to cyberattacks in the future?

Fundamentally two words sum it up: **Resilience** and **Recovery**.

First, **Resilience** is not about avoiding a cyberattack, it is about surviving it. NotPetya was a highly sophisticated nation-state–originated cyber weapon that impacted thousands of companies across the globe. You should assume that there is a scenario where a cyberattack will be successful and focus on being more resilient and quicker to recover

Being able to continue to do some form of business, even in the midst of a sophisticated cyberattack, is important for not only market perception but also employee engagement. A cyberattack can be a defining moment for an organization; it is typically a very public moment with a great deal of scrutiny from media, regulators, and the market. Customers can be lost or can become lifelong advocates; the response from suppliers and partners can make or break a relationship for years; regulators can be made sympathetic or adversarial; and markets can rise or fall.

For instance, in the absence of functioning IT systems, it is people who make the business work. People who have worked for the business for years and have a deep innate understanding of the business, the culture, and values. People who know how to navigate toward solutions. These people must be empowered in a cyberattack as they are key to surviving it.

While it should be assumed that a sophisticated cyberattack will be able to defeat even the most sophisticated technology controls, there is still a strong need for excellence in basic cyber hygiene. This will slow, rather than defeat, an attack and make recovery easier and faster. Cyber hygiene is, unfortunately, rather mundane and dull and surprisingly difficult to do well. For example, procedures such as IT patching must be done to a high standard, IT asset management must be exemplary, networks must be secured, and back-up must be world class. They all matter.

In the NotPetya attack the price of a good clean back-up was $30 Billion — the price of the company, as without it there would be no company.

Above all, IT systems must be designed to fail in a resilient manner. They should degrade gracefully under attack, protecting core functionality in order to keep the business ticking over. Core systems should be able to continue to function even if systems linked to or feeding them fail. Software concepts such as "priority display" — a technique protecting critical processes under stress and dating from the Apollo Space Program — seem to have fallen out of favor, but are now more relevant than ever.

The second is **Recovery**: Whilst an event such as NotPetya is uncommon, it is not unique, and there should be a realistic expectation that it will recur on a regular basis. There is plenty of evidence that this is indeed the case, with governments and healthcare and manufacturing sectors all being increasingly targeted by aggressive cyberattacks that have reduced business to pen-and-paper in a matter of minutes. Be good at getting back to normal.

Q5: So, if there is an inevitability about a high-impact cyberattack that will bypass technical defenses, how do you recover quickly and effectively?

(1) Be ready

Most organizations rehearse some sort of cyber incident, but they rarely go far enough. Businesses MUST rehearse for an uber-aggressive cyberattack that takes your business from normal to zero in 10 minutes, that trashes all technology you own, and takes you to pen and paper. Know how that feels. Know where your offline backups and your paper procedures are. Understand how your business can run in the complete absence of IT for an extended period, and what you would need to do to support this.

Picture what this would look like for your customers, and for your supply chain. Who could help? Who would you tell?

Do not think of this as a plan, but as a framework that gives you confidence that recovery is possible. This will save you days.

(2) Have the answer to the "what-ifs?"

A high-impact cyber event is a fast-moving incident with many unknowns. To the business, this will be the least familiar scenario for a business incident and a highly detailed response plan will not work well. Instead, invest time into thinking about the big questions that you may face in the recovery mode. This thinking will cost very little and will pay big returns.

Consider the following questions:

- What if we have to operate business in the complete absence of IT? *How would this work?*
- What if we have to restart a billion-dollar business from scratch? *Which system comes back first?*
- What if everyone is affected? *Most businesses will rely on help from others to restart, but what if the event is widespread and help is not coming?*
- What if we do not have a back-up? *Online back-ups are likely to have been destroyed and restoring a whole business from offline back-up is a monumental task. What if it cannot be done?*

(3) Understand how to respond to the incident

In a high-impact cyber incident of the nature of NotPetya, the rule book goes out of the window. That is not to say that there are no norms or frameworks that should guide you but recognize that things are different.

- *Fail-safe*: Recognize that in a high-impact cyber incident, security controls will have failed, and that your plight will be all over social media. This will attract fraudsters. Ensure that you have failed safe both in terms of people and systems — in that order.
- *Reset your risk appetite*: Appreciate how risk norms change in a high-impact cyber incident. Allow people to do things that would never be permitted on a normal day, as long as it helps and is legal.
- *Value and protect your people*: In the absence of technology, people will recover your business. Protect them from burnout. Provide for their needs. Allow them freedom. Understand that people react differently to this sort of event. Do not judge those that fail to rise to the occasion.
- *Communicate*: Whilst actual communication is most likely the responsibility of a media or communications function, a cyber event needs to be fully understood and someone who can make sense of a highly technical and complex situation will be in demand.

(4) Know when to reset to normal

Operating under extreme conditions can quickly become the "new normal," and people can become accustomed to working in new ways. It is important, however, to reset to normal, and there are a number of key tasks that should be planned for and executed.

- *Call it*: At some stage during the incident, the crisis mode must be exited. That is not to say that everything is back to normal, but that the recovery has sufficient momentum to be confident of success — the light at the end of the tunnel. At this stage, the organization must clearly communicate to its staff and customers that the crisis is over and that the transition back to normality has started. On a practical basis, this may include workforce-planning tasks, standing down crisis committees and, crucially, resetting behavioral norms.
- *Catch-up*: During the incident, some element of business will have been conducted but, in the absence of IT, may have been recorded on paper or inconsistently. Reconciliation of accounts, inventory, and orders will be an important but difficult task, requiring manual adjustments. During this stage, a focus on uncovering any fraudulent activity that has taken place should be a priority.
- *Celebrate success*: Whilst a recognition of the hard work and sacrifices that have been made by people to ensure the recovery is absolutely

appropriate, there can be dangers in establishing a "hero culture." Many people will have contributed to the recovery, often unseen and unnoticed, but equally, many people will have not been able to, by virtue of their role or geography. These people may be frustrated at having "missed the party" and celebration will only serve to increase their frustration. Additionally, there will be those who should have been able to help but fell by the wayside. They will need picking up again.

Q6: These are great lessons and takeaways for businesses, any final remarks?

A great proportion of the tasks listed above are only usually encountered (and required) in the heat of a major crisis or incident, under extreme pressure and time constraints. Being able to enter a crisis knowing that you have already thought about and prepared for these tasks is likely to be a considerable advantage.

At times like these, the elemental culture and core values of the business emerge and hold it together. This is not necessarily the nicely branded mission statement; it is what people *really* hold true for their company. In a situation where communication outside of the immediate building is really difficult, huge, high-risk decisions need to be taken at speed — the stakes are high. An organization that has the confidence in itself and its people will be able to do this, and that is key to a successful recovery.

6.5. Using the Gift of Hindsight

By analyzing real-world incidents, it is tempting to use the perfect vision of hindsight and to say that it would have been prevented by a particular cybersecurity control being in place, concluding that the solution is therefore to implement that control. However, this reactive approach is doomed to fail, and true insight requires a little more diligence.

The NotPetya cyberattack has a considerable history. Its origins lie in attack code (Eternal Blue and Eternal Romance) that was developed by a nation state (the US) around 2012, acquired and developed by a hacking group (Shadow Brokers), tested and improved by North Korea (WannaCry), further enhanced by Russia using code from France (Mimikatz), and delivered by a sophisticated hack on a Ukrainian software supplier (Linkos group — M. E. Doc). It contained 4 separate attack elements and used 13 discrete techniques to attack (Chiu, 2017), working at close to network speed.

However, the maritime supply chain was not the target of the attack, merely collateral damage, with Danish intelligence services registering the threat level to maritime as low just months before the attack.

In short, the attack was not foreseen, it was innovative, and standard technology approaches (such as patching) were largely ineffective. The logical conclusion should be that the next attack will be similarly unforeseen, innovative, and capable of defeating many technology controls — it will shock and it will succeed.

6.6. Conclusions

Cyberattacks on supply chains are becoming common occurrences and the "new normal" for businesses. The Mærsk incident reveals even the world's biggest company was caught off-guard. In the past, and in some instances still today, disasters such as these would be referred to as a "black swan" event because it was a rare, unpredictable, and unknown event. However, the new reality is cyberattacks are increasing, whilst we do not know when they will occur, we know they will occur, they will catch us when we least expect it and send shockwaves throughout the supply chain.

6.6.1. *Implications for global supply chains*

Cyberattacks can cause considerable economic costs not just to the companies that suffer these breaches but also to those who are part of the same supply chain. Estimates for the worldwide cost of NotPetya range up to US$10 billion (Greenburg, 2019), with Mærsk reporting the cost of the incident at around US$300 million.

Whilst Mærsk is acknowledged to have recovered relatively quickly, other companies hit by the attack, such as Merck and TNT Express, reported longer-term problems in their supply chain operations, with many costs not being noticed until after the damage had been done. This is further compounded by the increasing complexity of global supply chains and the speed and connectivity of operations required by companies to stay competitive as this case reveals; it was not only a firm-level impact but the wider supply chain had been impacted, particularly those that had limited information and tools available to manage these threats. The crisis and response by Mærsk reveals that organizations and their supply chains MUST be more resilient to cyberattacks that can cripple their supply chains, even if they are not directly affected by the attack. In addition to what we learn from this case, companies can prepare for potential attacks by applying appropriate supply chain risk-management tools and techniques both to reduce the likelihood of an intrusion and to deal with any disruption should an attack be successful. Every business that depends on a supply chain needs to build in cyber resilience.

The potential for disrupting the global supply chain is increasingly becoming an easy and highly lucrative mission not only for talented criminals, disgruntled employees, or hackers but also increasingly for nation states. Many military forces have critical supply chain dependencies on commercial suppliers, which present a soft target for a cyberattack in the case of a military conflict.

The resulting supply chain disruptions lead to financial losses as well as damage to brand reputation and organizational value. Additionally, high-profile cyberattacks that have crippled the supply chains of well-known companies reveal that the point of entry for these attacks is often through the weakest link in the chain. The networked and evolving configuration of the complex supply systems includes many modes of failure, and this stretches traditional chain-of-failure-event causality risk models beyond their practical applicability. Organizations currently do not have the resources to manage all potential losses derived from cyber risks or do not identify these risks often enough to adjust reaction plans to the risks as they emerge and change.

6.6.2. *Key recommendations*

Companies must therefore invest in supply chain resources and capabilities to improve cyber resilience. They must also embrace the reality that this often-unknown dimension of risk is the "new normal." A final point of consideration must also be placed on the displacement of threats, so for example, a change in security in one part of the supply chain may affect other parts. For instance, improving warehousing security could mean that thieves have shifted their attention to goods in transit. Ultimately, the design of supply networks should be at the forefront of any CEO seeking to improve their resilience.

De-risking the supply chain should be dynamic, linked to changes in the business model (such as M&A), but above all high on the corporate agenda. A flexible, resilient, and agile supply network that can be ramped up or down when the need requires it; strong partners who can take the reins in times of trouble; and dedicated and proactive supply chain risk management will all be helpful in surviving a cyberattack.

As supply chain industries digitize their operations and transport modes become connected to the Internet, the fragility of global supply chains in the era of the weaponized cyberattack is apparent. Resilience and recovery are our new watchwords.

References

Bichou, B. & Evans, A. (2007). Risk management in port operations, logistics and supply-chain security. In K. Bichou, M. G. G. Bell & A. Evans (eds.), *Lloyds Practical Shipping Guides*, Informa Law from Routledge.

Chiu, A. (2016). New ransomware variant "Nyetya" compromises systems worldwide. *Talos*, June 27. Available at: https://blog.talosintelligence.com/2017/06/worldwide-ransomware-variant.html. Retrieved date 27 January, 2021.

Digitisation in the Maritime Industry (2019). *Hellenic Shipping News*, June. Available at: https://www.hellenicshippingnews.com/digitalisation-in-the-maritime-industry/. Retrieved date 27 January, 2021.

Ghafur, S., Kristensen, S., Honeyford, K. *et al.* (2019) A retrospective impact analysis of the WannaCry cyberattack on the NHS. *NPJ Digital Medicine* **2**, 98. Available at: https://doi.org/10.1038/s41746-019-0161-6

Grant, A., Williams, P., Ward, N., & Basker, S. (2009). GPS jamming and the impact on maritime navigation. *Journal of Navigation*, **62**(2), 173–187. doi:10.1017/S0373463308005213.

Greenburg, A. (2019). *Sandworm — A New Era of Cyberwar and the Hunt for the Kremlin's Most Dangerous Hackers*, First Edition (New York, NY: Doubleday).

Hyppönen, M. (2018). A year after devastating NotPetya outbreak, what have we learnt? *The Register*, 27 June. Available at: https://www.theregister.co.uk/2018/06/27/notpetya_anniversary/. Retrieved date 27 January, 2021.

König, S., Rass, S. & Schauer, S. (2019). Cyber-attack impact estimation for a port. In J. C. Kersten, W. Ringle & M. Christian (eds.), *Digital Transformation in Maritime and City Logistics: Smart Solutions for Logistics, Proceedings of the Hamburg International Conference of Logistics (HICL)*, Vol. 28 (Berlin: epubli GmbH), pp. 163–183.

Lloyd's List (2020). Top 10 box port operators 2020. Available from: https://lloydslist.maritimeintelligence.informa.com/LL1135004/Top-10-box-port-operators-2020. Retrieved 27 January 2021.

Mikkelsen, R. T. & Khan, O. (2015). Cyber risk and resilience in the maritime industry, *Presentation at the 20th Annual Logistics Research Network Conference*, September 9 Derby, UK.

Rodrigue, J.-P., Comtois, C. & Slack. B. (2013) The geography of transport systems, In C. Comtois and B. Slack (eds.), Third Edition (London: Routledge).

Russell, W. & Waters, T. (2009). *Supply Chain Management: An Introduction to Logistics*, Second Edition (Omera: Palgrave Macmillan).

UNCTAD (2016). *Review of Maritime Transport 2016* (United Nations: Red Globe Press).

Talley, W. & Ng, M. (2013). Maritime transport chain choice by carriers, ports and shippers. *International Journal of Production Economics*, **142**(2), 311.

Stopford, M. (2009). *Maritime Economics*, Third Edition (Abingdon: Routledge).

White House (2017). Press briefing on the attribution of the WannaCry malware attack to North Korea. Available from https://kr.usembassy.gov/121917-press-briefing-attribution-wannacry-malware-attack-north-korea/. Retrieved 27 January, 2021.

White House (2018). Statement from the Press Secretary, February 15. Available from https://ru.usembassy.gov/statement-white-house-press-secretary-021518/. Retrieved 27 January 2021.

CHAPTER 7

The Role of Blockchain with a Cybersecurity Maturity Model in the Governance of Pharmaceutical Supply Chains

Stefan Kendzierskyj,[1] Hamid Jahankhani,[1] Farooq Habib,[2]
Arshad Jamal[1] and Murtaza F. Khan[3]

[1]*Northumbria University, UK*
[2]*Cranfield University, UK*
[3]*University of Law, London, UK*

7.1. Introduction and Background

The recent phenomenon of digital interconnectivity across global supply chains has increased their vulnerability to cyber threats more than ever before. Due to recent technological advancements and the growing importance afforded to data, the chain of custody and project management of logistical workflow can no longer rely on human competencies and interactive dashboards which aid the management of these combined ecosystems of manufacturer, distributer, and customer, through its cloud-based monitor and control workflow. Data can prove critical, for instance in the case of cyberattacks upon supply chains for critical national infrastructure (CNI) such as in healthcare. Supply chain is of course present in any industry, and this chapter will focus on the landscape of pharmaceutical supply chain and thereafter delve into a suggested hybrid framework detailing the benefits of a Cyber Security Maturity Model (CSMM). The framework assists in an end-to-end supply chain that ensures all those that sign up for the supply chain follow the CSMM framework to ensure effective monitoring, training, and compliance. Blockchain can then be used as the mechanism to enhance cybersecurity that allows tracking from origin all the way through to manufacturing and distribution, using smart contracts to prevent criminality, counterfeiting, falsification, and tampering.

7.2. Supply Chain: An Introduction

Supply chain risk management is an undeniable and continually moving measurement depending on a range of factors causing a great deal of concern. Supply chain decision-makers have the challenge and responsibility to assess risks with higher probability of disruption to the business and determine the best techniques to control the risks (Prakash *et al.*, 2018). Contemporary technological additions such as cloud-based monitoring systems have given rise to a much more interactive intelligence and, in combination with the Internet of Things (IoT) sensors, we have achieved real-time monitoring. This can prove instrumental, for instance, where the supply chain is moving temperature-controlled pharmaceutical drugs that need to have an ambient temperature to maintain potency.

Accorsi *et al.* (2017) claim that strategies exist to mitigate these risks; however, Prakash *et al.* (2018) argue that 35% of supply chain companies still fail to manage these risks effectively. The emergence of blockchain integration across supply chains has generated efficiencies relating to audit history, time-stamping, and milestone-triggered payment releases on smart contracts. Since the data is immutable, it can be reviewed at any point in time, with blockchain-assurance of its integrity. In addition to blockchain, there is clearly more that could and should be applied to an end-to-end supply chain in healthcare. Fundamentally, blockchain works in harmony with a hybrid framework in the form of CSMM that drives the compliance and regulation to the stakeholders of a supply chain ecosystem. The proposed CSMM is detailed later in this chapter.

7.2.1. *The importance of supply chain*

Supply chain has a much broader meaning than logistics (Hugos, 2011), i.e. a supply chain involves more than just the movement of the product. It involves the traditional logistics elements, as well as other functions including product development, marketing, customer service, and finance. The trends between these elements tend to be in an integrated relationship, looping into many ecosystems, since it can involve everything from gathering of raw materials to manufacturing, distribution, and retailing to end-users. Due to their enhanced interconnectivity, global supply chains are increasingly vulnerable to the risks arising from potential cyberattacks (Ribeiro and Ana, 2018). Therefore, appropriate risk management is vital and should ideally include the identification, assessment, analysis, mitigation, and contingency outlooks of those risks. Mindfulness in supply chain risk management denotes the ability to foresee the occurrence of disruption, since underestimation of this aspect can cause severe impacts to the supply chain organization (Ribeiro and Ana, 2018).

7.2.2. *Understanding supply chain risk*

In recent years, activities such as global outsourcing have increased risks in supply chain management, due to the interplay of customer demands, economic cycles, geographic locations, and similar aspects (Behzadia *et al.*, 2018). Natural events, crises in different economies, and illegal activities also influence these risks. Consequently, there is a necessity to study and generate control over these risks. This involves the development of measures to implement mitigation strategies and control (Tang, 2016). Nonetheless, some of those risks are inevitable and sometimes the cause of their occurrence is hard to establish due to the volume of labor involved within the supply chain (Trkman and McCormack, 2009). Many supply chain companies understand the importance of risk assessments and utilize various quantitative models to assess supply chain risks. However, little attention has been afforded to mitigate other risks, especially if it is assumed that the occurrence of those risks is rather unlikely (Behzadia *et al.*, 2018).

7.2.3. *Key reasons of supply chain vulnerability*

There are numerous moving parts to supply chains and related outsourcing companies, which often run on disparate and outdated network infrastructures, making them easy prey for cyber threat actors. According to Duncan and Data (2019), some of the reasons why supply chain organizations are vulnerable to cyber risk include:

- Organizations often disregard supply chain security as their problem;
- Smaller organizations may lack the means and incentive to invest in security;

- Supply chains expand the potential number of user targets, who can be undereducated about security;
- Services organizations in particular have access to the information of multiple businesses, thereby making them a lucrative target for cyber threats; and
- Lack of visibility and inability to extend and control cybersecurity-related policies of organizations across the supply chains.

Most security implementations fail because organizations do not implement proper processes and user education to complement their roll-out of security technology. The right balance is difficult to strike for large, security-mature companies for the aforementioned reason, while smaller businesses often do not give it as much consideration (Duncan and Data, 2019). Many supply-chain–related cyberattacks use malware as their preferred weapon, which often relies on user error to activate it inside a company (phishing and spear-phishing attacks are the most common entry methods). User-oriented malware such as "Trojans" and "Droppers" remains the steadfast favorite of criminals, while the rise of enterprise ransomware has grown by over 340%, from 2.8 million attacks in the first quarter of 2018 to 9.5 million attacks in the first quarter of 2019 (Posey, 2019).

7.2.4. *Pharmaceutical drugs and its counterfeit supply chain*

The issues around counterfeit/falsified drugs and their authenticity can have detrimental consequences on those connected along the supply chain to the patient. Deception and fraud relating to drug origin, expiry, and compound mixtures may conceal contamination and improper ingredients, thereby impacting dosage and potency, which can ultimately have disastrous consequences upon the end-user's health and wellbeing. There needs to be an implementation of a secure method to track provenance from raw materials to active pharmaceutical ingredient (API), to manufacturing, formulation, packaging, and distribution, in order to overcome this problem. Where the supply chains are sensitive to external pressures, there needs to be a positive momentum toward adopting blockchain as the layer to affect traceability, immutability, and time-stamping through its smart contract process. According to research undertaken by the World Health Organisation (WHO), there is evidence to suggest 10% of drugs worldwide are counterfeit, and this figure dramatically increases in developing countries to 30% (Mettler, 2016). Counterfeit drugs have no boundaries and range from multivitamin supplements to treatment drugs for cardiovascular disorders. They can have impure ingredients, improper dosages, and where the patient relies on the active ingredients for health preservation, these variables carry high risk for the patient. When blockchain is used, everything is time-stamped and recorded on the chain, including production date, location, and component origins. Ownership, in the case of transfer to other parties, is also transparent. Anything that is out of the chain is not verified and can be treated as forged until evidence is given as to the parameters set (or rules applied to smart contracts). Blockchain integration could be a viable solution to reducing the illicit trade of counterfeit drugs, thereby saving lives in one of the most impactful global supply chains. Figure 7.1 provides a representation of the pharmaceutical supply chain using blockchain and related methods of deploying smart contracts to ensure the capture of important milestone events.

The question remains though on what else can we use to enforce and make sure those entities that enter the supply chain adhere and genuinely want to collaborate to help reduce all risks to a minimum. This is what is proposed as a hybrid CSMM framework to complement the blockchain attributes discussed in later sections.

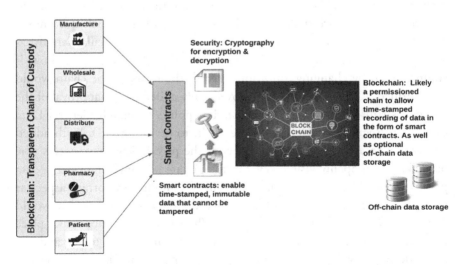

Figure 7.1: Transparent Chain of Custody Using Blockchain

7.3. Blockchain — A Disruptive Technology

Blockchain is said to be one of the most disruptive computing paradigms after the Internet (Swan, 2015). The technology is more than just a means of financial and economic trading — it looks to provide a consensus of trust, whereby transactions require storage by multiple parties who may be unknown and untrusted. Recently, different arms of the industry are starting to harness the technology to take advantage of its benefits, attributes, and methods of application, especially in order to provide a more auditable supply chain. The concept of blockchain was first circulated as a white paper (Satoshi, 2008) and created using a pseudonym under Satoshi Nakamoto. Blockchain technology has been quoted as allowing records to be "shared by all network nodes, updated by miners, monitored by everyone, and owned and controlled by no one" (Swan, 2015, p. 1). Blockchain is based on a decentralized system, i.e. a distributed ledger database where sequential inventory of transactions has identical copies shared and maintained by numerous individuals over network nodes. The multiple parties hold the consensus over the data and its validity rather than one individual. Under certain blockchain setups, there is also protection against network attacks since more than 51% of the blockchain network would need to be compromised. Immutability ensures that records in the chain contain exact information on creation, the cryptographic signature in the preceding record in the chain, and any arbitrary data. The signature (a hash which is a unique record identifier) has the cryptographic sequence of a particular length, as alphanumeric, which uniquely determines the digital entity. This is how, if compromised by changing a previous record, the break in the chain would be identified. Records cannot be removed, only added by the approval of the consensus (this is one of the consideration points to match General Data Protection Regulation (GDPR) as the "right to be forgotten"). With added encryption to each block, only keepers of the private keys have access (the pubic key is an openly visible key, but the private key only unlocks the data permissible on the blockchain). Auditability is another important aspect as transparency allows all stakeholders to see the data, something that would help improve the transparency of data. When new transactions take place between parties, these are broadcast to the network for all to see and the network miners will verify it. This collective verification will only allow the block to be added, and the "trustless" method works by not relying on any single entity to be the only authority to verify (as is the case for traditional, centralized models). There can be some limitations, such as rate of transactions and block size, but this is not a compelling issue since for our purposes blockchain may just be used for authenticating rather than holding data on the chain itself (Mettler, 2016).

7.3.1. *Consensus models*

Consensus is characterized as a general agreement of the state blockchain is in. This agreement is fundamental to demonstrate that a transaction recorded on blockchain is tamper-free and free from malicious influence. The consensus protocols are the primary rules of a blockchain, and the algorithm acts as the mechanism that the rules can be adhered to. Essentially, the algorithm is there to direct the steps to take, so compliance is achieved with the end result expected. There are differing consensus protocols and algorithms used that are dependent on what may be suited to deploy; however, these fall under Byzantine Fault Tolerance and Leader-based types (Curran, 2018).

7.3.2. *Attributes of blockchain and its benefits*

Blockchain is set to disrupt industry and help transform traditional methods and business models. While the benefits of blockchain are increasingly well understood across industries today, there is still room for specialist analysis and the integration of blockchain models into the existing supply chains. Many supply chain organizations, including healthcare, government, manufacturing, pharmaceutical, financial, and media/publishing, have already undertaken successful pilot programs and achieved higher returns than anticipated. There are many examples, but specifically looking at the pharmaceutical sector, Modum — founded in 2016 — was designed to help improve the pharmaceutical industry for supply chain monitoring (Schumacher, 2017). Traceability and compliance are difficult in current scenarios, and blockchain helps cut down on the paper trail and provide a more tamper-proof system that is auditable along its entire journey. This is particularly specific in the pharmaceutical industry where, in some regulation compliance, it is essential that deviations are reported in temperature, light conditions, humidity, etc., as IoT sensors monitor the temperature of the products and the sensor data and is transferred to the blockchain. A smart contract is initiated thereafter (this is the integrity and immutability the system offers) and the data recordings are compared and measured against the compliance requirement.

Should a deviation occur, a notification is released to the parties required to know and assess its consequences.

Surveys undertaken in industry indicate heavy support for blockchain, and this is undoubtedly the consequence of the severe problems associated with a centralized network, including those relating to interoperability, security, data integrity, and privacy. Another interesting benefit of blockchain technology is its decentralized nature — better protection is available against contemporary cyberattack models, such as the now infamous WannaCry ransomware attacks in 2017, as the blockchain would need to be simultaneously attacked by numerous sites rather than just one (Mattei, 2017a, 2017b). With increasing instances of identity theft and other cybercrimes, blockchain may also help safeguard sensitive user data.

The pharmaceutical industry is examining ways to improve its risk identification and mitigation processes by undertaking pilot studies on end-to-end verification. Some organizations looking to collaborate more closely have conceptualized the Good Distribution Practice (GDP) — a methodology of quality assurance ensuring that pharmaceutical products have consistent storage conditions under transportation; however, there is yet to be a unified GDP standard (IQPC, 2011). While this is certainly a promising development, there is a pressing need for a unified framework and complementary methodology to ensure regulatory compliance. The infiltration of counterfeit drugs into the pharmaceutical supply chain is a grave issue. The European Union Falsified Medicines Directive (EU FMD) updated Directive 2001/83/EC to offer more public health protection and introduced new rules to rigorously regulate the pharmaceutical supply chain. The Directive, effective from February 9, 2019, introduced safety features to enhance security with a Data Matrix code that comprised a unique identifier (UI) and tamper-evidence device (O'Mathuna, 2017). It provided an end-to-end verification serialization model, where the start point in the supply chain had the UI printed on the saleable unit and uploaded to European repositories. At the other end of the supply chain, the pharmacy would verify the tamper-evidence device and UI against the data on the European repositories, and if the match is correct, the medicines can be dispensed. This form of authenticity is most useful to protect the patient from receiving what might be falsified or counterfeit medicine. To further support this, a collection of national repositories called National Medicine Verification Systems (NMVS) would be connected via a European Medicines Verification System (EMVS) acting as a central connecting hub. Data can be uploaded to the EMVS and the UI is distributed from the EMVS to the NMVS. Thus, the local pharmacist can verify the UI data on their NMVS. The system presents a meaningful enhancement to security but is not harmonized with regard to FMD serialization requirements; the EU markets remain free to interpret the delegated regulations and their implementation (O'Mathuna, 2017). The motivation behind a centralized verification model is driven by the real consequences of inadequate oversight. Regulation and compliance must go further in the way of adding more security layers like blockchain, as well as the development of a harmonized framework, if they are to honor public trust and political accountability. The CSMM expounded in this chapter can ensure stakeholder compliance with centrally ratified rules and regulations in a secure and harmonized framework.

In not too dissimilar a fashion, Ireland's approach toward pharmaceutical supply-side regulation has been connecting to the Irish Medicines of Verification Organisation (IMVO) repository, thereby allowing authentication checks to be conducted prior to supplying the drugs to patients (IMVO, 2019). This harmonization operates through the additional layer of a barcode containing unique identifiers that are sent to the IMVO database. Thus, when a pharmacist scans the code and there is no match in the IMVO database, the drug can be classified as an exceptional event to investigate.

The above examples of verifying and checking authenticity go some way toward helping solve the issues of falsified drugs and criminal activity plaguing supply chains, but there are some areas where improvements can be driven in the shape of blockchain and a stronger framework to manage supply chain. A deeper understanding of the beneficial attributes of blockchain will inform how industry takes advantage of the technology available.

7.3.2.1. *Privacy and security*

The confidentiality, integrity, availability, and audit (CIAA) is subject to a lot of pressure, both internally through non-malicious behaviors, e.g. accidental loss of data, and outside vectors such as targeted malicious behaviors for the purpose of identity and data theft. The industry is trying to tackle this with the day-to-day traditional structures (the typical network security, compliance, intrusion prevention, and detection systems, training, etc.,) that help mitigate risk and have a continual cycle of lessons learned. But through an additional layer of blockchain, it can offer enhanced security with encryption and would increase the integrity with the use of a decentralized and distributed ledger system, which will offer good controls for a secure authenticated data interchange (Miles, 2017). Organizations take privacy seriously: e.g. Pokitdok, which is an API platform-as-a-service, is allowing users to interact with over 700 trading partners and use identity management to validate the partner transactions involved. This can help facilitate what was once data held in silos and now having seamless interaction — e.g. near-instant billing and insurance claim resolution (Engelhardt, 2017). It is also a good way to protect and track data interchange with respect to who is requesting and its permissions. Another similar idea is Patientory — a start-up that believes there is a need for more collaboration between providers and patients to allow more connectivity and transmisson of data securely using blockchain technology. It has also developed a mobile healthcare app to help patients keep track of their medical history, bills, pharmacy medications, insurance, etc. (Slabodkin, 2017). Interestingly patients can also connect with other patients with similar health problems, thereby allowing data interchange but in a secure fashion. For handling person-centric data, BurstIQ uses blockchain as an authenticated and permissioned interchange, connecting any data from any source (Preusler, 2020). The model allows researchers, businesses, and individuals to connect and share data. Individuals can decide if and when to share sell or even donate their data, accessed through their HealthWallet. This could cover electronic medical data and other such as diagnostic, behavioral, fitness, pharmaceutical, and smart data.

7.3.2.2. Procurement and contract process

The use of smart contracts properties of blockchain will help relieve most of the complex processes, negotiations, and supply chain issues by streamlining the process to provide efficiency and reduce costs, thereby allowing automated supplier contracts and analytics to maximize productivity and control (Holder, 2018).

7.3.2.3. Traceability

For supply chain, this is a cost-saving, efficient, and key aspect to provide transparency over the chain of custody and, in some cases, identify counterfeit processes, products, or records/transactions. The immutability, time-stamping, and proof of records end-to-end gives the industry confidence that the business model is untampered, single version of the truth and audit trail at any given point (Wattanajantra, 2019). The pharmaceutical industry is looking at the immense benefits offered. For example, "The Advanced Digital Ledger Technology" is a solution by iSolve that manages the life cycle of drug development and drug supply chain in the biopharma and healthcare industry by using blockchain as the mechanism to track, audit, and record all logistical movement of medications. Data sharing and transparency are key components to the system. There is a need to have meticulous tracking due to counterfeit and fraudulent drugs and medications. This issue is highlighted more in regions where regulation and legal frameworks are not mature or right controls and monitoring. Blockchain can handle the life cycle from development to distribution, so even something simple like expiry dates can be determined with accuracy, negating the chances of fraudulent relabeling by changing of dates (Engelhardt, 2017). iSolve also manages the acquisition of IP assets, raises funding, and advances drug development through Smart Market, where information is held in a secure repository and is trackable, immutable, and visible as a marketplace to investors and service providers.

7.3.2.4. *Supply chain logistics and chain of custody transparency*

Supply chain logistics has become increasingly complex over the years and, depending on the type of product, can involve hundreds of stages spread across a global geography where multitudes of paperwork should correspond accurately to all stages and payments made. It is this securing of the supply chain and knowing it is completely accurate and tamper-proof which gives blockchain its appeal. Applying technology to improve supply chain efficiencies is nothing new if we review how all the complicated logistics of freight is taken care of or how computing systems are used to handle the manual processes. Blockchain can be observed as just a technology mechanism to provide the confidence of knowing the data is maintained at 100% accuracy, is secure, and validates the sequence of events from start to the end. As well as all the entities that are involved in the supply chain process, it is also an important aspect for the end-user of the products to know that all is as it supposed to be and totally transparent (Pratap, 2018). It becomes very difficult to know if there are counterfeit issues, malpractice, criminality, etc., involved in any stage of the supply chain. Merely looking at documents that state the case as factual and accurate is not enough to determine if it has not been tampered with, or if it is of unethical practices/origins.

7.3.2.5. *Is blockchain really the new panacea?*

The question is asked because blockchain is still a relatively new technology for application to industry and the combination of type of blockchain used, consensus algorithm, size, etc. makes it difficult to conduct like-to-like comparisons. However, it can be observed there are some general themes that present the more negative or darker sides of blockchain as summarized below:

- **Scalability and Performance:** If data is stored on blockchain, then this may require significantly more computing power. However, in the case of the model proposed in this chapter, there is no data stored on blockchain due to the disadvantage of storage capacity, power, GDPR considerations, and cost. Processing power for transactions is another question, with comparison of typical credit card companies operating 24,000 transactions a second compared to bitcoin's 7 transactions per second. However, advanced research and development is ongoing in this area of processing for the transactions to be faster and cost-effective, so in the case for blockchain purposes, these can significantly change (Enchev, 2018).
- **Governance:** For hybrid blockchain consortiums, there is a swing toward some modified form of centralization. In the case of the proposed model, there has to be since the whole purpose is to reduce criminality and corruption and validate and monitor those that want to be part of the consortium, so some pre-entry qualification will take place by those stakeholders responsible for the consortium. That might appear as a conflict of decentralization reasons.
- **Legal Jurisdictions:** Blockchain nodes will span across numerous locations around the world, and there can arise conflict or difficulty to establish which jurisdictions laws and regulations would apply in a given dispute scenario (Salmon and Myers, 2019). This perhaps makes the large-scale production a variable factor to be aware of.

7.4. Unsafe and Counterfeit Medicines Case Study

As mentioned earlier, counterfeit drugs in the supply chain can create very serious implications, ranging from ineffective drugs and side effects, to life-threatening situations to end-users. In June 2019, a report uncovered how thousands of stolen medicines ended up in pharmacies and healthcare providers (Slawther, 2019). Many of these drugs were for serious conditions including epilepsy, schizophrenia, and cancer, to name a few. These stolen drugs are known as falsified medicines and become a risk to patients. Criminal gangs were able to able to divert stolen prescription medicines and sell them to wholesalers. Approximately 10,000 units of 25 different medicines had made its way into the UK supply chain. The criminality is of course an issue, but more dangerous is the problem of drugs being tampered with or not being stored at the correct temperatures required for the drug to be effective. Pharmaceutical companies take great care to store certain drugs at the correct temperature as it is known that, if not stored correctly, it can cause a breakdown of the drugs into other more dangerous compounds. At best case they are just ineffective drugs that will not treat the condition (that in itself can be life-threatening to the patient unaware of this) and increasing to worse scenarios of turning into these dangerous compounds.

As Slawther (2019) makes clear in the investigation, the wholesale and distribution network is open to abuse, and a practice known as "parallel trade" makes this easier for criminals to tamper with. Quite simply a drug's manufacturer can sell to the NHS at a nominal cost per drug batch, and for that same drug batch, the UK manufacturer can sell to a country in Europe for half that batch cost, and then that company in turn can also sell to another wholesaler in a different country; eventually the drug can be sold back to UK for a cost still lower than the original batch that went to the NHS. That UK wholesaler can then sell its drug batch at a lower cost and offer a cost saving for NHS. But all through that process of the drug batch changing hands, it can be subject to tampering or counterfeiting and records may not be trustworthy or kept up to date. In the report (Slawther, 2019), even reputable UK pharmacies such as Lloyd's Pharmacy were caught up in the problem of unknowingly supplying falsified drugs as their parent company Trident Pharmaceuticals had purchased these falsified drugs. The Medicines and Healthcare Agency (MHRA), the regulatory body to take care of safe drugs through its ratification process, seemed not well prepared to handle the allegations, although the evidence was overwhelming. The interesting aspect was how criminals took advantage of a system that was easy to manipulate, extort, and make lucrative money. There were several major thefts from 2011 to 2014, where thousands of critical medicines for serious illnesses went missing. Suspicions were raised when a German pharmaceutical wholesaler bought a batch of Herceptin (breast cancer drug) from a UK wholesaler and it was found to have been tampered and rendered as ineffective and useless as a treatment drug (Slawther, 2019).

The worrying aspect is when the MHRA were further questioned as this counterfeit operation came to light, they were not sure where or what has happened to the numerous other falsified drugs. Traceability did not exist, nor were there methods to audit exactly where the batches had passed hands and in what timescales. Storing drugs incorrectly and tampering with fake drugs likely means there have been other incidents besides the scandal uncovered in 2019 (Slawther, 2019). The case study is extremely valuable to support not just one attribute of blockchain but also make it a much more powerful solution to stop or make the tampering of the supply chain in pharmaceuticals difficult and provide that immutable experience. It also strengthens the case for a CSMM framework that makes it more difficult for criminals to enter the supply chain since there is a more stringent acceptance process, ongoing review, etc. (Slawther, 2019).

7.4.1. *Pharmaceutical blockchain framework to combat issues*

The case study in Section 7.4 strongly highlights the need for a technology such as blockchain to take care of the end-to-end chain of custody and ensure that all data is captured and immutable and drugs are traceable and can have full audit control, should there be any questions at the current or later time. All parties would have to conform to blockchain requirements so anything that was appearing as a drug that had "no history" should be assumed as a falsified drug unless otherwise strong evidence can be provided. In some ways, this can help drive the industry to follow better standardization and de facto compliance. It is helpful to know the definition of "substandard" and "falsified":

- **Substandard:** WHO defines a substandard medicine as an authorized medical product (WHO, 2017a) but one that did not meet the quality standards and was not a deliberate attempt by the manufacturer to defraud. This is more a problem of adopting good practices during manufacturing and a way to track and keep quality levels high.

- **Falsified Medicines:** WHO advises that these are deliberate attempts to fraudulently produce medicines that are not having true sources of materials or identity or may have been produced in unsanitary or unregulated conditions (WHO, 2017a). What is known as the API can have a mix of incorrect quantities, or ingredients that will have no effects, or worse in the form of substances that are contaminated. The aesthetics of the product look the same as the genuine product, making it impossible to distinguish them without some way of testing.

Other problems that exacerbate the situation are as follows (Ghanem, 2019):

- **Underreporting of incidents:** a consensus on understanding the definitions set by WHO for substandard/spurious/falsely labelled/falsified/ counterfeit (SSFFC) as there are different interpretations on how to classify them and record the data.
- **Poor detection methods:** more efficient detection methods are required to improve more accurate estimates and so help minimize issues with medicines or falsified and substandard types.
- **Global harmonization:** to prevent the manufacture of distribution of falsified medicines, more collaboration is needed between national and regulatory authorities and with the WHO and other non-governmental entities. This affects not just the low-to-middle-income countries (LMIC) that need the regulatory discipline but also the high-income-countries (HIC), as in Section 7.4 we discussed how falsified medicines infiltrated HIC supply chains, appearing in UK, Germany, and Finland.

The cases of falsified and substandard medicines appear frequently, and WHO signaled a problem in the area of antimicrobials in Africa, particularly an issue where malaria is endemic and the cause of child mortality (WHO, 2017b). The report estimated 169,000 children die from pneumonia and 158,000 die from malaria due to accessing these substandard and falsified antimicrobials. The degradation of the API will render the drug ineffective or other ingredients inert, thereby resulting in fraud.

7.4.2. *Smart contracts and blockchain*

There is nothing new in the concept of a contract to signal agreement, understanding, and a statement of what the engagement is, and this exists mostly in the form of paper-based contracts (even digitalized forms are facsimiles of the paper-based version). They may be stored with a trusted third party or on local servers. Usually the signature acts as proof of legality, but there are many supporting documents that act as the data that services the contract and these can be highly subject to being manipulated, data made more biased, or worse as counterfeited (even if held digitally as access can be breached, or the centralized method is not secure or trusted). However, smart contracts are converted code that address the issues traditionally faced with efficiency, as well as in certain use cases, reduce the cost of undertaking transactional activity or, indirectly, costs to validate if the data is true and untampered. A smart contract is a self-enforcing agreement run with a set of computer code that contains the approved set of rules that parties would agree in any normal transaction. The predefined rules have to be satisfied in order to be enforced as a transaction on blockchain by expediting, authenticating, and executing the conditions of an underlying agreement. Once enforced, it follows the concept blockchain provides of immutability (non-tampering), protection from deletion or any attempts to revise data, and therefore comply with what all parties agreed to and to which the majority consensus on the decentralized network can all audit and track. Smart contracts remain transparent for this reason and allow any form of transaction to take place without the need to have a middle-man or centralized authority to agree, thereby reducing the ability to make any process fraudulent. It is also very efficient, accurate, and precise, which means any future dispute or review can easily be settled.

7.4.3. *Pharmaceutical CSSM with blockchain*

Essentially, devising a blockchain framework to suit a supply chain revolves around the environment and what data interchanges and other parameters that may go beyond just security aspects. Therefore, a combination of methodologies is needed. In this section, a theoretical framework is presented where blockchain is supported by a CSSM that is the underlying structure supporting all organizations that would sign up to the requirements of such a supply chain framework. The framework then allows mechanisms such as blockchain to be more securely supported and further information governance procedures that will be applied to give direction that is specific to the pharmaceutical supply chain and can be documented under the Statement of Applicability (SoA). Within the supply chain, the SoA mandatory controls need be respected, followed, and audited, in addition to selecting those optional controls that enhance the model more directly and are specific to their environment. What additionally should be considered to ensure the continual review and amendment of the framework, as the supply chain evolves, is a methodology to monitor the SOA and organizations through, perhaps, models of Capability Maturity Model Integration (CMMI), Information Technology Information Library (ITiL), and other such types.

7.4.4. *End-to-end pharmaceutical framework combined with CSMM*

In Figure 7.2, a framework is suggested for the end-to-end pharmaceutical supply chain using blockchain as the underpinning mechanism to control the transparency, tracking, and audit trail. The model will help position typical current areas of concern and how this framework may help position and protect these points of the chain of custody where problems are encountered, and numbered points explained in Table 7.1. The underlying framework that all organizations sign up and agree to its requirements is the CSMM, which ensures compliance, diligence, and adherence to process. The end-to-end supply chain can then be secured with blockchain and its attributes, explained earlier in this chapter, complimented by a methodology that will monitor, audit, and check compliance through CMMI or a similar industry standard. This framework fits in with the earlier explained end-to-end verification models undertaken in Ireland (IMVO, 2019) and similar Euro models (O'Mathuna, 2017) but goes further than being just a means of verification. It applies a framework that encompasses cyber risk identification, how to plan and facilitate policies to match and incorporate it across the supply chain, the top-down approach to tackle risk treatment, and of course the very important continuous cycle of improvement. Tied into this is the monitoring and ongoing training that each organization in the supply chain should be undertaking to compliment the whole process and ensure to limit its identified risks. Interestingly, although this proposed framework focuses

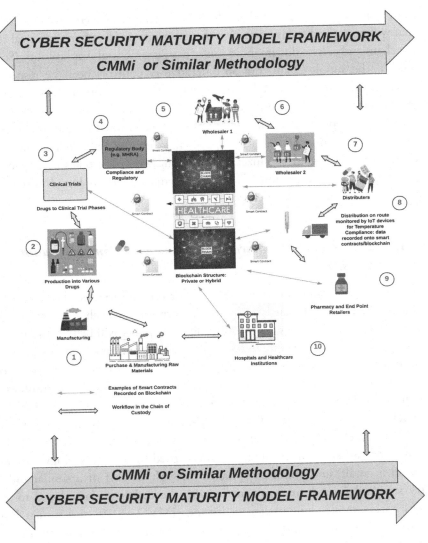

Figure 7.2:   CSMM/Blockchain Framework to Manage the Supply Chain of Drug Custody

on the pharmaceutical industry, it could also be applied to practically any industry where there are many moving parts in the supply chain, where it could be subject to forms of counterfeiting or similar, ethics are misaligned, or there is danger to end-users, e.g. in aviation, food processing, and timber production industries. The hybrid framework could also be used in various other industries.

Table 7.1: Blockchain and Chain of Custody across Pharmaceutical Supply Chain

Stage	Description
①	**Raw Materials:** At the start of the supply chain sourcing of raw material is initiated. At this stage, the potential risk of counterfeit/falsification is extremely high, since from this point the drugs may become dangerously ineffective or cause harm due to toxic or contaminated materials. If everything is captured on smart contracts, then it can be tracked as a "single version of the truth."
②	**Manufacturing/Production:** Industrial processes and production workflow should be captured to ensure correct methods, ambient temperatures, and other delicate processes and have the data captured and authenticated through blockchain. This will ensure a better standardized and compliant production takes place in regulated and sanitary conditions.
③	**Clinical Trials:** The phases within clinical trials requires careful consideration from outlined objectives in the protocols to informed consent and the various data that need to be captured regarding final reports and submissions and crosschecking the outcomes. There is also the issue of publication bias, cherry-picking, and selective reporting as issues in the current trials process and adoption of transparency is not deployed on a wide-scale basis.
④	**Regulatory Body (MHRA):** The role of regulatory bodies, such as MHRA, takes care of approval of regulating medicines, medical devices, and associated equipment with its main aim to safeguard public health. MHRA would issue a license (marketing authorization) to allow issue of medicines for treatment once full assessment has been undertaken by an evaluation team of experts. It would also empower MHRA to enforce a better code of conduct and transparency that blockchain offers.
⑤	**Wholesaler (1):** A wholesaler can purchase from a manufacturer and resell to another wholesaler in another country. The issue here is the lack of knowledge regarding the exact history and timeline of that drug batch. It would be far more credible if the whole history could easily be accessed utilizing blockchain to give confidence to other wholesalers purchasing the same batch, distributors that require to deploy to their customers and other stake-holders in the supply chain such as pharmacies, retailers, etc.
⑥	**Wholesaler (2):** The stage in the diagram gives idea as to how the same batch of contaminated drugs can be sold from one distributor to another and eventually even end up back in the country it originated from as shown in the case study in Section 7.4. Using smart contracts like other data interchanges on blockchain can help give security and confidence in the history of what is being purchased and also some form of protection if being sold onto another party.
⑦	**Distributors:** Ideally, with the possibility of so many drugs passing through many stages, it would benefit the supply chain to have them all recorded and tracked through smart contracts.

(Continued)

Table 7.1:   *(Continued)*

Stage	Description
⑧	**Logistics and Shipment:** Certain drugs being stored at the correct temperature is absolutely vital, otherwise the drug is rendered as useless and inert or can even cause danger due to compounds breaking down. If drugs are being stored as part of the manufacturing process or at a distributor, then these should have been recorded through blockchain throughout all stages of the journey.
⑨	**Pharmacy and End-point Retailers:** It is critical that end-points such as pharmacies know what they are providing to patients/users and possess all the backup data and legitimacy to ensure they are genuine products. That can be held as an entire history legacy for a pharmacy to review through the various milestones and data interchanges on smart contracts held on blockchain.
⑩	**Hospitals and Healthcare Institutions:** As in the case study, it is seen how counterfeit or falsified drugs made its way to the NHS hospitals in the UK after being legitimately purchased from a wholesaler that was not aware they were supplying falsified drugs through their supply chain.

Note: Numbers in circles correspond with stages in Figure 7.2.

Based on Figure 7.2, the details of the role of blockchain and issues regarding chain of custody across pharmaceutical supply chain are discussed in Table 7.1.

7.5. Remediation Blockchain and its Framework

Regarding how the traditional supply chain of custody could improve, blockchain offers a huge amount of remediation and solves many legacy issues that persist and are growing due to the revenue that can be gained from criminality. Practically every supply chain is a candidate for using blockchain even just for the reasons of deploying smart contracts since the method is highly efficient and tamper-proof.

It is useful to look at the drug and pharmaceutical supply chain to explore what potential remediation measures are available, since this will have several issues from beginning of manufacturing to retail and end-users. The extent of criminal involvement in operating the manufacturing and distribution of fake medicines and falsified and counterfeit drugs is huge and estimated to be up to US$200 billion annually; Isles (2017) and Lain *et al.* (2016) explain that Interpol seized 2 tons of falsified medicines in 13 Asian countries, and in August 2015, 150 tons in seven African countries. It is widely known that customs are seizing increasing quantities of falsified drugs, but the picture is thought to be a lot worse as data is not clear on the extent and tracking of even whether recalled batches were returned. Lain *et al.* explain there were 15 reported incidents (2005–2011) which helped stop 7 of these reaching patients. However, in one incident alone, 500,000 medicine packs reached patients, showing the lack of control in auditing and tracking all counterfeit drugs. With the increasing and exponential use of online activity, there is growth of users self-diagnosing on the internet and seeking solutions from online pharmacies. The growth and trend are seeing more prescription-type medicines such as antibiotics being procured. In 2015, more than 20 million falsified medicines with value of US$81 million were seized in an international investigation into online medicines (Lain *et al.*, 2016). Online pharmacies present a greater risk of distributing falsified medicines, with drugs being manufactured in unsanitary and unregulated conditions, using a dangerous and contaminated mix of ingredients, and selling this illegitimate stock through legitimate channels.

7.5.1. *Cyber risk standards*

A key part of understanding the cybersecurity risks and issues facing supply chains in the industry 4.0 context, involves reflecting on the following seven standards:

- *The FAIR (Factor Analysis of Information Risk)*: It enables the quantitative measurement and analysis of information risk in financial terms by applying the learning from existing quantitative cyber risk assessment models (e.g. Cyber VaR, RiskLens) (FAIR, 2017).
- *CMMI:* This model combines the 5-levels (i.e. initial; managed; defined; quantitatively managed; optimizing) of Capability Maturity Model (CMM). The main limitation of CMMI is that it does not provide any guidance regarding cyberattacks-related disaster management or post-disaster recovery planning (CMMI, 2017).
- *Common Vulnerability Scoring System (CVSS)*: CVSS entails a scoring system for comparative assessment of the severity of potential vulnerabilities pertaining to cybersecurity. A "modified base metrics" is employed to rank the potential vulnerabilities based on the mathematical approximation of the values attached to the respective severity. However, like CMMI, CVSS provides little guidance regarding disaster and recovery planning (CVSS, 2017).

- **The International Organization for Standardization (ISO)**: This promotes a range of international standards for managing recovery from cyberattacks: e.g. (1) ISO 27001 provides guidelines on how to establish an Information Security Management System (ISMS); (2) ISO 27031 facilitates the development and implementation of recommendations for cyberattacks-related disaster recovery (ISO, 2017); while (3) ISO 27032 enables the development of a collaborative approach between supply-chain participants to tackle cyberattacks in a coordinated manner.
- **National Institute of Standards and Technology's Cyber Security Framework (NIST)**: Under NIST, cybersecurity activities are divided into five distinct categories (i.e. identify, protect, detect, respond, and recover). NIST is the most advanced framework for recovering services compromised via cyberattacks by providing guidance related to recovery planning, improvements, and communications (NIST, 2014).
- **The Operationally Critical Threat, Asset, and Vulnerability Evaluation (OCTAVE)**: Informed by qualitative data, this framework offers guidelines for understanding and exploring the potential cyber risks through a series of workshops (Caralli *et al.*, 2007). Because of its departure from a quantitative approach, OCTAVE is unable to provide an objective measure of the three levels of recovery (high, medium, low) required from cyberattacks.
- **Threat Assessment & Remediation Analysis (TARA)**: TARA is a qualitative analytical model that applies threat matrix and standardized template to record system threats from cyberattacks. TARA promotes and somewhat facilitates the identification of appropriate recovery options, but fails to quantify the impact of cyber risks, which is crucial for deciding on appropriate recovery planning (Wynn *et al.*, 2011).

7.5.2. Statement of applicability

The Statement of Applicability (SoA) is an important basis for the treatment of the risks and direction of the mandatory and optional controls to deploy and covers the 10 clauses in ISO/IEC 27001:2013. It provides clear guidance on how to manage the risks and vulnerabilities and forms a basis of the monitoring and auditing process. It is a particularly important benchmark that all organizations in the supply chain can follow and adopt. It also means any new parties wanting to join the supply chain would need to have some level of understanding of these practices and be willing to undergo constant monitoring and evaluation of a cycle of continuous improvement.

7.6. IoT/Artificial Intelligence and Role with Blockchain

The increasing use of sensors and IoT devices across supply chain means a lot more structure and conformity are needed to ensure not just an end-to-end verification model as used by some examples described, but the method and framework to manage those that participate in the supply chain and new entrants understanding what they are signing up to. Tools and mechanisms such as blockchain all enhance that capability to offer better security, tracking, audit, and transparency. A strong Information Governance (IG) policy need to be set in place for the supply chain that has a clear purpose and scope as to what the policy should cover and defined roles and responsibilities. The Information Security Management System (ISMS) sets in place the policies and procedures to secure sensitive data and ensure risks are minimized. Included within the SoA, part of ISO 27001 procedures can comprise several controls that manage risk areas, which could include IoT devices as one of the controls.

There is a definite synergy and link between blockchain and IoT devices/sensors toward helping to increase the efficiency and transparency and reduce the negative effects of criminality. The devices can behave autonomously and can be attached to the network and collect and coordinate data based on parameters such as their location, identity, behavior, etc. Other IoT sensors collect extrinsic data based on their behavioral and environmental surroundings, such as temperature, humidity, lighting, deviations in speed, etc.

There are many practical uses of sensors, and again, if we think of the pharmaceutical industry, sensor tags on healthcare packaging can indicate if someone has physically tampered with the seal, collate data, and flag the issue. It is understandable how IoT is harmonious to blockchain since these sensors and devices do exactly what blockchain wants to enforce in its benefits of immutability, non-tampering, transparency, etc. There is also the question of how artificial intelligence (AI) can also bring enhancements and benefits to blockchain operations. AI is being explored in tandem with algorithms that can operate with data while in an encrypted state. Working in an encrypted state is always more secure than unencrypted. Perhaps AI data simulations on supply-chain attacks and vulnerabilities or further exploration on data mining supply-chain interactions can help resolve cybersecurity issues in the pharmaceutical industry.

7.7. Conclusions

The supply chain of custody has, over the years, became complex with the advancement of technology and globalization, where there are multiple partners and stages that can interact with a single supply chain. At any point, tampering, misuse, malpractice, criminality, and multitude of other negative factors can all affect organizations and users who are trying to behave in a legitimate way and have access to genuine products. The severity can depend on what the supply chain is, and it can damage the environment, ethics, and even individuals, as we have seen in pharmaceutical supply chains. Blockchain can heavily influence how a supply chain community can behave and adhere to the conditions that all legitimate businesses require. This can cover and comprise all the important ingredients that make blockchain an effective mechanism: covering aspects of privacy and confidentiality but allowing data interchange in a safe and secure manner, aiding traceability and audit trail, and devising new ways to combat the growing criminality that the pharmaceutical industry tends to attract. In addition, more emerging technologies are being used, such as complementing blockchain with IoT and sensors. This means there is an acute awareness as the product is being moved along the supply chain and traceability and audit trail should be fulfilled, both in the present and at any time required in the future if a dispute or investigation arises. Furthermore, blockchain and AI are complementary to each other as AI can analyze data and make predications to help blockchain become more efficient and secure, operating in an encrypted mode. Having a CSMM in place is, although a traditional type of frameworks/governance, still important to ensure control and audit of those who enter the supply chain consortium. This can ensure the right methodology and approach is taken by all stakeholders that sign up to the CSMM, and the benefits include monitoring, compliance, and prevention of poor discipline/procedures, a means to apply non-conformance advice and, if necessary, expulsion.

The combination of a CSMM and blockchain provides an alternative method that various industries using supply chain can review to optimize a solution that minimizes the criminality risk, ensures all involved are in compliance with the CSMM requirements as part of the supply chain, and works toward improving efficiency and safety and reducing the risk of harm to end-users. The framework can be applied in a similar way, as shown in this pharmaceutical case study and model, to other industries with a complex chain of custody. There are some questions over blockchain scalability across global mixed-entity participants and legalities where there may be some conflicts of responsibility, but the initial model of any such supply chain will likely be at a pilot stage before advancing to large-scale production. More research can be conducted to take forward a pilot based on the CSMM and blockchain model and tested with a broad mix of entity participants.

References

Accorsi, R., Bortolini, M., Baruffaldi, G., Pilati, F. & Ferrari E. (2017). Internet-of-things paradigm in food supply chains control and management. *Procedia Manufacturing*, **11**, 889–895.

Behzadia, G., Michael, O., Tavera, L. & Zhang, A. (2018). Agribusiness supply chain risk management: A review of quantitative decision models. *Omega*, September, **79**, 21–42.

Caralli, R. A., Stevens, J. F., Young, L. R. & Wilson, W. R. (2007). Introducing OCTAVE Allegro: Improving the Information Security Risk Assessment Process, Technical Report, Hansom AFB, MA.

CMMI (2017). What is Capability Maturity Model Integration (CMMI)®? CMMI Institute. Available at: http://cmmiinstitute.com/capability-maturity-modelintegration (Accessed 15 December 2019).

Curran, B. (2018). "What is Practical Byzantine Fault Tolerance? Complete beginner's guide? Available at: https://blockonomi.com/practical-byzantine-fault-tolerance/ (Accessed 29 December 2019).

CVSS (2017). Common Vulnerability Scoring System SIG, FIRST.org. Available at: https://www.first.org/cvss/ (Accessed 20 December 2019).

Duncan, R. & Data, D. (2019). How to secure your supply chain? *Network Security*, March, 18–19.

Enchev, S. (2018). The dark side of blockchain. Available at: https://hackernoon.com/the-dark-side-of-blockchain-46666adb8061 (Accessed 18 November 2019).

Engelhardt, M. (2017). Hitching healthcare to the chain: An introduction to block-chain technology in the healthcare sector. *Technology Innovation Management Review*, **7**(10), 22–34. Available at: http://doi.org/10.22215/timreview/1111 (Accessed 20 October 2018).

FAIR. (2017). Quantitative Information Risk Management. The FAIR Institute, Factor Analysis of Information Risk. Available at: http://www.fairinstitute.org/. (Accessed 15 December 2019).

Ghanem, N. (2019). Substandard and falsified medicines: Global and local efforts to address a growing problem. *The Pharmaceutical Journal.* Available at: https://www.pharmaceutical-journal.com/research/perspective-article/substandard-and-falsified-medicines-global-and-local-efforts-to-address-a-growing-problem/20206309.article?firstPass=false (Accessed 7 December 2019).

Holder, M. A. (2018). Essentials of blockchain and smart contracts in the supply chain. Available at https://supplychainbeyond.com/blockchain-smart-contracts-in-supply-chain/ (Accessed 29 December 2019).

Hugos, M. H. (2011). *Essentials of Supply Chain Management* (Hoboken, NJ: John Wiley & Sons, Inc.), pp. 2–39.

IMVO (2019). How will the system work in Ireland? Available at: https://www.imvo.ie/information1/index (Accessed 19 December 2019).

IQPC (2011). Pharma supply chain 360°. Available at: http://www.iqpc.com/media/8927/30913.pdf (Accessed 19 December 2019).

Isles, M. (2017). What's in a word? Falsified/counterfeit/fake medicines — the definitions debate. MA@POC. Available at: https://doi.org/10.5301/maapoc.0000008 (Accessed 8 December 2019).

ISO (2017). ISO — International Organization for Standardization. Available: https://www.iso.org/news/ref2451.html (Accessed 15 December 2019).

Lain Abril, J., Holt, D. W. & Wilson, R. R. (2016). Falsified medicines in the European Union and North America: What are we doing to protect public health? *Journal of Pharmacovigilance*, **4**, 213. Available at: doi: 10.4172/2329-6887.1000213 (Accessed 8 December 2019).

Mattei, T. A. (2017a). Privacy, confidentiality, and security of health. Available at: https://www.ncbi.nlm.nih.gov/pubmed/28647653 (Accessed 17 December 2019).

Mattei, T. A. (2017b). Care information: Lessons from the recent WannaCry cyberattack. *World Neurosurgery*, **104**, 972–974. Available at: https://doi.org/10.1016/j.wneu.2017.06.104 (Accessed 10 August 2019).

Mettler, M. (2016). Blockchain technology in healthcare: The revolution starts here. *IEEE 18th International Conference on e-Health Networking, Applications and Services (Healthcom)* DOI: 10.1109/HealthCom.2016.7749510 (Accessed 18 August 2019).

Miles, C. (2017). Blockchain security: What keeps your transaction safe? Available: https://www.ibm.com/blogs/blockchain/2017/12/blockchain-security-what-keeps-your-transaction-data-safe/ (Accessed 29 December 2019).

NIST (2014). Framework for improving critical infrastructure cyber security. Available at: https://www.nist.gov/publications/framework-improving-critical-infrastructure-cybersecurity-version-11 (Accessed 12 December 2019).

O'Mathuna, E. (2017). Viewpoint: EU FMD update and the impact on drug distribution. Available at: https://www.securingindustry.com/pharmaceuticals/

viewpoint-eu-fmd-update-and-the-impact-on-drug-distribution/s40/a5670/#. XftX8mT7Q2x (Accessed 19 December 2019).

Posey, B. (2019). Why enterprise ransomware attacks are on the rise. *ITPro Today*. Available at: https://www.itprotoday.com/security/why-enterprise-ransomware-attacks-are-rise (Accessed 22 December 2019).

Prakash, A., Agarwal, A. & Kumar, A. (2018). Risk assessment in automobile supply chain. *Materials Today: Proceedings*, **5**(2), 3571–3580.

Pratap, M. (2018). How is blockchain disrupting the supply chain industry. Available: https://hackernoon.com/how-is-blockchain-disrupting-the-supply-chain-industry-f3a1c599daef (Accessed 29 December 2019).

Preusler, C. (2020). Boosting transformation in healthcare: BurstIQ's HIPAA and GDPR-compliant global data network reimagines data management. Available at: https://www.hostingadvice.com/blog/burstiq-is-transforming-data-management/ (Accessed 1 March 2020).

Ribeiro, J. P. & Ana, B. (2018). Supply chain resilience: Definitions and quantitative modelling approaches — A literature review. *Journal of Computers & Industrial Engineering*, January, 15, 109–122.

Satoshi, N. (2008). Bitcoin: A peer-to-peer electronic cash system 2008. Available at: https://bitcoin.org/bitcoin.pdf (Accessed 18 August 2019).

Schumacher, A. (2017). Blockchain & Healthcare. 2017 Strategy Guide for the Pharmaceutical Industry, Insurers & Healthcare Providers. https://www.researchgate.net/publication/317936859_Blockchain_Healthcare__2017_Strategy_Guide (Accessed 05 October 2019).

Slabodkin, G. (2017). Blockchain remains a work in progress for use in healthcare. *Health Data Management*. Available at: ProQuest, https://search.proquest.com/docview/1914536464?accountid=12860 (Accessed 25 October 2019).

Salmon, J. & Myers, G. (2019). Blockchain and Associated legal issues for emerging markets. Available at: https://www.ifc.org/wps/wcm/connect/da7da0dd-2068-4728-b846-7cffcd1fd24a/EMCompass-Note-63-Blockchain-and-Legal-Issues-in-Emerging-Markets.pdf?MOD=AJPERES&CVID=mxocw9F (Accessed 12 December 2019).

Slawther, E. (2019). Italian Mafia diverted stolen medicines to UK phamacies. Available at: https://www.chemistanddruggist.co.uk/news/channel-4-dispatches-stolen-medicines-in-uk-pharmacies (Accessed 24 November 2019).

Swan, M. (2015). *Blockchain: Blueprint for a New Economy* (USA: O'Reily Media Inc).

Tang, C. (2016). Perspectives in supply chain risk management. *International Journal of Production Economics*, **103**, 451–488.

Trkman, P. & McCormack, K. (2009). Supply chain risk in turbulent environments — A conceptual model for managing supply chain network risk. *International Journal of Production Economics*, **119**(2), 247–258.

Wattanajantra, A. (2019). How blockchain traceability can improve supply chain management. Available at: https://www.sage.com/en-gb/blog/blockchain-traceability-supply-chain/ (Accessed 29 December 2019).

World Health Organization (2017a). Definitions of Substandard and Falsified (SF) medical products. Available at: https://www.who.int/medicines/regulation/ssffc/definitions/en/ (Accessed 12 December 2019).

World Health Organization (2017b). A study on the public health and socio-economic impact of substandard and falsified medical products. Available at: https://www.who.int/medicines/regulation/ssffc/publications/Layout-SEstudy-WEB.pdf?ua=1 (Accessed 14 December 2019).

Wynn, J., Whitmore, G., Upton, L., Spriggs, D., McKinnon, R., McInnes, R., Graubart, L. & and Clausen, J. (2011). Threat Assessment & Remediation Analysis (TARA) Methodology Description Version 1.0, Bedford, MA.

CHAPTER 8

Reducing Cybersecurity Vulnerabilities Through the Use of 12N QR Codes

Ron Lembke

University of Nevada, Reno

8.1. Introduction

Cybersecurity is, unfortunately, going to be an important issue for the foreseeable future. No matter how many advancements are made in computer security, there is a never-ending arms race between the bad guys in the black hats who want to steal information, and the IT professionals whose job it is to keep the bad guys out.

In this chapter, we will look at well-known cybersecurity breaches, vulnerabilities, how supply chains face a unique combination of vulnerabilities, and two ways that the new, ANSI-approved 12N QR codes may help reduce those threats.

8.2. Growing Cybersecurity Breaches

The largest data breach to date was suffered by Yahoo! in 2013–2014, when the records of three billion users were compromised. The attack was apparently carried out by a "state-sponsored actor" (Gallagher and Kravets, 2017). The Equifax hack of 2017 that exposed the personal information of 145 million Americans was apparently carried out by members of the Chinese military (Warzel, 2020).

Fortunately for most companies, the information stored on their devices is not sensitive enough or valuable enough to motivate a foreign government to want to steal it. However, that does not mean that malicious actors will not attack their devices.

In 2019, the number of organizations that reported suffering ransomware hacks increased by 41% (Popper, 2020), and the average ransomware payment was US$84,116. Europol called ransomware the "most widespread and financially damaging form of attack." Not surprisingly, spyware is a US$1 billion industry (Frenkel, 2020).

A 2020 report by Verizon found that nearly 40% of companies had their mobile security compromised (Rosenberg, 2020).

8.3. Retail Supply Chain Vulnerabilities — Target and Home Depot

Retailers are particularly attractive targets for hackers. They have valuable information, particularly in the form of credit card numbers. They also are geographically very widely dispersed. They have hundreds of stores spread around the globe and similarly complicated networks of suppliers. Payments need to be sent to suppliers, and point-of-sale terminals must communicate to credit card companies and banks on a non-stop basis.

In 2014, the Department of Homeland Security and the Secret Service estimated that the point-of-sale terminals at more than 1,000 businesses in the US were infected with malware that captures credit card and debit card numbers and forwards them to hackers. A study also found that most retailers are neither prepared for such attacks nor act quickly detect them (Perlroth, 2014).

In 2005, hackers broke into poorly secured wireless networks at two Marshall's stores in Miami and were able to access their payment systems, ultimately stealing 45.6 million credit card numbers over 18 months. This was possible, in part, because the parent company TJX was not yet fully compliant with industry security controls mandated by credit card companies, known as Payment Card Industry Data Security Standard, or PCI (Vijayan, 2008).

In November and December 2013, hackers stole 40 million credit card numbers from Target point-of-sale terminals (Perlroth, 2014), starting just before the busiest shopping day of the year, Black Friday, November 27, and continuing until Target personnel discovered it on December 13 (Kassner, 2015). The attack was made possible when a Pennsylvania HVAC contractor fell victim to a phishing attack, two months before the data theft began (Krebs, 2014). The HVAC company was using the free version of Malwarebytes Anti-Malware software, which does not offer real-time protection against threats and is only for personal, not corporate use (Krebs, 2014). An employee there likely had access to Target's Ariba billing system, and those credentials were stolen after the phishing attack allowed the hackers to install Trojan horse software on one of their computers. Once the hackers were logged into Ariba, they likely used a method known as SQL injection (described later) to gain access to other systems (Kassner, 2015).

In 2014, Home Depot suffered a security breach in which information about 56 million credit and debit cards were accessed by hackers (Newman, 2019), as well as 53 million email addresses (Soergel, 2014). It took Home Depot five months to become aware of the intrusion (Perlroth, 2014). The hackers began near Miami (Banjo, 2014) and targeted 7,500 self-check registers because they were clearly identified in their internal databases, while the 70,000 cash registers were only stored by an identification number (Soergel, 2014).

Stolen account information from a third-party vendor was used to gain initial access to Home Depot's computer networks. Once inside, the hackers used "custom-built malware" on self-checkout registers in the US and Canada. The malware was different enough in its design that it was not detected by their anti-virus software (Soergel, 2014).

Once they had access, hackers were able to move from a peripheral, third-party vendor system to the company's more secure main computer system by taking advantage of a vulnerability in the Windows operating system, which was patched during the attack. However, the hackers' access allowed them to move within the systems as if they were high-level employees (Banjo, 2014). In fact, the hack would have gone on longer, but the thieves tried to sell the stolen credit card numbers, and law enforcement was able to identify Home Depot as the source of the stolen cards and alerted Home Depot.

The most ironic aspect of the Home Depot hack is that, at the time, they were in the middle of a long-overdue upgrade to their security systems, including encrypting credit card numbers at the point of sale, and these upgrades were inspired by the Target hack. The CEO, Frank Blake, said,

"The irony was not lost on us. We believed we were doing things ahead of the industry. We thought we were well-positioned" (Banjo, 2014).

8.4. Cyberattack Strategies

Although hackers are continually updating their methods for breaking into systems, they can be broken into three major classes: guessing passwords, stealing passwords, or accessing a system without a password.

8.4.1. *Brute force attacks*

Brute force attacks involve attempting to gain entry by trying passwords with no knowledge of the user's other passwords or usernames. In 2014, multiple celebrities' iPhones were hacked, and private pictures were stolen. The hackers were able to get in by guessing passwords using automated software. Apple, at the time, allowed users as many attempts as they wanted to enter passwords or answer security questions. Hackers took advantage of this to attempt unlimited numbers of times and ultimately succeeded. Apple has since limited the number of attempts that can be made (Solomon, 2014).

8.4.2. *Compromised passwords*

Since 2017, more than 550 million passwords have been leaked, and a database of all of them exists (Winder, 2019). This database consists of usernames or email addresses and passwords. Many people are unaware that their credentials are now known to hackers, or may believe themselves to not be at risk, or may have only changed their password at a site that suffered a known hack. These users may not have considered that they have used the same username and/or email address and password at many websites. For hackers armed with this database, logging in as any of these users is trivial.

Hackers used this exact approach to log into the Twitter accounts of Facebook CEO Mark Zuckerberg and Google CEO Sundar Pichai in 2016 (Bradley, 2016; Greenberg, 2016). Fortunately for these tech executives, the hackers did not tweet anything malicious or change any passwords. They only did it to prove that anyone who uses compromised passwords is vulnerable.

In 2019, Google studied logins of users and found that approximately 1.5% of all logins involved web credentials that had already been exposed in known security breaches (Lakshmanan, 2019).

If anyone is determined to break into a particularly valuable account, it is likely they will have tools to automate the process of attempting to login to a system, and they will use these databases, in a so-called "dictionary" attack (Delahaye, 2019).

In 2018, it was estimated that 90% of the attempted logins to e-commerce sites were from hackers attempting to login using stolen data, a process known as "credential stuffing" (Detrixhe, 2018). These attacks are often successful, because this type of fraudulent activity costs the e-commerce sector US$6 billion a year (Detrixhe, 2018).

8.4.3. *Phishing*

The Home Depot attack would not have been possible without phishing. In phishing attacks, emails are sent to large numbers of individuals, with links that appear to be legitimate, impersonating trusted websites. These attacks may involve attempts to replicate the actual website, or appear to be from the legitimate website (called "spoofing"), or may have a domain name almost the same as the legitimate one, a technique called "domain spoofing." Some are "man-in-the-middle" attacks, where the victim enters their credentials at the legitimate website, and someone is in between, watching. The thieves watch the user enter their credentials, which they then use for fraudulent activities. The best defenses against phishing are anti-malware software, combined with education and reminding employees to be always vigilant and very careful when clicking links in emails (Swinhoe, 2019)

8.4.4. *Spear phishing*

The Yahoo! breach was possible through "spear phishing." In spear phishing, the emails are carefully tailored for a small number of individuals, chosen for their valuable financial information or high-level access to a network. In the case of Yahoo!, a high-level, "semi-privileged" employee was targeted (Gallagher and Kravets, 2017). A higher level of anti-malware software monitoring may be appropriate for these key personnel, who are high-value targets for hackers.

8.4.5. *Social engineering*

While spear phishing involves a targeted email, social engineering involves using other methods, such as phone calls, to gain access to a system. In such attacks, hackers may call an IT help desk, pretending to be a new employee attempting to login, and ask the desk for a temporary password (CISA, 2009).

8.4.6. *Supply chain hacks: Installing malware at the source*

One of the most troublesome types of hacks are so-called "supply chain hacks," in which hackers build a backdoor into the software that is shipped with electronic devices (Greenberg, 2019). In 2018, hackers were able to infect legitimate copies of the CCleaner software that is used to remove unwanted files from computers. The hackers first gained entry to one computer via stolen credentials and used this access to install keylogging software on other computers, which then allowed them to alter the CCleaner software so that when users downloaded it, the infected software forwarded information to the hackers, allowing them to infiltrate 11 other companies. (Newman, 2018). The infected CCleaner software was downloaded 2.27 million times (Greenberg, 2017).

Over the years, companies and individuals have become better about not clicking on phishing links and only downloading software from trusted hosts. These trends have made hackers' traditional routes for stealing data less profitable. However, a supply chain attack can yield them millions of infected computers, from people who have placed their trust in the infected software, downloaded from infected sources.

8.4.7. *SQL injection*

If you have ever wondered why you are not allowed to use certain characters in your user name or password, it is likely because of SQL injection attacks. SQL is the programming language used to manage large databases. In these attacks, hackers use forms on websites and insert malicious SQL code into the form. According to the Open Web Application Security Project (OWASP), SQL injection is the number one web application security risk (OWASP, 2020).

When a user enters data into a form, the response is sent back to the server for processing. Instead of entering plain text, if the hacker enters a valid SQL command, the server may be tricked into executing whatever command was entered. This could allow the hacker to do anything they want to with the server.

One way to prevent these attacks is searching for SQL command strings in the form data, and preventing any data containing those characters from being processed. These vulnerabilities were first discovered in 1998, but as of 2015, 17 years later, *Motherboard* magazine called it "The Hack That Will Never Go Away" (Cox, 2015).

8.4.8. *Distributed denial of service*

In a Distributed Denial of Service (DDoS) attack, the server of a company is prevented from providing its usual service, because the server is swamped with requests from data by computers distributed all over the world (Perlroth, 2016). These requests typically come from devices that have been infected with some type of malware, turning them into "zombies," that make up a "botnet." This allows hackers to remotely use the device to send large volumes of data requests from the target server, effectively shutting down the server (Zetter, 2015). In 2014, the FBI estimated that botnets had caused more than US$110 billion in losses for companies worldwide, and that more than 500 million computers are infected each year (Demarest, 2014).

8.5. Defending Against Cyberattacks

While the continued creativity of criminals means that there will never be an end to their ingenuity in finding ways to steal information, best practices can minimize the opportunities for hackers to access valuable information.

As many cybersecurity experts have commented, humans are often the weakest link in any IT process. There is an acronym for this: PEBKAC (Problem Exists Between Keyboard and Chair) (Ward and Wall, 2018).

8.5.1. *Do not use compromised passwords*

The easiest way to not fall prey to credential stuffing is to use a password that is not part of that database. The website haveibeenpwned.com allows users to see if their password, or one they are considering using, appears in the website's database of 550 million passwords.

In October 2019, Google added a feature to its Chrome browser that automatically checks, every time a password is entered, to see if the password has been compromised, by checking to see if it appears in the haveibeenpwned.com database (Chacos, 2019).

8.5.2. *Create stronger passwords*

Using strong passwords and usernames that are not easy to guess are standard security suggestions. Unfortunately, this advice is not always followed. At the time of the Equifax hack, the password for the portal to manage credit disputes had a username of "admin," with a password of "admin" (O'Flaherty, 2019).

In addition to avoiding passwords that have been known to be stolen, there are many steps a user can take to make a password harder to guess. For years, these tips have included adding numbers and other characters. More recent advice is to string together four or five random words, or create a string from the first letters of a series of words from a song or other source (Rezulli, 2020). For example, "The woods are lovely, dark and deep, but I have promises to keep," from the poem by Robert Frost, could become "TwaldadbIhptk." For greater security, the "l" or the "I" could be replaced by the numeral 1, or the "t" of "to" could be replaced by the numeral 2.

The longer the password, the harder it is for someone to find it by brute force, by trying all combinations of letters and numbers. If the password is built from upper- and lower-case letters, numbers, and 10 symbols, there are 72 characters to try in each spot. For a six-character password, there are 139 billion possible combinations. A 12-character password has 19 sextillion combinations (1.9×10^{22}). Suppose a hacker could try all of the six-character combinations in one second. In order to try all possible combinations of 12 characters at that same rate, would require 4,417 years. Longer passwords are much more secure.

8.5.3. *Password managers*

One of the difficulties of long passwords is, of course, remembering them. A string based on a song's lyrics or other phrase is not difficult to remember, but one involving other characters and numbers can be. Many browsers offer the user the ability to store the password securely in the browser. There are also many other password managers that securely store your password for other websites. However, if you lose the encryption key that top-rated 1Password uses, no one, not even the company itself, can get it back (Gilbertson, 2020).

8.5.4. *Careful use of free public WiFi*

One-fifth of companies who said their mobile devices had been attacked said the attacks happened on free public WiFi networks (Rosenberg, 2020). Such networks are a threat because anyone on the network can observe any unencrypted traffic. Also, hackers will sometimes set up free networks that appear to be hosted by the coffee shop, etc. but were created just for watching and capturing user information. FTP file downloads often use unencrypted connections, which means the username and password are visible to anyone else on the network (Geier, 2013).

Even more dangerously, hackers can see unsecured logins to websites and capture the session key, which allows them to directly use the website, without having to enter any login information at all, a process known as session hijacking (Geier, 2011).

8.5.5. *Vendor anonymity*

One unique aspect of the Target breach that is of particular note for supply chain professionals is that the Microsoft website contained a detailed description of how Target was using their security software. Hackers were able to learn all about the systems and security used by Target (Kassner, 2015).

Target's supplier portal also contained a publicly available list of some of their suppliers, one of whom then fell victim to the phishing attack (Kassner, 2015). Removing such public lists of vendors can help prevent those small vendors from becoming phishing targets. Because small companies are less likely to have sophisticated cybersecurity technologies and practices, they are more susceptible to attacks.

8.5.6. *Up-to-date security patches*

As surprising as it seems, major corporations holding vast troves of highly valuable information are not always following simple security best practices.

Every time a security patch is released, hackers reverse-engineer the patch to see what vulnerabilities the patch was designed to protect against. Anyone not immediately applying the patch is unprotected from such attacks.

The Equifax breach could have been totally avoided if Equifax had promptly applied a security patch supplied earlier by Apache. Failure to do so left the company vulnerable to such an attack (Warzel, 2020).

8.5.7. *Best practices to avoid SQL injection*

OWASP has white papers outlining best practices for removing SQL injection vulnerabilities at OWASP.org. These best practices are updated regularly, as new threats are identified.

8.5.8. *Encrypt valuable data*

Not only was Equifax not applying security updates as quickly as possible, they were not storing the data under encryption. The data was not encrypted, but stored as plain text. If the data had been encrypted, it would have been impossible to use, and therefore worthless (Warzel, 2020).

8.5.9. *Two-factor authentication*

Another common recommendation is to use two-factor authentication (2FA) also known as multi-factor authentication (MFA). Most frequently, this involves sending a text message to the user's known phone number, to ensure the person accessing the resource is the legitimate user.

The Target breach also could have been prevented if Target had followed the PCI recommendation of using 2FA for remote access to the network (Krebs, 2014).

8.6. The Importance of Up-To-Date Technology

Every time a software provider discovers another vulnerability in its software, an update, or patch, is released. Installing these as quickly as possible is of fundamental importance to maintaining security. This is true not only for the company running the server but also for the vendors and customers who use their computers to log in to the system.

Without up-to-date software, operating systems, and patches, suppliers and vendors are susceptible to all of the malware and phishing attacks described above.

8.6.1. *Operating system updates*

To protect against the recent wave of ransomware attacks, one of the first recommendations of experts is to make sure all computers have the most up-to-date versions of their operating systems and to always install any updates from your software vendors, as soon as they become available (McMillan, 2017). This is similar to the recommendation to update other software, but is more fundamental and, as we will see, more problematic. Operating system updates are more fundamental, because if the operating system is not up to date, then software patches cannot be installed.

Operating system updates can determine when a device has become too old for secure use, because once a device becomes too old, it can no longer run the latest version of the operating system, which means it can no longer run the safest, most up-to-date version of the software, and is therefore vulnerable to all of the weaknesses that have been or will be discovered. Rather than invest in new hardware, some companies unfortunately prefer to keep obsolete, and therefore insecure, hardware still running.

8.6.2. *Obsolete operating systems still in use*

Unfortunately, there are many, many individuals and companies still running obsolete operating systems, and therefore vulnerable to any manner of cyberattack.

Upgrading computers away from Windows XP and Windows 7 would seem like an obvious first step to take. Unfortunately, many small businesses lack the resources to frequently update their hardware. And often, large corporations are also slow to update because they need to check for compatibility issues with existing software (Ranger, 2017). As of 2017, Britain's fleet of submarines with nuclear weapons were still running Windows XP, three years after the last security update (Mizokami, 2016; Corfield, 2017).

One of the least appreciated threats may come from the fact that nearly 4% of computers worldwide were still running Windows XP in 2019, 18 years after its launch, and 14 years after it was replaced (Hruska, 2019).

This amounts to tens of millions of computers worldwide (Barrett, 2019). Once a company stops supporting software, no additional patches are released, and as more vulnerabilities are exposed, with no updates to stop hackers from exploiting them, anyone using the unsupported software is highly vulnerable to attack from any of these issues.

Although the number of computers worldwide running XP may be only 4%, in 2019, *Forbes* estimated that one in three companies is still running Windows XP on at least one computer. The last regular security update for XP was in April 2014 (Dellinger, 2019), although in May 2019, Microsoft released a patch for a significant vulnerability in Remote Desktop Services, which allows one computer to take control of another, but offered no specifics (Barrett, 2019). Microsoft said the vulnerability would have allowed infected machines to infect other machines and spread worldwide. The prediction was that, within 24 to 48 hours of the Microsoft announcement, hackers would figure out the vulnerability, and build a "worm," which can spread from one computer to the next, without the need of a human to click on a bad link (*Ibid.*).

This same article reports that 79% of companies were still running Windows 7, for which support ended in January 2020. The story also reports that half of the respondents "don't have a cybersecurity expert on staff" (Barrett, 2019). As of April 2, 2020, 10 weeks after Microsoft stopped supporting Windows 7, 26.2% of all computers worldwide (and 29.4% of all PCs) were still running Windows 7 (Keizer, 2020).

8.6.3. *Pirated operating systems*

In addition to the computers running out-of-date operating systems, another source of concern is the computers running illegal, pirated copies of their operating systems. In 2011, US President Barack Obama quoted Microsoft CEO Steve Ballmer, who estimated that only 1 customer in China, out of 10, was actually paying to use Windows (Brodkin, 2011). The other 90% were using pirated copies of the operating system.

Unfortunately for everyone, users of pirated software do not have access to security patches and upgrades. Their computers can be hacked or infected with malware and incorporated into botnets. The security of everyone, then, is at risk when large numbers of computers are running pirated or obsolete operating systems.

In 2012, Microsoft performed a study, in which they found that 59% of new computers sold with pirated versions of the operating system were already infected with malware, such as software that can remotely log users' keystrokes and spy on them through their webcams. More than 70% of them also had Windows Firewall disabled, making them vulnerable to attack (Kan, 2012).

Because of the collective global vulnerability represented by these computers with pirated operating systems, in 2015, Microsoft decided to offer free upgrades to Windows 10 and Windows 8.1 to anyone in China, even if they were using pirated versions of the operating system (Asay, 2015).

8.7. Supply Chain Cybersecurity Challenges

Clearly, IT and cybersecurity specialists have their challenges ahead of them. There is reason to believe that the challenges are even greater for supply chain IT. All of the above threats and solutions apply to all companies, but supply chain management is, by definition, boundary spanning. It is involved with all aspects of a firm: accounting, accounts payable, accounts receivable, invoicing, supplier relations, customer relationship management, etc. All of these functional activities have their own cybersecurity issues, but by being connected to all of them, supply chain activities must be alert to all of them.

Companies with global supply chains face additional challenges because of their global context. Vulnerabilities exist in every continent, in every language, in every culture.

8.7.1. Smaller suppliers in smaller cities

An unfortunate reality is that the cybersecurity challenges for supply chain management are likely to become greater.

China has made an active effort to encourage companies to move manufacturing operations to smaller cities in China (Magnier, 2016), counting on the industrialization of smaller cities to continue to expand the middle class and sustain the country's economic growth (Areddy, 2016).

Wages in China have been steadily rising, which has caused many companies to think about leaving China for cheaper labor in other Asian countries, further fragmenting an already widely distributed supply base (Bradsher, 2019).

The shift to smaller cities also mirrors a movement toward smaller companies. Small businesses in China account for 60% of the economy and 80% of the jobs (Batson, 2010). Unfortunately, smaller businesses are more vulnerable to cyberattacks, lacking the resources to invest in hardware, software, or cybersecurity expertise. Not surprisingly, as larger companies increase their defenses against cyberattacks, smaller companies are increasingly becoming the targets (Simon, 2019).

Having smaller suppliers generally means having more vulnerable suppliers, and having more suppliers means more opportunities for suppliers to be victim of an attack.

8.7.2. *Supply chain visibility*

At the same time, supply chain visibility is increasingly important. There is more interest in the sourcing history of products and supplies. Customers want to make sure that their diamonds are not "blood" diamonds. Companies have to ensure that their minerals are not conflict minerals and not sourced from dictatorial regimes. Customers also want proof that the products they buy are not the result of slavery or child labor.

Companies want to track individual food items' origins, to better target recalls, improving public health. At the upper end of the economic scale, affluent consumers want to trace the provenance of their food, to know that the gourmet products they are buying have really come from the places they are claimed to come from. Customers and companies want to make sure that food products were kept sufficiently cold throughout the cold chain, or that technology products were not subjected to significant shocks or drops.

Those efforts toward visibility will require more suppliers and supply chain partners to upload more data. One way to collect this information is through the IoT, in which automated devices upload information, often in real time, directly to a cloud-based system. From a security standpoint, every time another device is allowed to write to the database, it represents one more potential source of a security breach.

8.7.3. *Blockchain*

At the current time, many people have high hopes for the potential of blockchain as a solution for many of these data needs. With blockchain, only trusted parties who have been granted access may write to the distributed ledger. Once data is written to the blockchain, any subsequent attempts to alter the record will be discovered quickly and corrected. But again, the more people or devices who are granted access to a network, the more potential sources of unauthorized activity.

Even if the data is stored with perfect security, the weak link is usually a human. Every additional user is one more user who can fall prey to a phishing or spear phishing attack.

8.8. 12N Codes: One Label Does It All

12N codes are a new way to include multiple pieces of information in a single two-dimensional (2D) barcode.

8.8.1. *Limitations of one-dimensional barcodes*

Universal Product Codes (UPC) are the linear bar codes on consumer products that consumers are accustomed to scanning at retail stores. A UPC typically contains 12 digits, and when one is scanned, the point-of-sale terminal uses those 12 digits to look up all relevant information associated with that product. The individual UPC codes are assigned by GS1, a non-profit organization based in Europe. Companies are assigned a UPC prefix, and then individual UPC codes for each individual product. A 12-pack of a soda has to have a different UPC than an 18 pack of the same soda.

UPC codes are a specific type of one-dimensional (1D) bar code, but companies can use any of the other formats of 1D bar codes to store any product information they wish to store. Code 39 barcodes were invented by Intermec in 1974 and can store up to 39 alphanumeric characters (Allais, 2006). Code 128 barcodes can contain 48 characters (GS1, 2017), using 128 different ASCII characters. 128 barcodes have greater character density than Code 39 barcodes (Greico *et al.*, 1989). Formerly known as UCC 128 barcodes, in 1989, GS1 introduced the GS1-128 standard. 128 is an open standard, so anyone can generate a barcode following its rules, and the resulting bar code can be read by anyone with a scanner.

Unfortunately, 1D bar codes are quite limited. Firstly, they can store no more than 48 characters. Second, they are also very inefficient, space-wise. How small a bar code can be printed depends on the quality of the printing process and medium, as well as the resolution of the scanner that will read it. For practical purposes, 1D bar codes end up requiring a substantial amount of surface area, per character represented. Companies spend large sums to design the customer-facing appearance of their products. The last thing they would want to do would be to waste valuable "real estate" on their products by printing a long 1D bar code on it.

8.8.2. *QR codes*

Two-dimensional (2D) bar codes are a much more efficient way to present information. QR (quick response) codes were developed by Denso Wave of Japan for labeling automotive parts. The inventor, Hara Masahiro, was inspired while playing the game "Go" on his lunch break (Nippon.com, 2020). Denso needed codes capable of storing significant numbers of characters and being read quickly and easily. Denso patented the technology, but does not enforce the patent, allowing people all over the world to use it for free. In 1997, it was approved as an international standard by Automatic Identification Manufacturers International, and in 2011, it was approved by GS1 as a standard for mobile phones. It can store up to 7,089 numerical characters, or 4,296 alphanumeric characters (Denso, 2020).

QR codes found widespread acceptance as a marketing device. Customers could scan a QR code on an ad and quickly be taken to the advertiser's website. Unfortunately, users had to have a specialized QR reader, although now most major phone operating systems include QR reading functionality in the camera app.

A larger problem was that after scanning a QR code, the user was typically taken to a website that was not optimized for the dimensions of the user's cell phone. Everything was poorly aligned and unpleasant to navigate.

For most users, the novelty of scanning a QR code quickly wore off, and they became less effective as a marketing tool. In 2013, a brand advertising consultant named Alex Carantza posted a "helpful flow chart" to help people decide if they should use a QR code in their advertising or not. It says, "Should I use a QR code? → No. → But what if… → OMG NO" (Carlson, 2013). Although QR codes can still occasionally be found in advertising, they are far less common than they once were.

This does not mean that QR codes are no longer used. In China, the world's largest economy, an enormous volume of customer transactions are paid for using QR codes connected to users' Alibaba and Tencent accounts. Many phones had NFC chip readers, but to use those, vendors would have to purchase expensive NFC terminals. QR codes only require the vendor to print out a QR code, which is much more affordable (Chiu, 2018).

As a result, Chinese consumers pay for nearly everything via QR codes. You can rent a bike, order and pay for dinner, play a video game, or purchase food from a vending machine. In August 2019, the author was in Shanghai and saw a farmer selling sweet potatoes from a wagon on a busy street corner, not accepting any cash, only Alipay and Tencent's WeChat app.

In 2017, US$1.65 trillion worth of transactions were performed using QR codes in China (Wang, 2017). In 2019, Alipay processed US$50 billion of transactions every day. In a sign of continual innovation, in late 2019, both Alipay and WeChat began testing systems that allow users to pay, not by scanning a QR code, but simply by scanning their faces (Lee, 2019).

8.8.3. *12N Codes: Including many fields in one QR*

One major drawback of a QR code is that it can only contain a single field of information. The field can contain up to 4,296 characters, but it can only be one field of data. So, for example, a QR code cannot contain multiple URL addresses. If a company wants to give users the choice of two different websites to go to, it must present the user with two separate QR codes.

In 2013, the Reverse Logistics Association's (RLA) Standards Committee began developing a standardized system for storing multiple pieces of information in a single QR code (Lembke, 2015).

This effort was begun after a manufacturing company that was a member of the RLA related a challenge they were facing and needed a way to contain multiple pieces of information in a small space. They were sending laptops to be repaired in a distant country, and the paperwork would typically be lost in transit.

When the laptops arrived at the repair facility, because the paperwork was missing, the facility would have to test the laptop again, duplicating the earlier tests and incurring unnecessary expense. Because of national Internet restrictions at the repair facility, as well as security concerns, the manufacturer could not give the repair facility the ability to log in to the manufacturer's systems. Thus, the repair facility had no way to access the information about which repairs were needed for each laptop.

What the manufacturer wanted was a small sticker that could be placed on each device that could contain the repair instructions for each device. After the repairs were made, a similar sticker could be put on the device, telling what repairs were made and detailing any required test results after the repair.

The RLA Standards Committee began developing a standard to meet these needs. After gathering feedback from many member companies, a draft of the standard was presented to the American National Standard Institute (ANSI) Accredited Standards Committee MH10.

In July 2016, the MH10 Accredited Standards Committee approved the request from the RLA to create a new Data Identifier. The committee gave the RLA the 12N Data Identifier. 12N is thus part of the ANSI-approved global Data Identifier Standard.

This ANSI approval is technologically agnostic, meaning that 12N codes can be used in any data format. 12N codes can be stored in QR codes, 1D barcodes, RFID tags, printed out on stickers, or stored in Data Matrix barcodes, the other common 2D barcode, more commonly used for industrial applications.

The 12N standard is an open standard, which means there are no royalty fees to be paid to generate, print, or scan a 12N code.

8.8.4. *Generating 12N codes*

Leaving the technical details aside, to create a 12N barcode, a company creates a string of characters that contain the desired information. The first few characters are mandatory, so the scanner can know the barcode conforms to the ANSI standard. Those are followed by the characters "12N," so the scanner knows the barcode follows the 12N standard. Then, in front of each piece of information, a Field Identifier (FI) tells the scanner what the next information represents.

For example, one FI could tell the scanner that the next block of text is the name of the company. The next FI could inform the scanner that the next information is a product number, or a serial number, or the gross weight of a shipment, or the net weight of the contents, etc.

More than 200 FIs have already been created, and the RLA has a very simple process for requesting the creation of a new FI, if a company discovers the need for an FI that has not yet been created.

Each FI is four characters. At present, all FIs use a capital letter in the first character, and numbers in the remaining three positions, which provides

26,000 possible combinations. This would seem to be more than enough for the foreseeable future. If the first character is kept as an upper-case letter, and the remaining three characters are allowed to be numbers or upper-case letters, 1,213,056 different FIs could be created.

Once a company has identified the FIs they want to include in a 12N code, and the data to be used for each FI, the actual 12N code has to be generated. Many companies will want to include the serial number of the item in each 12N code. This will make it possible to read the serial number and identify an exact unit of a product with a quick, simple scan. At the retail point of sale, the serial number of each unit can be captured and stored for granular inventory tracking.

However, including the serial number means that the 12N codes for each unit must be different, and that means that the company must be able to generate new 12N codes for each unit as it comes off the assembly line. At a minimum, the time to generate and print each successive 12N code must be shorter than the time between completing successive units.

Each 12N code must exactly follow the requirements of the broader ANSI standard as well as the particulars of the more complicated 12N standard. The technical specifications for creating a 12N code currently fill a 50-page document (Lembke, 2017).

As an open standard, anyone may generate their own 12N codes. However, given the complexity of the requirements, and the time pressure of including serial numbers, rather than developing their own software for generating 12N codes, most companies will want to license software. The RLA Standards Committee has worked closely with Informission Solutions, who have developed a software suite that allows a company to generate 12N codes quickly and easily, and connects to their ERP systems to download product information. It also allows them to store a library of 12N codes they have generated and modify them for reuse.

8.8.5. *12N benefits to customers*

12N codes can provide customers or potential customers with any kind of information. A 12N code could contain the manufacturer's suggested retail price, nutritional information, or any other useful information. 12N codes can also contain multiple URLs, so a 12N code on a package could provide a links to videos and websites to answer any user questions. They can also contain phone numbers for the user to click on to call, or email links to request information.

A 12N code on the back of a TV or other device could provide links for downloading the manual, quick start sheet, or wiring diagram. It could provide links for customer support, or to purchase compatible accessories.

In addition to providing basic product information, 12N codes can also play an important public health safety role. For items with a lot code or date code, 12N codes could significantly reduce the effort required to find out if a particular item is involved in a recall.

Without 12N codes, capturing the serial number of an item as it is sold requires alerting the retail associate of the need to scan a second 1D barcode, which means additional labor cost. Using a 12N code means that the serial number of every single item could be captured, for no additional cost, using a single scan.

Single-scan serial number capture could allow a retailer to associate the individual item with the purchaser's rewards account, for automatic warranty registration. It also provides a significant theft deterrent. If someone steals an item and tries to return it for cash or store credit, the retailer can deny the return, stating they believe the unit has been stolen, having no record of its sale.

8.8.6. *Customized, updatable web links*

If a URL is included in a 12N code, the longer the URL, the more characters that have to be stored in the 12N code. Increasing the number of characters means more dots are required in the QR code, which means more space will be require when the QR is printed. To keep the size as small as possible, a URL shortener should be used. For example, the URL for the user manual for the author's television is more than 100 characters long. Using a URL shortener like Bit.ly, the URL can be reduced to 14 characters.

A URL shortener also future-proofs the website. If the company changes the file structure on their website, an old URL will no longer successfully take the user to the desired file. But if the 12N code contains a shortened URL, the destination can be updated to the new file location. So no matter how old, a 12N code can always be directed to the proper location.

URL shorteners are helpful for giving users an easy to remember URL. Google used to provide a URL shortener, but because they assume communications will be increasingly electronic, where shortening is not beneficial, they discontinued the service.

However, URL shortening offers many advantages with 12N codes, and a specialized URL shortening service has been created for 12N codes at http://12N.io.

8.8.7. *12N code security features*

The 12N standard also allows a high degree of security and control over who can access each piece of information. By default, any field is open to the public, so anyone with a consumer scanner will be able to read it.

However, when a label is created, the company can designate whether a field should be readable by a consumer scanner, a professional scanner, or an enterprise scanner. Data set as professional will not be available to consumers, but only to service professionals, such as field repair agents, customer service personnel, repair facilities, etc. Finally, data marked as enterprise is only displayable on scanners to employees within the manufacturer or original equipment manufacturer (OEM) organization.

Data records that are for professionals may or may not be encrypted. The unencrypted professional designation will be useful for data that is neither secret nor proprietary but is not likely to be of interest to consumers.

For greater security, asymmetric public key encryption may be used on any or all of the data in a 12N code. Additionally, private key encryption may also be applied to any data in the 12N code.

Thus 12N codes provide the user with the ability to provide literally any information they desire to their users in a very compact form, with any level of security and encryption that they desire.

8.9. More Secure 2-FA Using 12N QR Codes

In the remainder of this chapter, we will focus on ways to reduce supply chain vulnerabilities through 12N codes.

8.9.1. *2-FA vulnerabilities*

As mentioned earlier, one frequent recommendation for cybersecurity is 2FA, in which the user confirms their identify by receiving an SMS text message, typically consisting of a six-digit number, and entering that code into a box on the website. If a hacker is trying to break into a website, the thinking goes, they will not have possession of the legitimate user's phone, so by entering the correct number, the person accessing the system has proven they have the legitimate user's phone, and therefore must be the legitimate user.

2FA definitely provides greater security than single-factor authentication, but is not perfect. The major attack strategy is SIM swapping. A subscriber identity module, or SIM card, is the small chip that stores your international mobile subscriber identity number (IMSI) and provides it to the cellular network. In SIM swapping, hackers bribe an employee, or use personal information gained from data breaches, to convince the person's phone carrier that they are the person, and have the phone number assigned to a new SIM card, and receive the 2FA codes (Cipriani, 2020). According to Allison Nixon from the security firm Flashpoint, unfortunately, "If a skilled SIM hijacker targets you, there's realistically not much you can do to stop them" (Barrett, 2018).

An alternative to using SMS texting is to use an authentication app such as Google Authenticator, or Authy, which tie the authentication to your physical device, not to your phone number. If someone tries to SIM-swap you, they still will not receive your 2FA messages (Barrett, 2018).

In 2018, security expert Kevin Mitnick demonstrated a process in which a phishing email can create a man-in-the-middle attack that hacks 2FA. When the user clicks on the link, the hacker has setup the phishing email to take the user to the legitimate site, and it does not allow the hacker to see the six-digit encryption key, but it does allow the hacker to capture the user's login name and their password, and also the session cookie or session key, the same type of vulnerability discussed above with public WiFi networks. Once the hacker has the session key, they can access the website as the user, not to mention having the login and password for future access (Biggs, 2018).

Hackers have also written malware that, once on your machine, will capture the authorization tokens and perform malicious transactions while your machine is idle (Grimes, 2018). Some websites also allow unlimited attempts to enter the 2FA passcode number, which would allow anyone to break it using the brute force method (*Ibid.*). Hackers have also figured out how to reroute 2FA calls and SMS texts to intercept the messages, so the user is unaware of the hackers' login, and receive the digits (Matteson, 2019).

In November 2019, the FBI issued a warning to IT professionals about these security vulnerabilities in 2FA. They still recommend 2FA as secure, but wanted to alert people to these vulnerabilities (Cimpanu, 2019).

To summarize, determined hackers can perform a SIM swap on a user; with a phishing email, they can gain the user's login, password, and session key, without the user's notice; and can intercept SMS 2FA text messages. Clearly, security improvements are needed. As we will detail later, we believe 12N 2D barcodes offer security improvements.

8.9.2. *12N enhanced 2-FA*

12N offers the opportunity for enhanced 2-FA. Rather than texting a six-digit code, a website can present an encrypted 12N code, based on a private key stored on the user's phone, perhaps based on the previous transaction.

The user would scan it with their phone, decrypt the message, and send an encrypted response to the website. Only a user whose phone contains the proper key can thus be authenticated.

The greatest weakness of traditional 2FA is SIM swapping. But if the user scans an encrypted 12N code, taking control of a user's phone number (via SIM swapping) will do the hacker no good. To access the protected account, the hacker needs the encryption key, which is stored securely on the user's device and not accessible via SIM swap.

2FA based on encrypted 12N codes would also provide some protection against phishing. If hackers sent a phishing email, trying to access a website that required an encrypted 12N response, they would not be able to generate a 12N QR that matched the encryption key held by the user.

8.10. Avoiding the Need for User Logins

As we have seen, the majority of the security vulnerabilities come down to human mistakes or inattentiveness.

In January 2018, residents of Hawaii were awoken by a false warning of an incoming missile attack. The island's Emergency Management Agency said they had not been hacked, but an employee pressed an incorrect button. A photo from their Twitter account in July 2017 shows their operations officer in front of several monitors, and a post-it note clearly says "Password" and a readily legible password. Authorities say this was not the password to the system that sent the alert, but it brought their practices under scrutiny (Leswing, 2018).

For years, security experts cautioned users against writing their passwords down on paper. But recently, the consensus has shifted to say that writing down passwords is not bad, per se, assuming that the written passwords can be kept safe. The trouble is that many users, like the Hawaiian employee, leave them in plain sight.

Every time a person has to login to a website to access or input information, that connection represents a risk. Every user account represents a risk for phishing and/or stolen passwords. In many cases, it may be possible to remove the need for users to log in to a company's server, by providing suppliers or customers the information they need via a 12N code.

8.10.1. *Doing away with user logins*

The situation that lead the RLA to create 12N codes provides a perfect example. If a 12N code provides all the information required for a transaction, there is no need for the recipient to log in to the company's website. The recipient can obtain all the required information from a 12N code. In the case of the laptop repairs, all the information about test results and the details of the repair can be contained in another 12N code that can be printed and returned to the manufacturer with the device.

The more suppliers or partners a company has, the more passwords and logins that are required to be kept safe. When the communication flow is one-way, and involves the physical shipment of an item from a facility controlled by the first party to the supplier, a 12N code can accompany the item, and provide all of the necessary information. If after processing, the device will physically travel from the supplier to the larger company, again, a 12N code can accompany the item, providing the information to the company.

Even if the item is not going to the supplier from an OEM, if the item is originating from a larger, higher-tier supplier, 12N codes could still reduce risk. The larger supplier can access the OEM's system and generate the 12N codes that provide the lower supplier with the needed information. This removes the need for the lower supplier to access the OEM's information systems.

Similarly, even if the item is not going directly back to the OEM, but to a larger supplier, 12N codes can be used in lieu of logins. 12N codes can transport the information to the larger supplier, who can then be entrusted to enter the information into the system.

As we saw earlier, smaller firms are less likely to have strong security practices or large security budgets. Using 12N codes reduces the number of firms that must log in to the system and the number of logins, reducing overall cybersecurity exposure.

8.11. Summary

In this chapter, we have looked at ways to reduce supply chain cybersecurity threats. We began with the numerous ways hackers attack information systems, including the special vulnerabilities that retail supply chains represent. We have also looked at recommended ways to minimize these vulnerabilities.

Next, we have presented an overview of ANSI/MHI 12N codes, which provide companies a very secure and efficient way to pass information to a customer or retail partner using QR codes, Data Matrix codes, or RFID.

Finally, we have presented two ways that 12N codes offer supply chain cybersecurity benefits, by allowing 2FA using encrypted QR codes and by removing the need for individuals to log in to a company's information systems altogether.

References

Allais, D. C. (2006). *AIDC Memoirs* (Mukilteo, WA: PathGuide Technologies, Inc). Available at: https://aidc100.org/wp-content/uploads/2018/07/Allais-_David_ Memoirs.pdf. Accessed February 12, 2021.

Areddy, J. T. (2016). Overproduction swamps smaller Chinese cities, revealing depth of crisis. February 17. Available at: https://www.wsj.com/articles/overcapacity-swamps-smaller-chinese-cities-revealing-depth-of-crisis-1455738108. Accessed February 12, 2021.

Asay, M. (2015). Microsoft gives up on charging for Windows in China. *Tech Republic*, March 20. Available at: https://www.techrepublic.com/article/micro-soft-gives-up-on-charging-for-windows-in-china/. Accessed February 12, 2021.

Banjo, S. (2014). Home Depot hackers exposed 53 million email addresses. *Wall Street Journal*, Nov. 6. Available at: https://www.wsj.com/articles/home-depot-hackers-used-password-stolen-from-vendor-1415309282. Accessed February 12, 2021.

Barrett, B. (2018). How to protect yourself against a SIM swap attack. *Wired*, August 19. Available at: https://www.wired.com/story/sim-swap-attack-defend-phone. Accessed February 12, 2021.

Barrett, B. (2019), Microsoft's First Windows XP patch in years is a very bad sign. *Wired*, May 15. Available at: https://www.wired.com/story/microsoft-windows-xp-patch-very-bad-sign/. Accessed February 12, 2021.

Batson, A. (2010). Rising Wages Rattle China's Small Manufacturers. Wall Street Journal. August 1. https://www.wsj.com/articles/SB100014240527487033149 04575399111408113090. Accessed February 12, 2021.

Biggs, J. (2018). Hacker Kevin Mitnick shows how to bypass 2FA. *TechCrunch*. May 10. Available at: https://techcrunch.com/2018/05/10/hacker-kevin-mitnick-shows-how-to-bypass-2fa/. Accessed February 12, 2021.

Bradley, T. (2016). Poor security choices come back to haunt Mark Zuckerberg. *Forbes*. June 6. Available at: https://www.forbes.com/sites/tonybradley/2016/06/06/ poor-security-choices-come-back-to-haunt-mark-zuckerberg/#3d60607ed8a9. Accessed February 12, 2021.

Bradsher, K. (2019). One Trump victory: Companies rethink China. *The New York Times*, April 5. Available at: https://www.nytimes.com/2019/04/05/business/china-trade-trump-jobs-decoupling.html. Accessed February 12, 2021.

Brodkin, J. (2011). Ballmer to Hu: 90% of Microsoft customers in China use pirated software. *Computerworld*, January 21. Available at: https://www.computerworld.com/article/2512502/ballmer-to-hu--90--of-microsoft-customers-in-china-use-pirated-software.html. Accessed February 12, 2021.

Carlson, N. (2013). Here is a helpful and hilarious flow chart to help you decide whether to use a QR code. *Business Insider*, April 9. Available at: https://www.businessinsider.com/here-is-a-helpful-and-hilarious-flow-chart-to-help-you-decide-whether-to-use-a-qr-code-2013-4. Accessed February 12, 2021.

Chacos, B. (2019). Google's new Password Checkup tells you if your accounts can be compromised. *PC World*, October 2. Available at: https://www.pcworld.com/article/3442722/googles-new-password-checkup-tells-you-if-your-accounts-can-be-compromised.html. Accessed February 12, 2021.

Chiu, K. (2018). How the QR code conquered China. *Abacus News*. Available at: https://www.abacusnews.com/who-what/how-qr-code-conquered-china/article/2136537. Accessed February 12, 2021.

Cimpanu, C. (2019). FBI warns about attacks that bypass multi-factor authentication (MFA). *ZD Net*, October 7. Available at: https://www.zdnet.com/article/fbi-warns-about-attacks-that-bypass-multi-factor-authentication-mfa/. Accessed February 12, 2021.

Cipriani, J. (2020). SIM swap fraud: What it is, why you should care and how to protect yourself. *Cnet.com*. Available at: https://www.cnet.com/how-to/sim-swap-fraud-what-it-is-why-you-should-care-and-how-to-protect-yourself/. Accessed February 12, 2021.

CISA Cybersecurity and Infrastructure Security Administration (2009). Security Tip (ST04-14): Avoiding social engineering and phishing attacks. October 22. Available at: https://www.us-cert.gov/ncas/tips/ST04-014. Accessed February 12, 2021.

Corfield, G. (2017). HMS Windows XP: Britain's newest warship running Swiss Cheese OS. *The Register*, June 27. Available at: https://www.theregister.co.uk/2017/06/27/hms_queen_elizabeth_running_windows_xp/. Accessed February 12, 2021.

Cox, J. (2015). The History of SQL injection, the hack that will never go away. Motherboard, Tech by Vice. November 20. Available at: https://www.vice.com/en_us/article/aekzez/the-history-of-sql-injection_the-hack-that-will-never-go-away. Accessed February 12, 2021.

Delahaye, J-P. (2019). The mathematics of hacking passwords. *Scientific American*, April 12. Available at: https://www.scientificamerican.com/article/the-mathematics-of-hacking-passwords/. Accessed February 12, 2021.

Dellinger, A. J. (2019). Survey finds one in three businesses still run Windows XP. *Forbes*, July 31. Available at: https://www.forbes.com/sites/ajdellinger/

2019/07/31/survey-finds-one-in-three-businesses-still-run-windows-xp/. Accessed February 12, 2021.

Demarest, J. (2014). Taking down botnets. Statement before the Senate Judiciary Committee, Subcommittee on Crime and Terrorism. July 15. Available at: https://www.fbi.gov/news/testimony/taking-down-botnets. Accessed February 12, 2021.

Denso Corp. (2020). History of QR code standardization. Available at: https://www.qrcode.com/en/about/standards.html. Accessed February 12, 2021.

Detrixhe, J. (2018). Hackers account for 90% of login attempts at online retailers. *Quartz.* July 18. Available at: https://qz.com/1329961/hackers-account-for-90-of-login-attempts-at-online-retailers/

Frenkel, S. (2020). How Jeff Bezos' iPhone X was hacked. *New York Times,* January 22. Available at: https://www.nytimes.com/2020/01/22/technology/jeff-bezos-hack-iphone.html. Accessed February 12, 2021.

Gallagher, S. & Kravets, D. (2017). How did Yahoo get breached? Employee got spear phished, FBI suggests. *Ars Technica,* March 15. Available at: https://arstechnica.com/tech-policy/2017/03/fbi-hints-that-hack-of-semi-privileged-yahoo-employee-led-to-massive-breach/. Accessed February 12, 2021.

Geier, E. (2011). Seven free network apps for rooted androids. *PC World.* September 26. Available at: https://www.pcworld.com/article/240596/seven_free_network_apps_for_rooted_androids.html. Accessed February 12, 2021.

Geier, E. (2013). Here's what an eavesdropper sees when you use an unsecured Wi-Fi hotspot. *PC World,* June 28. Available at: https://www.pcworld.com/article/2043095/heres-what-an-eavesdropper-sees-when-you-use-an-unsecured-wi-fi-hotspot.html. Accessed February 12, 2021.

Gilbertson, S. (2020). The best password managers to secure your digital life. *Wired,* February 1. Available at: https://www.wired.com/story/best-password-managers/. Accessed February 12, 2021.

Greenberg, A. (2016), Meet OurMine, the 'security' group hacking CEOs and celebs. *Wired.* June 27. Available at: https://www.wired.com/2016/06/meet-ourmine-security-group-hacking-ceos-celebs/. Accessed February 12, 2021.

Greenberg, A. (2017). Software has a serious supply chain security problem. *Wired,* September 18. Available at: https://www.wired.com/story/ccleaner-malware-supply-chain-software-security/. Accessed February 12, 2021.

Greenberg, A. (2019). Supply chain hackers snuck malware into videogames. *Wired,* March 23. Available at: https://www.wired.com/story/supply-chain-hackers-videogames-asus-ccleaner/. Accessed February 12, 2021.

Greico, P. L., Gozzo, M. W. & (Chip) Long, C. J. (1989). (Palm Beach Gardens, FL: PT Publications).

Grimes, R. A. (2018). 11 ways to hack 2FA. *CSO,* May 15. Available at: https://www.cso online.com/article/3272425/11-ways-to-hack-2fa.html. Accessed February 12, 2021.

GS1 (2017). *Education & Training: How to Label Your Cases and Pallets with GS1-128 Barcodes* (Lawrenceville, NJ: GS1 US).

Hruska, J. (2019). Microsoft Windows XP is finally dead, nearly 18 years post-launch, *ExtremeTech,* April 11. Available at: https://www.extremetech.com/computing/289440-microsoft-xp-is-finally-dead-nearly-18-years-post-launch. Accessed February 12, 2021.

Kan, M. (2012). Microsoft: Most PCs running pirated Windows in China have security issues. *Computerworld,* December 13. Available at: https://www.computerworld.com/article/2493787/microsoft--most-pcs-running-pirated-windows-in-china-have-security-issues.html. Accessed February 12, 2021.

Kassner, M. (2015). Anatomy of the Target data breach: Missed opportunities and lessons learned. ZDNet.com. February 2. Available at: https://www.zdnet.com/article/anatomy-of-the-target-data-breach-missed-opportunities-and-lessons-learned/. Accessed February 12, 2021.

Keizer, G. (2020). Windows by the numbers: Windows 7 holds fast as pandemic upends everything. *Computerworld,* Apr 2. Available at: https://www.computerworld.com/article/3199373/windows-by-the-numbers-windows-7-holds-fast-as-pandemic-upends-everything.html. Accessed February 12, 2021.

Krebs, B. (2014). Email attack on vendor set up breach at Target. *KrebsOnSecurity,* February 12. Available at: https://krebsonsecurity.com/2014/02/email-attack-on-vendor-set-up-breach-at-target/. Accessed February 12, 2021.

Lakshmanan, R. (2019). Google study says people are still using old passwords after being compromised. August 16. Available at: https://thenextweb.com/security/2019/08/16/google-study-says-people-are-still-using-old-passwords-after-being-compromised/. Accessed February 12, 2021.

Lee, Y. N. (2019). Forget the QR code. Facial recognition could be the next big thing for payments in China. *CNBC,* November 19. Available at: https://www.cnbc.com/2019/11/19/tencents-wechat-china-may-soon-use-facial-recognition-for-payments.html. Accessed February 12, 2021.

Lembke, R. (2015). Labeling standards: RLA members welcome the new "sQRrl" codes. *Reverse Logsitics,* March, Edition 73.

Lembke, R. (2017). SQRL Codes: Standardized quick response for logistics, using the 12N data identifier. Reverse Logistics Association. Available at: https://rla.org/resource/12n-documentation. Accessed February 12, 2021.

Leswing, K. (2018). A password for the Hawaii emergency agency was hiding in a public photo, written on a Post-it note. *Business Insider,* January 16. Available at: https://www.businessinsider.com/hawaii-emergency-agency-password-discovered-in-photo-sparks-security-criticism-2018-1. Accessed February 12, 2021.

Magnier, M. (2016). How China is changing its manufacturing strategy. *The Wall Street Journal,* June 7. Available at: https://www.wsj.com/articles/

how-china-is-changing-its-manufacturing-strategy-1465351382. Accessed February 12, 2021.

McMillan, R. (2017). How to protect yourself from ransomware. *Wall Street Journal,* May 14. Available at: https://www.wsj.com/articles/how-to-protect-yourself-from-ransomware-1494793417. Accessed February 12, 2021.

Mizokami, K. (2016). Britain's doomsday nuke subs still run Windows XP. *Popular Mechanics,* January 21. Available at: https://www.popularmechanics.com/military/weapons/a19061/britains-doomsday-subs-run-windows-xp/. Accessed February 12, 2021.

Matteson, S. (2019). Why 2-factor authentication isn't foolproof. *Tech Republic,* August 15. Available at: https://www.techrepublic.com/article/why-2-factor-authentication-isnt-foolproof/. Accessed February 12, 2021.

Newman, L. H. (2018). Inside the unnerving supply chain attack that corrupted CCleaner. *Wired,* April 17. Available at: https://www.wired.com/story/supply-chain-hackers-videogames-asus-ccleaner/. Accessed February 12, 2021.

Newman, L. H. (2019). The worst hacks of the decade. *Wired,* December 23. Available at: https://www.wired.com/story/worst-hacks-of-the-decade/. Accessed February 12, 2021.

Nippon.com (2020). The little-known story of the birth of the QR code. February 10. Available at: https://www.nippon.com/en/news/fnn20191214001/the-little-known-story-of-the-birth-of-the-qr-code.html. Accessed February 12, 2021.

Perlroth, N. (2014). Home Depot data breach could be largest yet. *The New York Times,* September 8. Available at: https://bits.blogs.nytimes.com/2014/09/08/home-depot-confirms-that-it-was-hacked/. Accessed February 12, 2021.

Perlroth, N. (2016). Hackers used new weapons to disrupt major websites across U.S. *The New York Times,* October 21. Available at: https://www.nytimes.com/2016/10/22/business/internet-problems-attack.html. Accessed February 12, 2021.

O'Flaherty, K. (2017). Equifax lawsuit: 'Admin' as password at time of 2017 breach. *Forbes,* October 20. Available at: https://www.forbes.com/sites/kateoflahertyuk/2019/10/20/equifax-lawsuit-reveals-terrible-security-practices-at-time-of-2017-breach/#558ec2563d38. Accessed February 12, 2021.

OWASP (2020). Top 10 web application security risks. Available at: https://owasp.org/www-project-top-ten/. Accessed March 3, 2020. Accessed February 12, 2021.

Popper, N. (2020). Ransomware attacks grow, crippling cities and businesses. *The New York Times,* February 9. Available at: https://www.nytimes.com/2020/02/09/technology/ransomware-attacks.html. Accessed February 12, 2021.

Ranger, S. (2017). Windows 10 has finally overtaken Windows XP in businesses. *ZDNet,* July 24. Available at: https://www.zdnet.com/article/windows-10-has-finally-overtaken-windows-xp-in-businesses/. Accessed February 12, 2021.

Rezulli, K. A. (2020). 7 tips to create a hack-proof password you'll actually remember. *Newsweek,* February 8. Available at: https://www.newsweek.

com/7-tips-create-hack-proof-password-youll-actually-remember-1486319. Accessed February 12, 2021.

Rosenberg, J. M. (2020). At risk for cyberattacks. *Reno Gazette Journal*, March 15, 1D, 3D.

Simon, R. (2019). A small business with no working website, felled by a cyberattack. *The Wall Street Journal*, June 2. Available at: https://www.wsj.com/articles/a-small-business-with-no-working-website-felled-by-a-cyberattack-11559490543. Accessed February 12, 2021.

Soergel, A. (2014). 53 million email addresses stolen in Home Depot hack. *US News & World Report*, November 7. Available at: https://www.usnews.com/news/newsgram/articles/2014/11/07/53-million-customer-email-addresses-leaked-in-home-depot-hack. Accessed February 12, 2021.

Solomon, B. (2014). Apple admits celebrity photos were stolen in targeted attack. *Forbes*, September 2. Available at: https://www.forbes.com/sites/briansolomon/2014/09/02/apple-admits-celebrity-photos-were-stolen-in-targeted-hack/#569bebef3e1a. Accessed February 12, 2021.

Swinhoe, D. (2019). Man is a man-in-the-middle attack? How MitM attacks work and how to prevent them. *CSO*, February 13. Available at: https://www.csoonline.com/article/3340117/what-is-a-man-in-the-middle-attack-how-mitm-attacks-work-and-how-to-prevent-them.html. Accessed February 12, 2021.

Vijayan, J. (2008). One year later: Five takeaways from the TJX breach. *Computerworld*, Jan 17. Available at: https://www.computerworld.com/article/2538711/one-year-later--five-takeaways-from-the-tjx-breach.html. Accessed February 12, 2021.

Wang, S. (2017). Why China can't get enough of QR codes. *CNN.com*, September 8. Available at: https://money.cnn.com/2017/09/08/technology/china-qr-codes/index.html. Accessed February 12, 2021.

Ward, M. & Wall, M. (2018). How can we stop being cyber idiots? *BBC.com*, November 2. Available at: https://www.bbc.com/news/technology-45953238. Accessed February 12, 2021.

Warzel, C. (2020). Chinese hacking is alarming. So are data brokers. *The New York Times*, February 10. Available at: https://www.nytimes.com/2020/02/10/opinion/equifax-breach-china-hacking.html. Accessed February 12, 2021.

Winder, D. (2019). Ranked: The world's top 100 worst passwords. *Forbes*, December 14. Available at: https://www.forbes.com/sites/daveywinder/2019/12/14/ranked-the-worlds-100-worst-passwords/#7523793069b4. Accessed February 12, 2021.

Zetter, K. (2015). Hacker lexicon: Botnets, the zombie computer armies that earn hackers millions. *Wired*, December 15. Available at: https://www.wired.com/2015/12/hacker-lexicon-botnets-the-zombie-computer-armies-that-earn-hackers-millions/

CHAPTER 9

Cybersecurity Challenges in Logistics

George Moakley

Founding Fellow, ASU W.P. Carey School of Business,
Internet Edge Supply Chain Lab

9.1. Introduction

In 2018, according to *BusinessWire* (2019), the logistics industry reached a value of US\$ 4,730 billion. Everything around us has been moved, multiple times, from sourcing as raw materials through various entities refining and processing these materials to finished products acquired by individuals or businesses. Logistics companies typically compete primarily on price, and their cost-containment strategies create a number of interesting security discussions as we consider the implications of the Fourth Industrial Revolution empowered by Internet of Things (IoT), edge intelligence, machine learning (ML), and 5G.

First, there are traditional cybersecurity challenges. Logistics businesses employ traditional, centralized information systems maintaining proprietary core competency information such as routing information, subcontractor agreements, and so forth; traditional cybersecurity challenges apply to all of this. Second, there are novel attack planes. Instrumentation applied to shipments and/or vehicles by logistics companies or their customers become cybersecurity targets. Malefactors may wish to monitor them, disable them, or compromise them to generate bogus information, reveal sensitive information, damage in-transit shipments, etc. The mere presence of such instrumentation creates risk; e.g. if there are a series of trucks parked for the night, the one emitting detectable status updates, even if the updates are encrypted, has already revealed it is likely to be carrying valuable cargo. Third, there are opportunities to apply instrumentation as a physical security solution, including various strategies for theft detection or prevention and to detect smuggling attempts.

9.2. Foundation

Understanding cybersecurity challenges in logistics requires a shared understanding of key applicable megatrends and how they will affect the evolution of logistics. This discussion will presume a baseline understanding of key technologies or that the reader will access any of a number of readily available resources explaining them. The following thumbnails are intended to address the relevance of these technologies to logistics cybersecurity.

According to Meola (2018), "The **Internet of Things**, (emphasis added) commonly abbreviated as IoT, refers to the connection of devices (other than typical fare such as computers and smartphones) to the Internet." For the purposes of our discussion, the relevance of IoT is the opportunity to bring Internet connectivity to logistics entities, including freight (at any level of grouping from individual items through the shipment level), pallets, shipping containers, vehicles, roll-on/roll-off trailers, forklifts, etc. Any object involved in logistics *could* be granted an IP address, and, as an industry, we are just beginning to think through *which* objects *should* be given an IP address. For what it is worth, the answer to that question will depend on the perspectives of the various interested parties, including warehouse operators, freight carriers, fleet operators, etc.

"**Edge intelligence** (emphasis added) is a new approach to data collection, storage, and processing," according to Cox (2018). Edge intelligence builds on IoT and refers to computing solutions involving distinct computational engines outside the cloud or datacenter. Traditional computing solutions are centralized, bringing data from a variety of sources (including IoT-enabled things) to cloud or datacenter resident line of business (LOB) or analytical systems for processing. Intelligent edge solutions do not "move" computing to the edge; they add complementary computing at the edge. In so doing, edge intelligence makes things and spaces "smart," smart enough to become active participants in business process automation.

Note that this is not the same as Client/Server or Three-Tier solutions; such solutions distribute a computational context across platforms. Edge intelligence involves multiple, distinct computational contexts interacting with each other.

Edge intelligence models are typically applied when the volume of valuable data exceeds what can realistically be transmitted to a centralized system (e.g. vehicles can generate a terabyte of raw data per hour), when latency cannot be tolerated (e.g. a vehicle evaluating whether to take evasive action cannot wait for cloud-based analytics), or when communications links are expensive, constrained, or unreliable.

The smartness of "smart" things can refer to anything from the ability to provide derivative information to creating the opportunity to delegate decisions to "smart" things.

Here is a simple example. Consider an IoT-enabled tire on a fleet-managed truck:

(1) Providing an Internet address to the tire pressure gauge creates the opportunity to periodically collect a current pressure reading. Such readings improve safety, fuel efficiency, and feed centralized analytic engines regarding tire life, driver habits, etc.

(2) Providing an Internet address to the tire pressure gauge *and* some local processing create the opportunity to sample tire pressure repeatedly (e.g. every few seconds) in order to provide an average and a standard deviation. The average is a better-quality result than periodic snapshots, and the standard deviation of the pressure readings will increase as the tire thins with wear, creating additional analytic opportunities such as projecting tire life to further improve safety and optimize tire replacement scheduling.

(3) Providing additional intelligence to the tire pressure gauge could create opportunities for ML (see below; e.g. patterns revealing information about road conditions, driver habits, load optimization, etc.) or even the ability to delegate to a tire the ability to continuously regulate its own pressure to further optimize safety, fuel economy, and tire life.

It would be unlikely for such sophistication to be cost-effective for a tire, at least in the near future, but the thought experiment is suggestive of the opportunities to revolutionize business computing as various components involved in logistics operations move beyond provision of an IP address and are made "smart" enough to become active participants in the business operations in which they are involved.

"**Fifth-generation wireless (5G)** is the latest iteration of cellular technology, engineered to greatly increase the speed and responsiveness of wireless networks." According to Rouse (2020), 5G brings more to bear than higher bandwidth. 5G facilitates IoT by supporting far higher concurrent device density and facilitating more machine-to-machine communications. More concurrent devices matters for logistics, considering the number of objects that will be assigned IP addresses, and facilitating machine-to-machine communications will enrich our ability to build edge intelligence solutions for logistics.

ML refers to Machine Learning. According to Hao (2018), "Machine-learning algorithms use statistics to find patterns in massive amounts of data." For the purposes of this discussion, ML refers to the process of detecting patterns in data that correlate with interesting events. For example, if we employ edge intelligence to continuously monitor accelerometer readings from an instrumented shipment, we may discover that particular patterns precede damage to sensitive freight. This would create the opportunity to program an edge intelligence solution to raise an alert when such patterns are detected before damage occurs.

The Fourth Industrial Revolution was originally described by the Nicholas Davis in a 2016 World Economic Forum report, referencing the First Industrial Revolutionary shift from hand production to machine production, the Second Industrial Revolutionary shift using railroads and telegraphs to accelerate the movement of material and ideas, and the Third Industrial Revolutionary shift to a digital economy.

In that context, one could think of this Fourth Industrial Revolution as having started with mainframes, but the term has recently been gaining international traction as the confluence of IoT and edge intelligence, bolstered by 5G and ML, are starting to facilitate a substantial upheaval by extending automation to business activities that have not yet been digitized (sometimes referred to as OT [Operational Technologies]).

Much of the logistics industry consists of such business activities.

9.3. Waves of Digitization

To put this in perspective, it is useful to think of the history of business computing as successive waves of automation, with each wave extending digitization to business activities that had not yet been digitized.

The first wave of automation occurred when mainframes automated bulk calculations, including core financials like general ledgers, actuarial tables, and so forth.

The next wave occurred when minicomputers (now servers) were installed to automate departmental computing functions such as inventory management, order processing, accounts receivable, customer relationship management, etc. These solutions largely automated record keeping, accessing, and updating databases. Over time, they created new classes of problems (e.g. reconciling records overlaps like "customer") that were addressed through Enterprise Resource Planning (ERP) solutions that integrated these departmental functions.

The next wave occurred when personal computing devices (initially PCs, now supplemented by smartphones and tablets) automated personal productivity with applications including email, spreadsheets, and word processing.

The next wave occurred when the World Wide Web introduced the Internet Browser, abstracting the complexity of the Internet with a graphical user interface. From a business computing perspective, the web automated the dissemination of information to prospective customers, suppliers, and partners, and e-business automated routine business transactions.

Thinking of the history of business computing as waves of automation can certainly result in lively debates about how to position cloud computing and social media, whether to segregate PCs from smartphones and tablets, and so forth. Regardless of those details, thinking of the history of business computing as successive waves bringing automation to business activities that had not previously been digitized, eliminating some jobs, creating others, and creating industries with profound improvements in productivity, is extremely useful, especially considering the scale of the logistics industry.

This next wave of business computing, the Fourth Industrial Revolution enabled by IoT, edge intelligence, 5G, and ML/artificial intelligence (AI), is just beginning to drive the next massive upheaval in business computing. The heart of this next wave is edge intelligence; the ability to make things and spaces "smart" enough to become active participants in business process automation. There will be winners and losers, as jobs are created and lost. There will be experimentation; a variety of solution concepts will be tried, with costly failures and successes so transformative as to become as presumed to be part of any business as ERP systems have become.

From a cybersecurity perspective, these waves are important to understand for three reasons. First, each wave brings information technology to a new set of business activities. The security challenges of the previous waves still apply, but these new activities, in addition to transformational productivity advances, also create novel attack planes. For example, adding minicomputers for departmental computing to the pre-existing mainframe automated business activities like order processing, created the opportunity to compromise those orders. Adding PCs for personal productivity applications created the opportunity to introduce malware to departmental computing functions through personal email attachments, infected USB drives, etc.

Second, the tried and true security solutions of each wave cannot be applied to the next wave, in part due to the novel attack planes just described, but also due to economies of scale. Companies with one or a few mainframes eventually added hundreds or thousands of servers, and thousands to tens of thousands of PCs, smartphones, and tablets. We can expect these companies to add millions of items to their IoT deployments. Just as when PCs first reached the business computing market, the typical licensing fees for a minicomputer-based security tool was higher than the PC's total cost, and did not support features for such novel concerns as USB drives, security solutions designed for PCs and personal devices will be neither effective nor affordable for IoT. Third, and finally, thinking of the history of business computing as successive waves of digitization also teaches us that the productivity gains of each wave are simply too compelling to ignore.

Security experts might prefer that people and companies wait to deploy until after security risks and strategies are worked through, but history suggests that, as with previous waves, while pioneers may suffer, stragglers will lose competitive ground. So, we should expect companies to build solutions, malefactors to exploit them, and to read some very interesting headlines over the next few years.

With that in mind, the rest of this discussion will explore logistics cybersecurity in terms of traditional challenges, novel attack planes, and opportunities, recognizing that clear understandings of each will not be achieved for some time. Therefore, it is not the intent of this discussion to offer anything definitive regarding a subject area that is still rapidly evolving; rather, it is the aspiration of this discussion to help readers frame their thinking about the subject area in order to be as ready as possible to deal with challenges and opportunities as they emerge.

9.4. Traditional Cybersecurity Challenges

Given the scale of the global logistics industry, it is, unsurprisingly, complex and diverse. However, for the purposes of this discussion, we will use an up-leveled, simplified view that, though it ignores some of the richness of the industry, provides an adequate foundation for understanding cybersecurity concerns.

The term "logistics" will be considered as the movement of materials, whether by internal processes or any of a variety of service providers, from one point to another, sometimes involving intermediate way points and through a variety of owned, leased, or chartered vehicles.

In the aforementioned waves of automation model, some logistical processes were automated before the current technology wave began, including:

(1) Managing movement of material within a point of origin, waypoint, or destination by a cloud-based or on-premise inventory/warehouse management module of an ERP system.

(2) Route planning and tracking for the movement of material between origin, waypoints, and destination. Note that when the movement of materials is performed by a service provider such as a freight forwarder or 3PL, functions such as route planning and tracking, management of assigned or chartered vehicle capacity, and the presentation of tracking information are usually core competencies of the service provider, and the information systems supporting these core competencies are usually proprietary and guarded.

(3) Management of assigned or chartered vehicle capacity

(4) Presentation of tracking information, often through a web portal or smart device app

As the logistics processes that have been automated through well-understood information systems best practices, these logistics processes are also subject to traditional cybersecurity challenges, ranging from denial-of-service attacks, ransomware (e.g. a Canadian courier company reported a ransomware attack while this chapter was being written), intellectual property theft (e.g. compromising the information systems supporting freight company core competencies), and so forth. Such cybersecurity challenges and best practices are thoroughly discussed in the literature, and they are cited here primarily to distinguish them from the novel attack planes and physical security innovations to be discussed below.

9.5. Novel Attack Planes

Some years ago, at a security conference, an executive from a cybersecurity company spoke about cybersecurity for cars, then a futuristic topic. He said all the traditional cybersecurity challenges would apply; people would hack cars to break into them physically or to steal their owners' identities through monitoring of network traffic between cars and supporting services. However, he said, beware of novel attack planes. Imagine, he said, if you were to hack a car driving during rush hour on a crowded multilane highway and took control of the radio. Who, he asked, secures a radio? Imagine if you hacked that car and suddenly turned the radio volume to full, startling the driver and causing an accident costing, perhaps, dozens of lives. One can, and should, think about novel attack planes, because malefactors certainly will. One can think them through and take steps to thwart them. However, one should also, unfortunately, accept two things based on the history of prior automation waves:

(1) As diligent as the industry may be, the odds are excellent that malefactors will see unforeseen opportunities.
(2) The industry will move forward with the next wave of automation despite the risk because the business benefits simply cannot be ignored.

Thinking through novel attack planes requires cross-referencing the aforementioned simplified logistics model with the two primary next-wave automation opportunities created by emerging technologies. These two opportunities include fundamentally re-engineering solutions for processes already digitized and digitizing business processes that have never been digitized.

A simple, albeit extremely valuable, example of fundamentally re-engineering a currently digitized solution would be addressing the frequent human errors made during the movement of material within a point of origin, waypoint, or destination. DeHoratius (2012) noted that "Through direct observations and interviews with retail employees, we identify numerous errors that occur within the retail distribution center and how such errors create a mismatch between actual and recorded store inventory." Humans frequently either neglect to accurately update a location record for a moved item or fail to correctly relocate an item as directed by inventory/warehouse management systems. What if we made the space "smart" enough to always "know" where things are? What if, instead of relying on humans, error-prone when bored with repetitive tasks, we, instead, empowered the space to always know the "actual" location of every asset, and to repeatedly ensure that "location" fields were kept current with "actual" location? Such asset tracking need not be limited to the assets managed by the facility; they could also apply to the equipment used to manage the facility (e.g. forklifts, roll-on/roll-off trailers, containers, rail cars, trailers, etc.) One way to accomplish this would be through RFID tagging and strategically placed readers. Note that this would not simply be replacing a bar code scan with an RFID scan, but through the strategic placement of the readers and a certain amount of edge logic and frequent scans that update location fields with "actual" location. For example, the number of times a tag is not detected before concluding that the asset has been removed depends on the level of interference that might affect a successful read; an even better approach is to ensure strategic reader placement such that an asset no longer detected at one location would have been noticed as it moved past other readers. Such re-engineering options do not tend to be rich opportunities for novel attack planes because the underlying business process has been digitized through an earlier generation of technology.

Removing an RFID tag and leaving it in place to avoid/delay theft detection is certainly a possibility. Similarly, RFID tags could be obscured by covering the tag with something that interferes with the RFID signal to facilitate theft, but the timing of the last known scan of the tag would provide valuable information about when it was obscured. The RFID readers and/or the edge platform that processes their scan results would be another attack plane; falsifying reads and/or their processing could also avoid/delay theft detection. Spoofing RFID reads to create confusion and/or misinformation about asset locations, whether managed assets moving through the facility or facility equipment assets used to operate the facility, could force waste/cost for a customer by, essentially, aggravating the "misplaced" asset problem the re-engineered solution intended to address. Denial-of-service attacks involving floods of false reads could be similarly used.

Eavesdropping would be unlikely to be of much benefit unless it revealed the location of a particular asset, but that would require knowing the RFID assigned to the particular asset, suggesting this is an unlikely eventuality. A ransomware attack affecting the RFID readers and associated edge intelligence platforms could effectively obscure knowledge of warehoused assets. More transformative solutions, with more novel attack planes, would involve digitizing processes that have not, to date, been digitized.

The most obvious opportunity is to make freight "smart," either directly or through the vehicles carrying the freight. Understandably, innovations are initially applied to the highest-dollar shipments, but decreasing prices are expanding their application. For the purposes of this discussion, no distinction will be made between making the carrying vehicle or the freight "smart."

A number of industries depend on the transportation of materials sensitive to environmental challenges: e.g. food and pharmaceuticals have temperature sensitivities; some biological products generate volatile organic compounds (e.g. ripening fruit generates ethylene that can reduce shelf life; pathology samples may generate degradation byproducts); complex devices have shock, tilt, vibration, and moisture sensitivities; logistics companies also routinely ship munitions, hazardous chemicals, money and precious metals, live animals and plants, and so forth.

Early shipment integrity strategies were not sophisticated. An analog device (e.g. a "tip and tell") might indicate that a shipment was subjected to a tolerance exceeding shock; the absence of remaining dry ice on receipt would be an indicator that temperature thresholds were breached in transit. Some companies simply hired observers to monitor loading and unloading of sensitive and/or expensive freight.

There are three key trends to understand with regard to increasingly sophisticated solutions. The first is the proliferation of electronic sensory capabilities replacing analog devices, such as thermal sensors, accelerometers (shock, tilt, vibration), photosensors, moisture sensors, and increasingly sophisticated chemical sensors (e.g. volatile organic compounds, or VOCs, to detect the byproducts of shipment integrity degradation. One can envision extremely sophisticated shipment instrumentation, including active containers monitoring a substantial number of discrete microclimates. The second is the shift from integrity verification on arrival (i.e. inspecting sensory logs to determine whether in-transit excursions compromised the integrity of the shipment) to active monitoring (i.e. intelligent devices that raise an alert when a threshold is being approached to facilitate corrective action before shipment integrity is compromised). The third is the emergence of electronic records (e.g. blockchain) to facilitate trusted exchange of information about shipment integrity.

Monitoring or modifying communications with actively monitored freight would create opportunities to facilitate theft or inflict damage. Eavesdropping on status messages from instrumented freight is unlikely to be of great concern, but the existence of messages, even if effectively encrypted, would be suggestive of freight value. A prospective thief deciding which container to rob would likely choose the one emitting status messages even if those messages cannot be understood. Spoofing events from instrumented freight might prove tempting, either to initiate costly unnecessary mitigation procedures through false warnings concerning excursions or to mask excursions through false reassuring messages that circumvent a needed intervention. Freight monitoring instrumentation might also be updated with fallacious thresholds intended to enable damage or spoilage.

One could envision false warnings being used as part of a greater theft strategy if they resulted in a vehicle stopping to facilitate intervention and thereby create an opportunity for theft. Another possibility would be to spoof messaging that redirected in-transit freight from safe routes to a more favorable location for hijacking. Spoofing events could also mask theft by simulating ongoing status updates for a shipment that has, in reality, been hijacked.

Electronic records supporting trusted exchange of information about shipment integrity open potential novel attack planes. The employment of blockchain technology can create a false sense of security; while it is true that blockchains themselves are extremely difficult to compromise, the systems that write to, or read from, trusted blockchain records can be targets, creating the risk that a solution will involve highly trustworthy storage of falsified records.

This has been an exploration of novel attack planes as the next wave of automation brings information technology to logistics industry business processes that have not yet been digitized and create the opportunity to fundamentally re-engineer the kinds of solutions already deployed.

It is not, and could not, be comprehensive. It is in the nature of information technology waves that novel attack planes will be discovered, and exploited, by malefactors as we move forward.

9.6. Physical Security Innovation

The next wave of digitization creates novel opportunities to improve physical security. Shipments made smart enough to manage themselves can definitively record when excursions happened, allowing clear assignment of responsibility to reduce liability management costs. Sensors can be deployed to detect radiation or the chemical signatures of explosives. Theft protection options include sensors that detect attempts to compromise the integrity of a shipment. Light sensors can be used to raise an alarm if light levels increase when if light levels increase unexpectedly (e.g. someone is opening the shipping container). Similarly, contact sensors activated when a container door is closed can generate an event if the container is opened prematurely. Sensors coordinating through a mesh network can be used in a variety of ways. For example, if contact is lost with a sensor, that subset of the shipment may have been stolen (or left behind). If all but one accelerometer is heading north, then the one heading south may have been stolen.

Freight can be made smart enough to monitor their GPS readings compared to a downloaded route, manage the level of diligence applied to higher risk subsets of the route, and record and raise alerts for route deviations, even when the freight cannot currently connect with cloud resident services.

Smuggling detection options include more sophisticated applications that detect inconsistencies between the accelerometer readings across a shipment. If all of the accelerometer readings report concurrent movement away from the center of a shipment, then something may have been inserted in the shipment (smuggling). If the motion of all the sensors relative to each other changes during, for example, a turn, that may indicate a change in the overall shipment mass due either to theft or smuggling.

Finally, the instrumentation used to make freight smart enough to monitor itself can also be used to raise an alarm and facilitate recovery. Sensors attached to freight could, when contact is lost, begin to periodically emit a tracking signal to guide investigators.

9.7. Call to Action

Novel attack planes in logistics, whether the re-engineering of business processes already automated or bringing information technology to operational processes never before digitized, involve the deployment of edge intelligence and sensory technology and attempts to compromise such edge intelligence through preventing or compromising the behavior of, or communications between, these edge intelligences and line of business systems.

It is, therefore, imperative that such edge intelligence and sensory deployments be designed with security management in mind, within the practical limitations referenced above; specifically, just as the security tools used for minicomputers were prohibitively expensive for PCs and personal devices, the security tools since developed for PCs and personal devices will be prohibitively expensive for edge intelligence and sensor deployments. Cost effectively hardening these deployments will be challenging.

Edge intelligence deployments will, in order to scale, require provisioning and FOTA/SOTA (Firmware/Software Over The Air) solutions as well as remote manageability. Such provisioning and manageability solutions must include security management capabilities, including monitoring them for malware and establishing trust relationships for distinguishing between valid and spoofed sensory readings and/or events declared on the basis of sensory readings.

Two things are certain. One is that the productivity opportunities created by this next wave of automation are too compelling to ignore. The logistics industry needs to acknowledge the risks of this wave, and conferences should include speculative security tracks to explore novel attack planes and novel physical security opportunities. The other certainty is that we can expect interesting headlines in the years to come.

References

Businesswire (2019). The global logistics market reached a value of US$ 4,730 billion in 2018 and will continue to rise by 4.9% by 2024. *ResearchandMarkets.com*, https://www.businesswire.com/news/home/20190703005488/en/, Accessed 3 July.

Cox, L. (2018). At a glance — Edge intelligence. *Disruptionhub.com*, Accessed 22 October.

Davis, N. (2016). What is the Fourth Industrial Revolution? *Weforum.org*, Accessed 19 January.

DeHoratius, N. (2012). Inventory record inaccuracy in retail supply chains. *Wiley Encyclopedia of Operations Research and Management Science*, https://onlinelibrary.wiley.com/doi/10.1002/9780470400531.eorms0431.pub2, 15 October.

Hao, K. (2018). What is machine learning? *Technologyreview.com*, Accessed 17 November.

Meola, A. (2018). What is the Internet of Things? What IoT means and how it works. *Businessinsider.net*, Accessed 10 May.

Rouse, M. (2020). 5G. *Searchnetworking.techtarget.com*, Accessed June.

Index

Printed in the United States
by Baker & Taylor Publisher Services